A Clinician's Guide to 12-Step Recovery

Mark D. Schenker

W. W. Norton & Co.
New York • London

For information about permission to reproduce
selections from this book, write to Permissions,
W. W. Norton & Company, Inc.,
500 Fifth Avenue, New York, NY 10110

For information about special discounts for bulk purchases, please contact
W. W. Norton Special Sales at specialsales@wwnorton.com or 800-233-4830

Manufacturing by Quebecor World Fairfield
Book design by Paradigm Graphics
Production manager: Leeann Graham

Library of Congress Cataloging-in-Publication Data

Schenker, Mark D.
A clinician's guide to 12-step recovery / Mark D. Schenker.
p. ; cm.
"A Norton professional book."
Includes bibliographical references and index.
ISBN 978-0-393-70546-1 (hardcover)
1. Substance abuse--Treatment. 2. Twelve-step programs. I. Title.
[DNLM: 1. Alcoholics Anonymous. 2. Substance-Related
Disorders--rehabilitation. 3. Recovery of Function. 4. Self-Help
Groups. WM 270 S324c 2009]
RC564.S322   2009
616.86'06--dc22   2008037699

W. W. Norton & Company, Inc.,
500 Fifth Avenue, New York, N. Y. 10110
www.wwnorton.com

W. W. Norton & Company, Ltd.,
Castle House, 75/76 Wells St., London W1T 3QT

1   2   3   4   5   6   7   8   9   0

For Linda Glaser Schenker

And to Molly Schenker, David Kornblith and Havi Glaser

Contents

Acknowledgments

FIRST OFF, THIS BOOK would not exist if it were not for the clients and patients who have allowed me to work with them and learn from them. I'm particularly grateful to the members of the Alumni Group mentioned in Chapter One, who were quite patient with my learning curve.

I'd like to thank the many colleagues and friends who have offered encouragement and support in the course of my writing this book. I'm especially grateful to the members of 12-Step Fellowships who have reviewed various parts of the manuscript and corrected my more egregious errors of omission, commission, and interpretation. Without their input this book would be far poorer in content and execution. Of particular help, in no particular order, have been: Richard Levine, Michael Roeske, Sam Hartman, Vincent Morello, John Meaney, Dale Goldberg, Molly Layton, Susan Blank, Stanton Peele, Rudolf Moos, Sharon Hartman, and Anita Litwack. All have read sections of the manuscript and have offered supportive, challenging, and/or factual feedback. Deborah Malmud has been steadfast in her presence and support as editor and I'm grateful for her willingness to engage in this process. Vani Kannan and Kristen Holt-Browning were quite helpful in the logistical details of getting this project completed. Mark Fowler was a beacon of insight into the workings of the publishing industry.

This is also an opportunity for me to thank those teachers and mentors who have been influential in my overall professional and personal development and who have helped me move into a position where such a project was possible. These include: Morris Schwartz, Gordon Fellman, and Larry Rosenberg at Brandeis University; Jay Efran, Tom Shipley, and Marsha Weinraub at Temple University; Chuck Anderson, Bill Greenfield, Grace Strauss, Barney Dlin, Harry Aponte, and Tom Benfield. Jay Efran has been a particularly influential mentor, both in his example as a dedicated psychologist and friend, and in his ability to challenge every damn premise I can think of, and to help see new patterns in old backgrounds.

Of course, without Linda Schenker and Molly Schenker, none of this would be possible. They are my clear white light. Linda is particularly impressed that I've completed this without major disruption in our blissful life. It helps that we no longer have a typewriter. From a bit further distance both David Kornblith and Havi Glaser have enriched my life to a degree they can hardly imagine.

Thanks to you all.

Chapter 1

The Nature of the Problem

And one more thing: none of us would be here today if somebody hadn't taken time to explain things to us, to give us a little pat on the back, to take us to a meeting or two, to have done numerous little kind and thoughtful acts on our behalf. So let us never get the degree of smug complacency so that we're not willing to extend, or attempt to, that help which has been so beneficial to us, to our less fortunate brothers.

—Dr. Bob Smith

THE WORLDS OF PSYCHOTHERAPY AND ADDICTION RECOVERY have long been uneasy bedfellows. Most rehabilitation programs offer both 12-step treatment and psychotherapy, but they are not integrated either in theory or in practice. While intuitively there would appear to be a clear connection between these two areas, in fact, they remain uncomfortable allies, and sometimes not even that. There are a number of historical and philosophical reasons why this is so.

People in recovery from drug and alcohol addiction are often wary of professionals who have no personal experience of addiction and recovery. For the majority of these people, "recovery" is synonymous with 12-step programs such as Alcoholics Anonymous (AA) or Narcotics Anonymous (NA). The very essence of these programs is found in the experience of alcoholics and addicts helping each other to stay sober, not in help from trained professionals. For a novice therapist (and more than a few seasoned clinicians) there are few more dreaded questions to be asked by an addicted client than, "Are you in recovery yourself?" The apprehension, and all too often the reality, is that this question will be followed by a dismissal of the therapist's usefulness or disparagement of his or her "book learning."

1

Furthermore, many addicts and alcoholics have had disappointing experiences in psychotherapy, based on therapists' attempts to treat addiction as if it were a symptom of some other disorder (whether it be depression, anxiety, or some presumed underlying conflict), rather than recognizing addiction as a primary disorder in its own right. This points to the inadequate level of training in addictions treatment across all the human service professions. Each school of psychological thought has made an effort to fit addiction into its own constructs, from the analytic concept of oral fixation to the cognitive view of expectancies and negative beliefs. The view of addiction as an independent and primary disorder has only recently become recognized as a legitimate position.

Finally, the medical profession, due to a history of misunderstanding addiction and inadequate training, has often exacerbated these problems with inappropriate medications (early members of AA referred to their comrades who were addicted to prescribed medications as "chewing their booze"). It is still common to hear of a client experiencing anxiety in early recovery and being treated with benzodiazepines, beginning another cycle of addiction.

On the other hand, the mental health profession has been guilty of ignoring addicts and alcoholics altogether, and patronizing practitioners working within the recovery model—an early article referred to AA, somewhat disparagingly, as "folk psychotherapy." The belief that addiction is a product of other underlying factors is embedded in the professional world as strongly as it is in the layperson's mind. Alcoholics and addicts have been seen as poor prospects for therapy (and deadbeats when it comes to paying, to boot), which creates a vicious cycle of avoidance and stereotyping.

A male patient in his early 50s was referred to an addiction intensive outpatient program (IOP) for his drinking problems following a suicide attempt. When assessed in the drug and alcohol program, he reported that his suicidal ideation was secondary to his despair over not being able to manage his drinking. He further disclosed that he had been in outpatient psychotherapy with a psychologist for several years. His presenting complaint in psychotherapy was also to deal with his addiction, but the therapist, operating from a traditional psychodynamic model, saw the drinking as a symptom of his underlying depression. For several years, they explored the patient's conflicts and depression, and the patient continued to drink. When he would remind the therapist that his primary concern was about alcoholism, the therapist would reiterate that the drinking was only the superficial manifestation of underlying problems, and that this was the primary focus of treatment. Although well meaning, the psychologist's beliefs allowed the addiction to continue to worsen, until the patient's despair led to his suicide attempt. Fortunately, the attempt was mild and the patient was able to accept a referral to the addiction IOP, where he was oriented to AA and encouraged to attend meetings. Once again, he was fortunate to connect well with the fellowship, and he had little trouble maintaining sobriety. However, after several months, he reported that he was still depressed. This time, with his drinking problem out of the way, his depression was responsive to a combination of supportive psychotherapy and antidepressant medications (which had been discouraged previously because of his drinking).

As noted earlier, formal training in this area has been virtually nonexistent in the mental health field. Several surveys have found training in addictions treatment to be sorely lacking. Chiert, Gold, and Taylor (1994) reviewed course offerings and faculty interest in substance abuse in psychology programs, comparing three time periods (1978–1979, 1984, and 1991–1992). They found minimal differences across these three periods in the percentage of schools offering courses in this area (42%, 37%, and 38%, respectively) and only a slight trend in the percentage of courses that were elective (100%, 97%, and 95%). In 1992, although 52% of programs offered placements in drug and alcohol treatment settings, only 8.1% of students (15% in the programs offering them) availed themselves of these opportunities. Ratings of the adequacy of training were also low.

Annavi, Taube, Ja, and Duren (1999) found that 74% of psychologists surveyed had had no coursework in substance abuse in their graduate education. This stands in contrast to a survey of a separate cohort of clinicians in which 38% of their clients had substance abuse issues and 42% were at risk; 77% of the clinicians had at least one client with a drug or alcohol diagnosis and 83% had at least one recovering client.

More recently, Harwood, Kowalski, and Ameen (2004) reviewed training across several mental health professions. Apart from the specialty of substance abuse counselors, formal coursework in substance abuse was a relative rarity. The percentage of clinicians surveyed reporting formal coursework in this area was as follows:

Marital and family counselors: 53%
Professional counselors: 49%
Psychologists: 30%
Substance abuse counselors: 69%
Social workers: 38%

The figures for training in internships were even lower. Training via continuing education programs was somewhat higher for all disciplines, but 60% of psychologists and 57% of social workers had had no continuing education training in substance abuse whatsoever in the past year.

These findings stand in stark contrast with the observations of Miller and Brown (1997), who proposed that psychologists are particularly well-qualified to treat addiction. They pointed out that our treatments for addiction are largely psychological in nature, that addictions appear to respond to general laws of human behavior, and that therapist empathy, which is a component of general psychological training, is one of the most important therapeutic variables found in the treatment of addictions. The authors also pointed out that, given the prevalence of these problems in society in general, and particularly in clinical populations, some training in this area should be required. They also noted that one of the biggest obstacles is a lack of relevant training in graduate education, but they ignored the more general underlying biases against working with this population.

Within the area of training for substance abuse treatment, AA and NA, in particular, have been treated with skepticism and suspicion by professional practitioners. Some see them as cults or feel they interfere with psychotherapy ("diluting the transference" was the way one early supervisor put it) and steer clients away from it. When attention is given to "the program," it is often to reduce it to more familiar psychological constructs, such as group dynamics and symptom substitution. Bill Wilson's reliance on Carl Jung and William James in formulating his ideas is often cited by psychologically-minded writers, as if they are grown-ups claiming credit for a precocious child. One practitioner I know places alcoholic patients in a double bind in his referrals to AA—if they are successful, the problem is resolved, and they may then be amenable to psychotherapy; if they are unsuccessful, they were not motivated.

For its part, AA has been somewhat reluctant to subject itself to more rigorous scientific scrutiny, relying instead on periodic membership surveys and anecdotal evidence. Their reasons for this stance are understandable from their perspective, but it leaves questions about the actual outcomes of participation in the program. Much of the research has been done on 12-step facilitation (Nowinski & Baker, 1992), a modality in which such participation is encouraged and resistance is defused, but which is one step removed from actual AA participation; it serves as an analogue to actual AA involvement. Random assignment is difficult to achieve and, more significantly, violates one of the core precepts of the program—that it is a program of attraction.

This chasm is unfortunate for all concerned. Psychotherapy has a great deal to offer recovering people, if it can incorporate 12-step insights, rather than work on parallel, or counterproductive, areas. Addicted persons, particularly those with concomitant mental health problems (such as depression or marital conflicts) can benefit from psychotherapy that complements the very real work that can occur in the recovery process. Psychotherapy can assume a valuable role in motivating patients to seek recovery, in handling resistance to the process, negotiating lifestyle conflicts, exploring intrapsychic and interpersonal conflicts that can significantly impair progress, and addressing any related or even unrelated issues that emerge with sobriety.

On the other hand, the mental health professions are missing a bounty of knowledge, wisdom, and technique that can be gained from a better understanding of the 12-step concepts of addiction and recovery. Certainly, the intimate personal knowledge of addiction that a recovering counselor conveys, and the manner in which he or she conveys it, provide tremendous potential for learning by more formally trained mental health clinicians. Many mental health professionals have attended an AA or NA meeting and come away with a profound respect for the clinical skills of the meeting chair and members in general.

Furthermore, some very real advances in general psychological understanding have their roots in addiction treatment settings. I am thinking specifically of Miller's work on motivational interviewing (Miller & Rollnick, 2002) and Prochaska and DiClemente's work on stages of change theory (Prochaska, DiClemente, & Norcross, 1992). These innovations have far broader implications and usefulness beyond the addictions treatment world. Although these valuable insights are finding their way into addictions programs and enhancing interventions and treatment planning, they are only slowly gaining credibility in the larger world of mental health and psychiatric treatment, where they are equally relevant.

Psychological writers on AA, even those who have shed valuable light on its workings, have tended to reduce the phenomenon to more familiar psychological constructs. AA has been described and explained in terms of Winnicott's transitional objects (Speigel & Fewell, 2004), shift in epistemological stance (Bateson, 1972), affect regulation (Khantzian, Halliday, & McAuliffe, 1990), shared dependency, group dynamics, and so on. Rarely has the fellowship been accepted on its own terms.

Such study has been useful in helping us analyze and understand the mechanisms by which AA and the other 12-step fellowships (TSFs) operate. Unfortunately (in addition to fostering the professional–lay therapist split), these perspectives do not help us to utilize the knowledge of the program and do not provide a guide to understanding it on its own terms. These are academic perspectives, with little direct value to those engaged in clinical practice. These views do not reach the people who may benefit the most from them.

The primary purpose of this book is not to analyze the program but to make it more accessible, to serve as a guide to what you might encounter in attending a meeting, or what clients might deal with in working the program themselves. There is certainly plenty of room for those who wish to study the program—some may wish to analyze the program in its component parts for the sake of assessing the effective elements, or to relate it to more philosophical or spiritual traditions. However, this volume is designed to help the clinician learn about the fellowship as it exists today, in its fullness. These lessons are equally valid whether working in a private practice or in an addiction treatment program.

While we are increasingly aware that AA and NA are only two of many options for recovery (Volpicelli & Szalavitz, 2000), these programs remain among the most highly accessible and potentially beneficial avenues available. Given the ubiquitous nature of TSFs, and the lack of training provided in professional schools, it is important that clinicians become aware of the nature of this fellowship. Working in partnership with such an influential and potentially powerful movement for personal change benefits both sides of this partnership; clinical breakthroughs in psychotherapy are reinforced and enhanced in "the rooms," while issues that emerge in the struggle for sobriety and recovery can be processed in greater depth in the intimacy of the therapeutic relationship. It is a common clinical experience to see a patient make transformative changes in his or her life over the course of working the program above and beyond gaining a stable sober lifestyle, and in addition to the work done in individual therapy.

Unfortunately for the clinician entering this field (or for a more seasoned one who has not had exposure to it), few resources are available for guidance on this issue. Most frequently, AA and NA are referenced in surveys describing more general approaches to treating addiction. In such articles, the general background and principles are summarized, but the actual process of working with clients involved in these programs is rarely addressed. Each clinician is left to work through similar difficulties without any formal set of guidelines or understanding of the basic principles involved. A number of books dissect and elaborate on 12-step principles, but these generally presume the reader's familiarity with the fellowship and are often aimed at recovering people themselves, not at practitioners.

For a mental health practitioner encountering this field for the first time, the alternate worldview and apparent foreign language of this treatment can be jarring, to say the least. One of the biggest bones of contention is the concept of powerlessness, a cornerstone of the AA program. To a mental health clinician, for whom empowerment is usually assumed as an unspoken core value, the concept is anathema. To an addictions counselor, the acknowledgment of powerlessness over alcohol is the beginning of a shift in consciousness and the relationship to alcohol (Bateson, 1972; Brown, 1985). Later on, it might even be the key to spiritual insight (Kurtz & Ketcham, 1992). Although there are some ways to bridge this difference (limiting the concept to refer only to the loss of control over one's alcohol intake, for example), fundamental shifts are necessary to fully incorporate this concept and its many implications.

A patient was referred to an IOP for her alcohol and marijuana abuse by her mental health therapist, within a managed care system. She was doing well in her recovery program and began attending AA regularly. Her mental health therapist, while quite competent, did not understand the perspective of the TSF. In particular, the therapist had issues with the concept of powerlessness that is so central to the AA worldview. As this issue was explored on both sides of the fence, the client was caught between two widely diverging worldviews. Ultimately, she chose to leave AA and work on empowerment issues, a clinically valid goal, but one that left her less supported in her recovery work and vulnerable to relapse to substance use.

Another potential obstacle for mental health clinicians is the spiritual nature of the program. Religion and spirituality are uncomfortable topics for many mental health clinicians. Again, there have been many attempts to soft sell this aspect of 12-step programs, or to water it down. However, there are few ways around the spirituality at the core of the program without losing one of its most powerful elements. Those who have benefited the most from AA are usually those who have found a way to incorporate the "spirituality of imperfection" (Kurtz & Ketcham, 1992) into their lives in a broader manner than relating it only to alcohol. The distinction between spirituality and religion is frequently made, and is often blurred by the commonly used language, but it is important to reinforce this distinction rather than gloss it over. The evangelical Christian roots of AA may not be essential to the program, but they are quite obvious to any observer or participant. In such a prominent position, these references can deter those who reject religious overtones (including, initially, Bill W., the co-founder of AA).

Other areas of difference in values and technique include the common use of groups and the relative devaluing of individual insight-oriented therapy, the blurring of traditional therapeutic boundaries, and the central role of self-disclosure. Any of these can present a major crisis in orientation for a newcomer to the substance abuse treatment field.

There are places where psychotherapy and recovery coexist. A cogent argument has been made that all such treatment should be integrated, rather than compartmentalized or sequenced (Minkoff, 1989, 2001). While this is certainly a laudable goal, the exact mechanics have not emerged, with the current best practices still best described as peaceful coexistence.

More often, however, the integration of these modalities is poor or nonexistent. Most addictions and dual diagnosis programs must provide a description of their program philosophy and modalities for licensing or accrediting agencies. By and large, such descriptions match the confusion of the field, in that the role of psychotherapy is touted but not explicated. A typical program description might state, "We use a variety of modalities to address the denial of the patient, including gestalt, humanistic, cognitive and 12-step," which does little to provide a real picture of the workings of the treatment. A patient may attend a group on the progression of addictive disease (or worse yet, a process group without any specific focus), then go to an individual therapy session in which childhood issues or current relationship problems are discussed. The link between these issues is never spelled out and indeed may be unclear even to the clinicians.

> At one point early in my career, I conducted daily group therapy on an inpatient addiction treatment ward in a psychiatric hospital. The group was an open one, in which no topic was specified and frequent silences were the norm. Often, people would spend time talking about the damage wrought by their addiction or their resolve to beat it. Sometimes the talk was boring, sometimes deeply moving. However, I recall thinking on a near daily basis, "What does this have to do with their addiction?" My answer to myself was that if they felt better, they would not have as much of a reason to get high. After all, greater minds than mine had designed this program and they must have had a reason. Even then I knew that I was on thin ice with these answers, and it was only significantly later that I realized what was the proper role and structure of group therapy in an addiction setting (and that this was not it).

There are distinct challenges to this task. Addictions treatment and traditional psychotherapy speak substantially different languages. There are differences in values and in practices, both explicit and unstated. In general, there has been a far greater effort to train addictions practitioners to understand mental health issues (O'Connell & Beyer, 2002) than vice versa. For a mental health clinician to learn to understand this area, it is important to learn to accept it on its own terms; the language, the concepts, and the practices must be seen as valid in their own right, and worth understanding. It is far too easy to view the fellowship as a paraprofessional group or adjunctive (albeit a useful adjunct) to therapy, and to not take it seriously, or to translate its approach into more familiar psychological terms. There will be time and place for this, both later in the book and after this task has been assimilated. Analysis of AA is a valid and necessary activity, but it must be based on a full understanding of what it believes and how it works. For now, I encourage you to take this material in with an open mind, and to see the phenomenon of addiction from a somewhat different, and perhaps less familiar, vantage point.

My own experience in the field is typical and instructive. My entire training in substance abuse in graduate school consisted of one class on substance abuse in a semester survey course on psychopathology. AA was mentioned but was portrayed as an oddity, a curiosity. I had no training in it during an internship at a large inner-city psychiatric department; despite encountering addicted patients on a regular basis, substance abuse was rarely referenced as a problem to be addressed.

In my first job in an outpatient drug treatment clinic, I was told we worked on a psychotherapy model and we simply conducted therapy as usual. The treatment was probably identical to that provided in the mental health clinic upstairs—the distinction was that all our referrals had drug problems. However, our sister outpatient program, an alcoholism clinic, featured recovering individuals as therapists. AA meetings were held on the premises several times a week, and I could see, through the cloud of cigarette smoke, that they were crowded and animated. Initially, I was put off by therapy conducted with the door open, by therapists who openly spoke of seeing their clients outside of the clinic, and who read from a thick blue book (which I presumed to be a Bible). I was chagrined to see that their clients came back more frequently and seemed to be getting better to a larger degree than ours. What was going on?

In my next position, in an addictions ward of a psychiatric hospital, I became a little more closely acquainted with what was going on. Here the 12-step program was explicitly endorsed and was the center of the clinical program, with structured activities built around the steps and the program. AA or NA meetings were held daily, with attendance required. One evening, when a client cancelled an outpatient appointment and I had an hour to kill, I decided to go upstairs and check out the AA meeting. It was a revelation to me. In contrast to the relative vagueness with which I was conducting my own groups and individual sessions, these meetings had clear focus, established values, and a level of honesty that was bracing and refreshing. I found the figure and ground shifting in my work—the AA program became the central vehicle for personal change, with the psychotherapy as an adjunct.

It did not hurt that I was the first professional staff member to attend one of the meetings, and this one event branded me as more understanding and knowledgeable than my fellow psychologists and psychiatrists. This effect lasted for months, long after that particular cohort of patients had left the program. I recommend this "technique" to anyone working in such a setting.

My "training," at this point, was largely based on what I learned from the recovering therapists and from the clients themselves. There was little in the professional psychology literature to help me understand and use the approach I was learning by observation and osmosis. I actually started to look through that thick book, which turned out to be the Big Book of Alcoholics Anonymous. The pithy sayings of the AA program started to seem like nuggets of wisdom rather than maudlin clichés. It appeared that there was no possible situation that had not been anticipated with an aphorism. (I became convinced of this when a member of one of my groups reported that he wanted to reconcile with his girlfriend who was still drinking. One of the old-timers in the group muttered, "Beneath every skirt there's a slip.")

Several years later, I ran another outpatient program with a more refined sense of treatment goals and strategies. While working largely by the seat of our pants, we implemented a structured program, blending a specific, focused approach to addiction treatment, based on the work of James Milam (Milam & Ketcham, 1983) and Ron Rogers and Scott McMillin (1989), with more generic psychotherapeutic interventions. Clients attended our program 3 nights a week for 7 weeks, then 2 nights a week for 10 weeks. Following this, a number of clients requested further contact, so we created a weekly "alumni group," which was intended to be a general Yalom-styled group therapy. It was in this group that I learned about the power of the 12-step fellowship.

Initially, we had set out the requirements for membership, which were simple enough: completion of our (or an equivalent) program and regular attendance at 12-step (or equivalent) meetings. What I witnessed, however, was greater than the sum of these parts. By virtue of self-selection, the group consisted of highly motivated individuals, all of whom were highly invested in the TSF. Most evenings, after the group ended and I finished my paperwork, I would leave the office only to find them continuing the meeting in the parking lot. For the most part, I realized that my role was to listen and learn. I absorbed the lingo. I observed dramatic transformations. I witnessed true fellowship in action and was impressed and inspired.

I will never forget the evening in which one member of the group showed up and reported that he had relapsed. The member, understandably demoralized, reported on the circumstances of his drinking. The group displayed an understandable degree of concern and compassion, yet did not coddle him or excuse his behavior. Without any overt coordination, tasks were assigned—before the end of the group his wife was called, a ride was arranged, his car was driven home, and so on. I had no reason to doubt that he was in excellent hands and required little input from me.

In this context, I glimpsed the power of the fellowship, and the kinds of personal changes, above and beyond the simple (and necessary) attainment of sobriety, that were possible with this program. Although in recent years I have expanded my view to include other options for recovery in addition to the TSF, I have always understood how valuable and central it is. I believe that an understanding of the TSF is essential to anyone working with addicts and alcoholics in any setting, regardless of the theoretical orientation of the program or of the individual. It seems to me a disservice that so much of the current psychological literature in the field makes scant, or disparaging, reference to the TSF. I also recognized that some of the lessons of the fellowship had larger implications for psychotherapy and for life itself.

On my first day of my graduate school program, the director of clinical training, Jay Efran, gave a little speech, which I later learned was a traditional part of each class's orientation. He described the debate about whether psychology was more properly seen as a branch of biology or philosophy; he contended that one's undergraduate major was the primary determinant of where one stood on this issue. "And that's why I can't understand how anybody can learn psychology without a solid grounding in electrical engineering," he concluded. On this same basis, I feel that a solid grounding in the TSF is essential to understanding addiction and addiction treatment and can provide a far-reaching enhancement of one's therapeutic work in any area.

Early on in my career in the addictions treatment field, I attended a workshop on group work with addicted people. The one thing I remembered clearly afterward was the leader's admonition: "If you are going to work in this area, you must learn to speak the language of recovery and of the AA program." This may have been the most valuable piece of training I have had in this area. This book is an attempt to convey not only the language, but also the insights of the recovery program, in an effort to enhance the work of therapists and the lives of their clients.

Chapter 2
Background and Basics

In late 1934 I attended a patient who, though he had been a competent businessman of good earning capacity, was an alcoholic of a type I had come to regard as hopeless.

—Dr. William Silkworth
Alcoholics Anonymous (2001)

THERE IS A GREAT DEAL OF AMBIGUITY about the nature of AA and other TSFs. Much of this reflects ambiguity within the writings of the fellowship itself (Wallace, 2006) or differences in application and interpretation among various TSFs. One common interpretation is that they are "self-help" groups. Another views them as "mutual aid societies." In some literatures, AA can be found as a "treatment modality"; in Project MATCH, this was operationalized as "12-Step Facilitation" (Nowinski & Baker, 1992), a manualized treatment designed to encourage client engagement in the fellowship. There has also been reference to AA as a social movement, and much has been made of Aldous Huxley's description of Bill Wilson as "the greatest social architect of the 20th century" (Cheever, 2004).

As noted, there is even some ambiguity within the fellowship as well. Bill Wilson, while generally avoiding the use of the term "disease" (in an attempt to minimize controversy and avoid stepping on the toes of the medical profession), did use the terms *illness* and *malady* (Wilson, 1960); he generally was occupied with describing the nature of the alcoholic rather than being bothered to categorize the disease (Kurtz, 1982). Similarly, he made reference to "this band of alcoholics" and "the fellowship." In a similar fashion, he may have been attempting to avoid petrifying the movement by avoiding painting it into a corner. There is also an important distinction to be made between AA as a fellowship and AA as a program of recovery.

Perhaps this is not surprising, given the loose format and anarchic structure of AA itself. The fellowship provides guidelines, not dogma. Members (there are no requirements for membership except "a desire to stop drinking" and there are no membership lists, pledges, or membership cards) are free to interpret these guidelines in any way that works for them. Every meeting is autonomous, with membership free to structure it however feels best for that particular group. AA members on vacation in other parts of the country (or world) have commented on regional differences in practice and tradition in meetings and in membership, and yet there is a great deal of commonality and welcome in any meeting that one would drop in on. While this provides a positive degree of flexibility in accommodating a diverse membership, it makes generalizations about the fellowship much more difficult. It can be said that there may be as many versions of AA as there are AA members.

One thing is clear—AA is not a form of "treatment." While at times in the course of its history the movement came close to lending itself or its name to actual treatment programs (Kurtz, 1989; White, 1998), it has clearly differentiated itself from any formal role as a treatment program. In fact, the distinction between AA as a fellowship or program of recovery and its application in treatment settings has created a certain sense of tension and conflict, especially for AA members who also work in the field. The pervasive application of 12-step concepts in treatment settings is not an official extension of AA or NA, despite their assistance and cooperation with such activities (such as conducting meetings within treatment programs). There is a clear distinction between the activities of AA and the activities of programs utilizing TSF concepts as their foundation. This is a subtle distinction that is often lost in the public mind and, at times, in practice.

The easiest point of access to AA is a historical one. By understanding AA as it evolved, the current principles and practices make sense and come into clearer focus. Although much of AA functions in a condition of apparent anarchy, its historical roots have been well documented and preserved by the fellowship itself in its literature (*AA Comes of Age, Pass It On*, and in the Big Book itself), as well as by other observers (Cheever, 2004; Kurtz, 1989; White, 1998). A film (*My Name Is Bill*, starring James Woods and James Garner) also provides a fairly accurate depiction of the events of the early days of the fellowship, and a recent off-Broadway play (*Bill W. and Dr. Bob*) covers much of the same material. All of the above are highly recommended to readers of this volume.

Furthermore, familiarity with "the bedtime story" (as Bill called it) is essential for anyone working with this population. This story is part of the mythology of the fellowship and is a staple of conversation among novices and veterans alike. The story is repeated, like a favorite fairy tale or legend, and provides comfort and recognition for all members and friends of the program. Awareness of the background of AA is an important tool in demonstrating clinical competence in this area.

In the simple version of this story, AA began with a meeting between Bill Wilson, an alcoholic New York stock trader struggling to remain sober, and Dr. Bob Smith, an alcoholic proctologist, in Akron, Ohio, in 1935. In fact, the historical roots of AA begin long before this legendary meeting. As Bill White (1998) documents in his brilliant history *Slaying the Dragon*, there were recovery movements in America for at least 100 years prior to the formation of AA. Some have been widespread and influential, and most of the elements of AA were anticipated, either individually or in combination, in various of its predecessors. The Washingtonian movement, in the 1840s, emphasized "experience sharing" in much the same manner as AA speakers today share their "experience and hope" in telling "what it was like, what happened, and how it is now"; they also suggested ongoing service to other suffering alcoholics. The Sons of Temperance and the Order of the Good Templars pioneered the principle of anonymity in their secret meetings. The Water Street Mission and the Salvation Army stressed the central role of spiritual conversion and rebirth in coming to terms with one's alcoholism. Just as Henry Ford's enduring legacy is the implementation of the assembly line, not the Model T itself, one of the startling breakthroughs of Bill Wilson and AA was its ability to structure the program to survive the death of its founders. Bill can be seen as a brilliant synthesizer more than as a creator from whole cloth.

Ernest Kurtz (1989), in his scholarly history of AA, identifies four pivotal events in the history of the program. The first is the treatment of a man named Rowland H. by Carl Jung, which occurred around 1931. The second was a visit by Ebby T., a childhood friend, to Bill Wilson in November 1934, introducing him to the Oxford Group. The third is Bill's spiritual conversion experience in December 1934 and his subsequent reading of William James. The fourth is Bill's pivotal meeting with Dr. Bob Smith. I review these events, although not in this order. (In keeping with the AA tradition of anonymity, I refer to AA members other than Bill Wilson and Bob Smith by first name and last initial only).

In most depictions, the story of AA is the story of Bill Wilson, and we will abide by this, mostly accurate, narrative thread as the logical way to hold these events together. Bill Wilson (often referred to within the fellowship as Bill W. or simply Bill) was a Vermonter who found his way to New York City, following a stint in the army during World War I. Brought up in a stereotypically stoic Vermont household in a respected family, Bill demonstrated intelligence and determination, but also social awkwardness. These traits were exacerbated by his father's alcoholism and ultimate abandonment of the family, and by his mother's later abandonment of Bill and his sister to pursue her own life and career. Bill was subsequently raised by his maternal grandparents, who were well intentioned but ill prepared to raise a young man of Bill's sensitive temperament. His grandfather was a stoic man who displayed little ability to nurture his grandson so as to reduce his sense of loss and isolation.

Bill suffered a nervous breakdown following the sudden death of his sweetheart when he was 19 years old. He fell into a profound depression, and was barely able to speak or function. He failed classes and flunked his entrance exams to college (Cheever, 2004). He floundered for nearly a year. This was to be the first of many depressions in his life, which haunted him even into his later sobriety.

In Vermont, despite a secure upbringing, he felt himself the outsider, particularly in relation to the rich and sophisticated New Yorkers who vacationed in the vicinity. Ultimately he married one of these New Yorkers, Lois Burnham, and their futures were intertwined for the rest of their lives, through good times and awful. Bill was brought up in a temperance household and early on took a pledge to abstain. He had seen what alcohol had done to his father and to his family. His early experiences with alcohol occurred largely in the context of his introduction to a more sophisticated social world in New York, primarily through his wife, who hailed from a socially prominent family. Bill soon learned that a drink or two could transform him from a shy hick to a popular raconteur. He described his first drink (in New Bedford, Massachusetts, at age 21):

> Lo, the miracle! That strange barrier that had existed between me and all men and women seemed to instantly go down. I felt that I belonged where I was, belonged to life; I belonged to the universe; I was a part of things at last. Oh, the magic of those first three or four drinks.
>
> (Alcoholics Anonymous, 1984, p. 56)

In New York, Bill found success on Wall Street, primarily by providing field analyses of companies and making recommendations to brokerage houses based on his firsthand observations. This information was often gleaned from conversations with company workers in local bars. It is unclear if his choice of vocation was made to facilitate his addiction or if it was simply an unhappy coincidence.

Bill's descent into alcoholism was both steady and devastating. The once-prosperous Wall Street mover and shaker eventually had the mortgage to his house (formerly his wife's family home) foreclosed. Each of his promises to his wife for sobriety was followed by a dramatic relapse. The inscriptions in their family Bible can serve as a partial chronicle of Bill's personal struggle and their marital strain. They are emblematic of many similar desperate struggles (in Delbanco and Delbanco, 1995):

> To my beloved wife that has endured so much let this stand as evidence of my pledge to you that I have finished with drink forever.
> Bill October 20, 1928

Thanksgiving Day 1928. My strength is renewed a thousand-fold in my love for you.

To tell you once more that I am finished with it. I love you. Jan. 12, 1929

Finally and for a lifetime. Thank you for your love. September 30, 1930

Bill went through a series of medical treatments for detoxification, but rarely maintained sobriety for any significant period of time. Whether in celebration of specific events or out of despair, he relapsed repeatedly and severely. They survived thanks to Lois's small jobs and her family's largesse. Eventually, all connected with him assumed that he would require institutionalization. Bill wrote, "I had been overwhelmed. Alcohol was my master," (Alcoholics Anonymous, 2001, p.8).

In the Big Book of Alcoholics Anonymous, Bill describes his first encounter in a journey leading to his sobriety and his founding of the fellowship (although this corresponds to Kurtz's second founding event). Following one of his detoxes, and during a period of unemployment, Bill found himself drinking at home. He received a visit from a longtime friend and old drinking buddy, Ebby T. For once, Ebby refused a drink, and appeared to Bill to be "fresh-skinned and glowing." Bill, relieved that he would not need to share his gin, asked what this was all about. Ebby replied, with a smile, "I've got religion."

The religion that Ebby brought to Bill that day was in the form of the Oxford Group, a fundamentalist Christian group that sought to reestablish the values of early Christianity. The Oxford Group was founded in 1908 as the First Century Christian Fellowship. It flourished in the 1920s and 1930s under the leadership of Frank Buchman in Great Britain and Sam Shoemaker in the United States. (Much later, it would morph into a group called Moral Rearmament, blending conservative religion and politics.) The relevant features of the Oxford Group were their insistence on surrendering to God's will, taking personal inventory and sharing this inventory with another, making restitution for harm that had been done, and the practice of selfless giving to others. Although there was a distinct elitist element to the group (it sought out and displayed membership by celebrities and notables), they had taken a particular interest in working with alcoholics, who seemed responsive to their methods. To some measure this was attributable to their insistence on viewing tangible signs of change rather than simple professions of faith—many Oxford Group members spontaneously made such efforts as quitting drinking and smoking.

Ebby described the practices of the Oxford Group, in terms that will be familiar to all who are acquainted with the TSF. Ebby suggested that Bill admit that he had been licked, that despite his best efforts, he had been unable to control his alcohol intake—alcohol had won. The answer, Ebby suggested, was that Bill turn his will over to God. Bill found himself wondering, viewing his friend's sobriety, if the religious people were, in fact, right after all. However, the most important breakthrough for Bill came in Ebby's suggestion that Bill was free to choose whatever conception of God he might feel comfortable with. Bill, a skeptic at best, somehow found that this suggestion began to melt away his resistance.

At this point, it is necessary to return to the first link in Kurtz's chain of events. Preceding this meeting, Ebby himself had been inspired by his friend Rowland H. A desperate alcoholic, Rowland had journeyed to Switzerland for treatment with Carl Jung, the former disciple of Sigmund Freud. He was in treatment for a year but soon relapsed to alcoholism. Upon returning to Zurich to meet with Dr. Jung again, Rowland was surprised and dismayed to hear Jung tell him that there was nothing further that medical science could offer him, and that his only hope lay in the possibility of a religious conversion, however unlikely such a happening might be. In later correspondence with Jung, Bill described this conversation as "the first link in the chain of events that led to the founding of Alcoholics Anonymous" (Kurtz, 1989, p. 8). (In later years, questions were raised about the authenticity of Rowland's meetings with Jung, although more recent research suggests that the meetings did occur, although the dates may be off.)

Subsequently, Rowland found help in the Oxford Group, which offered him a spiritual conversion experience and allowed him to maintain extended sobriety for the first time. In the spirit of the Oxford

Group's belief in service to others, at one point he learned that his old friend Ebby T. faced institutionalization as a result of his alcoholism. Together with a friend, Rowland intervened, had Ebby released to his custody and introduced Ebby to the Oxford Group. Fortunately, Ebby was amenable (after all, it was better than life in an institution) and was able to establish his own sobriety. It was a few months later that he decided to reach out to his own "hopeless" pal, Bill Wilson. (It is sad to note that Ebby suffered numerous relapses in his later years, but Bill never rejected him and continued to refer to him as his first sponsor.)

After Bill's meeting with Ebby, he attended an Oxford Group meeting. Despite his cynicism, he was impressed that he did not drink again that evening, despite walking past numerous bars. Eventually, returning to drink, he attempted to blend what he had learned at the meeting with his own experience. He went, yet again, to Towns Hospital, to place himself in the care of Dr. William Silkworth, who was known as "the little doctor who loved drunks." Dr. Silkworth had been evolving his own theory of alcoholism, likening it to an allergic reaction to alcohol. One afternoon, in desperation, Bill followed Ebby's advice and appealed to God to save him from himself. What followed, in Bill's words:

> Suddenly the room filled up with a great white light. I was caught up into an ecstasy which there are no words to describe . . . it burst upon me that I was a free man. . . . A great peace stole over me and I thought, "No matter how wrong things seem to be, they are still all right. Things are all right with God and his world."
>
> (Alcoholics Anonymous, 1990, p. 63)

After this spiritual experience, Bill never drank again. Dr. Silkworth, who had read William James's book *The Varieties of Religious Experience*, provided reassurance that he had not gone insane and lent the book to Bill. Bill viewed "ego deflation at depth" as the core conversion experience that alcoholics must experience to be able to shed the chains of addiction.

Bill, with Lois in tow, embarked on a mission to convey this message to other alcoholics. Night after night, he brought drunks home to be fed, bathed, and put to bed. Day after day they left, only to return to drinking. His preaching was not effective in helping restore them to sanity, although he was later to realize that it was most useful to him in his quest for ongoing sobriety.

Eventually returning to employment on Wall Street, Bill found himself in Akron, Ohio, in May 1935, negotiating a corporate buyout. One afternoon, waiting for word about the deal, he found himself eyeing the bar in his hotel and realized that an unhealthy urge was slowly growing within him. Feeling isolated, he decided to see if he could contact another alcoholic to talk to. He realized that to save himself he must carry his message to another alcoholic (Alcoholics Anonymous, 2001). He called a number of local churches with his unusual request and eventually reached Mrs. Henrietta Sieberling, who arranged a meeting with a local "hopeless" drunk, Dr. Bob Smith.

Smith reports that he approached the meeting with impatience ("Dr. Bob's Nightmare" is one of the personal stories in the Big Book). As a long-standing alcoholic, he had been preached to by the best and anticipated more of the same. He put a 15-minute limit on the conversation going in. To his surprise, Bill said that the meeting was not to benefit Dr. Smith—it was to benefit himself. They talked for over 6 hours and to his own amazement, Dr. Bob stopped drinking (temporarily, as it turned out). Dr. Bob attributed this change to the talk. "He was the first living human with whom I had ever talked, who knew what he was talking about in regard to alcoholism from actual experience" (Alcoholics Anonymous, 2001, p. 180). Bill did not try to convert or pressure him, but presented him with the experience of his own alcoholism, an experience they shared and which bound them together.

Dr. Bob relapsed several weeks later while at a medical convention. He delayed restoring himself to sobriety until he could complete a surgery that had been scheduled—he knew that the shakes would not help. He took his last drink on June 10, 1935, which is regarded as the founding date of Alcoholics Anonymous.

This new partnership was not yet a fellowship. Bill and Dr. Bob spent much of the summer at Bob's home in Akron discussing their discovery and its implications. They recruited new members one by one and were delighted to discover that their method worked for others as well as themselves. Eventually, a small group of recovering alcoholics formed in Akron, later in Cleveland, and, upon Bill's return home, in New York. By 1937, they had 40 sober members; by 1939 they had 100. It was hardly a movement, but the momentum was growing.

Initially, much of this work occurred in the context of the Oxford Group and followed their steps. Eventually, the alcoholic contingent found it necessary to make a break with the parent group. For one thing, the Oxfords were bent on proselytizing and sought prominent names to attract others; the alcoholics were concerned with preserving their anonymity. Although the Oxfords had initially supported the inclusion of alcoholic members, as their numbers grew, they were viewed as more of a liability. Also, it became obvious that the alcoholics responded better to persuasion than to the coercive missionary style of the Oxford group. The split was cordial but appears to have been met with relief on both sides.

In response to the group's desire to codify the process, Bill set to work on a set of steps to encapsulate the method. Much of the 12 steps that emerged was based on the steps of the Oxford Group, which had provided the cocoon from which AA emerged. Initially, Bill articulated six principles of recovery:

1. We admitted we were powerless over alcohol.
2. We got honest with ourselves.
3. We got honest with another person, in confidence.
4. We made amends for harms done others.
5. We worked with other alcoholics without demand for prestige or money.
6. We prayed to God to help us to do these things as best we could. (White, 1998)

Over time, and in response to considerable feedback from other members, the list grew to the familiar 12 steps. As Bill described the process, he wrote them in a rush in one evening, and they required little subsequent revision. The most significant changes were in the way that the references to God were framed: first by substituting the phrase "a Power greater than ourselves" and second by adding the phrase "[God], *as we understand him.*"

Eventually, in an attempt to spread the word, Bill began to write a book to describe the process of recovery that he and Dr. Bob had developed, and to provide case examples to inspire others. Over the course of 1938 and 1939, Bill, with continuous feedback from other AAs, wrote what we now know as the Big Book of AA, formally titled *Alcoholics Anonymous*. Then, as now, the book consisted of a first section of program description and a second section of case histories. Over the years, newer stories have been added and substituted, but the first section has remained largely intact.

The Big Book (so called because it was originally printed with thick paper and in large print to make it more accessible to alcoholics with unsteady hands and vision) did not set the world on fire. It was not reviewed favorably in the medical press. Sales were slow and the fellowship floundered financially, buoyed by loans from members and sympathizers.

The first great boost in AA membership followed an extraordinarily positive article about the group in the *Saturday Evening Post* in March 1941 by Jack Alexander. The office was flooded with requests for information. The Alexander article is credited with a quadrupling of the AA membership to 8,000 by the end of the year.

Growth since that time has been exponential. Recent data from the AA Web site gives an estimate of over 2 million members in 100,000 groups based in 150 countries. Despite this expansion, the program remains free and open, with no central leadership or binding policy.

What are the lessons to be derived from this story (Alcoholics Anonymous, 1984)? Quite simply, one is that facing alcoholism on one's own is a losing proposition—alcoholism will win. Second is that acknowledging the fact of one's addiction opens the path to taking constructive action. Third is that preaching and cajoling addicts is not an effective strategy to change their behavior. The fourth is that by teaming up with others with the same affliction, change is possible. The fifth is that a spiritual approach can work to end the cycle of addiction.

Basic Principles of Alcoholics Anonymous

It is useful to contrast the AA model of addiction with other common models. Rogers and McMillin (1989) have identified several other prevailing models. The dry moral and wet moral models view alcohol itself as the culprit. The former presumes that alcohol will eventually seduce anyone who indulges in it and is inherently evil; the latter places the blame on the alcoholic for his or her irresponsible use of a dangerous substance. (Prohibition is the logical response to this ideology). The psychoanalytic model views alcoholism as a manifestation of underlying psychological conflicts, often enough related to improper weaning and a resultant oral fixation. Other related psychological models emphasize an underlying addictive personality or inadequate coping skills. The family model locates the problem in the interactions within the family; the alcoholic is expressing that conflict in his or her drinking. In all of these paradigms, the addiction itself is viewed as a symptom, not as a problem in and of itself.

In the view of AA, the nature of alcoholism remains somewhat vague, perhaps purposefully so. As Ernest Kurtz (1982) has pointed out, Bill's primary focus was on understanding the dynamics of the alcoholic, not on speculation about the origins of the disease. Bill variously refers to alcoholism as a craving, a malady, an illness, an affliction, or "a seemingly hopeless state of mind and body," and disavowed presenting a medical analysis. The closest we come to a formal definition comes in Dr. Silkworth's preface to the Big Book, "The Doctor's Opinion" (Alcoholics Anonymous, 2001, p. xxviii), in which he states that "the action of alcohol on these chronic alcoholics is a manifestation of an allergy; that the phenomenon of craving is limited to this class and never occurs in the average temperate drinker." This definition of alcoholism as "an allergy coupled with a craving" has become embedded in the mythology of AA. The disease concept of alcoholism is implied here but never specifically articulated, and it was not until 1960, with Jellinek's publication of *The Disease Concept of Alcoholism*, that this idea crystallized in the literature and in the public mind.

However, other views of addiction are implied within the TSF, and one is that addiction is a spiritual disease. No specific mechanism is identified for this problem, but the language used clearly indicates the spiritual underpinnings of the disorder. This can be understood in a literal religious sense, but Bill was clear in cautioning that the spiritual approach was not the same as the religious one. Prior to the strict invocation of anonymity, Bill Wilson published one article under his own name, based on a talk he gave to the New York Medical Society (Wilson, 1944), in which he provides an early, and simplified, presentation of the AA program. In it he states, "The alcoholic's basic trouble is self-centeredness . . . he has forgotten the brotherhood of man." (p. 1806). One way to view his approach to spirituality is to see it as a form of humanism, that alcoholism reflects a lack of "honesty, humility, unselfishness, tolerance, generosity, love, etc." (p. 1806). While the spiritual roots of addiction may be vague, clearer is the spiritual path prescribed for recovery.

The third view of alcoholism found within AA is a psychological one. Many of Bill's descriptions focus on psychodynamic issues and utilize much of the psychodynamic language prevalent in the heyday of Freudian psychoanalysis. AA writings are full of references to alcoholic immaturity (it is no coincidence that the first book of AA history is titled *AA Comes of Age*), character defects, and "self-will run riot." Despite the spiritual orientation and disavowal of earlier psychological constructs, Bill's view of alcoholism is largely borrowed from psychological sources. Indeed, he was open about his correspondence with Carl Jung about Rowland H. and his reading of William James following his "hot flash" experience.

The most important distinction of AA's conception of alcoholism from its predecessors is in the focus on alcoholism as the primary issue. Despite any underlying causes or determinants, alcoholism is seen as a primary disorder in its own right. Instead of working on underlying problems, the alcoholic is to deal directly with alcohol itself. Instead of approaching the disorder with a functional analysis ("Why am I drinking?"), he or she is encouraged to take a structural view ("How does my drinking work?") in order to gain a perspective on it that might be useful in arresting its progress.

It is also helpful to consider the appraisal of William White (1998), who felt that the founders of AA were not seeking scientific certainty but were searching for "metaphorical truths." Their view of addiction was based, at least in some small part, on the need to find a language that would be marketable to the average alcoholic. Their interest in why people became alcoholic was much less important than working on a pragmatic solution to this problem. It is remarkable, then, how much of their thinking is compatible with modern conceptions of addiction (Erickson, 2007).

Abstinence (Sobriety)

AA is unequivocal in its insistence that abstinence, or sobriety, is the foundation of further growth and is key to arresting the progression of the disease. Efforts at moderation are generally seen as misguided, and are signs that the individual has not fully absorbed the message, and has not fully surrendered. While the Big Book offers advice for those uncertain of their alcoholism on controlled drinking, this is widely seen as a rhetorical suggestion, and that for the true alcoholic, sobriety is the only resolution of the problem.

As clear and central as this is in the case of AA and NA, where the rest of one's life can easily be spent without indulging in drugs or alcohol, the notion of abstinence becomes more elusive in the case of "process" or behavioral addictions, such as sex, eating, gambling, and so on. Abstinence requires a more circumspect definition in these cases.

It might be easier to view abstinence in the case of behavioral addictions as "abstainence," for example, abstaining from destructive or compulsive behaviors. A person with a compulsive eating disorder certainly must continue to eat, but may be able, within some parameters, to distinguish between healthy, sustaining nutrition and binge eating to satisfy addictive needs. This often presents a more difficult judgment call for both patient and clinician, more difficult than simply whether the patient has ingested drugs or drunk alcohol (although even this question is not always as clear as it may seem).

> Several female members of an IOP group went out for lunch after a morning group session. The next day they mentioned, in passing, that several of them had enjoyed the snapper soup at the restaurant.

28

> The therapist asked if they had put a few drops of sherry in the soup, as is the common custom. Several had done so, without thinking about it. "Then you were not sober yesterday," the therapist pronounced. A heated debate ensued about the relevance of a mere few drops of sherry versus the intent of avoiding all forms of alcohol at any cost.

Abstinence is frequently distinguished from recovery. In this view, abstinence (equivalent to sobriety) is the simple state of not using addictive or mind-altering substances. Recovery is a further state of making changes to one's thinking, lifestyle, and behaviors, marked by honesty and humility about oneself and one's condition. Abstinence without recovery is often referred to as the "dry-drunk" state—sober, but still stuck in the same rut of behaviors and attitudes that marked one's addictive state. Generally, it is assumed that this is an unstable state, likely to lead back to active addiction. Abstinence and recovery, therefore, are different from each other but are intimately related. In a circular fashion, abstinence is a necessary precondition for recovery, but recovery is necessary to maintain stable sobriety.

Recovery: Change in Personality and Lifestyle

Alcoholism is so integrally woven into the fabric of the alcoholic life that it is impossible to remove it without changing a great deal more of the context of the addiction. This would include changes in lifestyle, cognitions, habits, attitudes, values, and so forth. In many ways, these changes are far more difficult than the act of attaining initial sobriety.

> A patient who had had several prior rehab experiences for alcohol and heroin dependence presented for treatment stating, "It is easy for me to get sober. I have to learn how to *stay* sober."

Without such changes, the individual's sobriety is seen as precarious, and most likely temporary. The goal of the TSP is not simply to achieve sobriety, but to help the person work a more lasting program to ensure their ongoing sobriety. Within the TSF, the nature of this program concerns personal and spiritual development.

Honesty

One of the most fundamental principles of the AA program is its insistence on honesty. Honesty is seen as essential in relations with others and, more important, with oneself.

One aspect of the role of honesty is the active acknowledgment of one's addiction to alcohol or drugs. This contrasts with the use of denial or defense mechanisms to avoid facing the realities of one's addiction. This is an honesty that finds its expression in the 1st Step of AA ("We admitted that we were powerless over alcohol . . . "). A more profound expression of honesty is found in later steps (4, 5, 8, 9), in which the recovering addict is asked to come to terms with past behaviors and make amends when appropriate. Although this may appear to be tenuously related to alcohol or drug use per se, it is a core element in the way of living that is basic to the 12-step lifestyle. It is notable that in the Big Book, the only ones who are deemed unable to benefit from the program are those who are born "constitutionally incapable of being honest with themselves" (Alcoholics Anonymous, 2001, p. 58).

Humility

The other foundation principle for AA is humility. On a simple level, this refers to an acknowledgment of one's powerlessness over drug or alcohol use. The acceptance of this state can trigger a tremendous psychological struggle or can be met with relief. It is often easier to accept the "unmanageability" of the First Step than the word *powerless* in the sentence (which is ultimately the cause of the unmanageability).

With this realization, however difficult it may be, often comes a deeper realization of one's humility in the face of the complexities of life. One of the famous AA aphorisms is an admonition to "accept life on life's terms," the logical outcome of Bill's statement, "First of all, we had to quit playing God" (Alcoholics Anonymous, 2001). This acceptance can provide a type of spiritual calmness. Harry Tiebout (1949, 1953), Bill Wilson's psychiatrist and an early supporter of AA, described this as "surrender" and felt that some form of surrender was essential to the conversion experience central to AA.

Although the original invocation of anonymity in the fellowship was to avoid social stigma, a deeper meaning became even more relevant. Anonymity was seen as a way to keep one's ego in check, a way to remain humble (Alcoholics Anonymous, 1989). Anonymity itself was a sort of spiritual exercise.

Two events in the history of AA illustrate the depth of the conviction about the importance of this tradition. Early on, Charles Towns, proprietor of the hospital in which Bill had his "hot flash," offered the fledgling organization an opportunity to take over the operation of his hospital and to make Bill a salaried therapist. Although he was tempted to accept this offer (it would relieve his personal financial problems and would give AA a legitimacy he craved), through the workings of the group conscience and with much contemplation, the offer was refused (Kurtz, 1989; White, 1998).

A more personal crisis was faced by Bill when he was offered an honorary doctorate by Yale University in 1954. As much as he desired this degree for personal validation, and as a way to further the prospects of AA, he ultimately decided to refuse the degree on the principle of anonymity, even though Yale was willing to grant the degree to him as "W. W." (Cheever, 2004).

Issues of humility and spiritual surrender will be discussed in greater depth in Chapters Three and Six.

Spirituality

The role of spirituality is central to the TSF approach and to the worldview underlying it; it is also one of the more controversial aspects of TSFs and the most difficult to convey. Efforts have been made to soft pedal this aspect of the program, yet they miss an essential element. At its roots, historically and in practice, the 12-step program is a deeply spiritual one.

For Bill Wilson, the key to achieving sobriety was the experience of a spiritual conversion. He had such an experience in the course of his contacts with the Oxford Group and at Towns Hospital. This was the experience described by Dr. James in *The Varieties of Religious Experience*, predicted by Dr. Jung, and which loomed as the last hope for desperate alcoholics. This experience was predicated on "hitting bottom," in the same way that a drowning man will unconditionally grasp onto anything that promises survival, however improbable it may seem.

In one view, the entire structure of AA is designed to help facilitate spiritual conversion experiences in its members. Although Bill's experience of his "hot flash" was sudden and overwhelming, he later acknowledged that most people reach this point gradually, and that sudden conversions like his own were relatively rare.

Twelve-steppers go to great lengths to distinguish their spirituality from religious belief. Bill himself was fed up with organized religion and agnostic about faith in general when he had his "hot flash" in Towns Hospital. He was quite clear when developing his program that he needed to speak to the disillusionment of the alcoholic who had been let down by organized religion. We recall Bill's relief at Ebby's suggestion that he choose whatever God suited him. The concept of the "Higher Power" was developed as an alternative to the more conventional conceptions of God and allows a free choice for each AA member.

On a deeper level, the spirituality of the program may be best embodied in the aforementioned aphorism: "Accept life on life's terms." At the root of this is a profound acceptance and appreciation for the mystery of life. Rather than seeking to understand the world on a logical or rational level, AAs are encouraged to simply let go and see things for what they are. By no longer "playing God" (Alcoholics Anonymous, 2001) we see the world in a more realistic and humbling light. By accepting our limitations (Kurtz, 1982) we become free to experience ourselves as an integral part of the universe, as both unique and commonplace.

In this view, the spirituality conveyed in AA is more related to the mystical traditions of most religions than to any of the dogmatic or liturgical aspects. This association has been made explicitly (Ash, 1993; Gregson & Efran, 2002) but is more typically found in the everyday humility and good works of the daily operation of the program. By reaching out to other suffering alcoholics, each AA reaffirms his or her own frailty and dependence on others. In a sense, AA spirituality may be viewed as a home-grown American form of Zen Buddhism, in which everyday consciousness contains its own transcendence, and down-to-earth pragmatic actions are the key to liberation (Suzuki, 1988).

Fellowship

While AA itself is often referred to as a fellowship, the interpersonal aspect of this fellowship is important to highlight. At one level, TSFs function as social groups, in which simply gathering together is a mechanism for sharing hope and support. Many meetings are followed by a group trip to a diner or coffee shop to continue the discussion or to embark on an entirely new discussion. Some AA groups sponsor explicitly social events, such as dances, camping trips, and bowling contests. In this aspect, AA provides an alcohol- and drug-free milieu and an alternative to the typical venues for socialization in our society.

Once again, the notion of fellowship has a deeper aspect, one in which a deeper sense of connection between members is experienced and acknowledged. Remember that the first AA meeting, between Bill and Dr. Bob, was simply two alcoholics finding each other, recognizing that each one had at last found someone else who understood his own plight, and feeling acknowledged by the other. This kind of personal affirmation is key to understanding the power of the fellowship.

In many cases, the fellowship alone, without working any other aspect of the program, such as the steps, is sufficient to maintain sobriety. In other cases, the fellowship is an important hook to keep new members coming back long enough to begin to take a more active role in their own recovery.

A young man reported back to his treatment group about attending his first Cocaine Anonymous meeting. He felt conspicuous and self-conscious and followed the lead of other group members. Each member stated his or her name as they went around the circle, and he did so as well. He noticed a piece of paper being circulated, with each member writing something on it. When it came to him, he saw that it was a list of names and phone numbers. He added his name and number and passed it on to the person sitting next to him, who handed it back to him. "No, this is for you," he was told. He experienced this act as an incredibly moving gesture of inclusion and support.

An interesting perspective on this phenomenon was offered by Ernest Kurtz (1982). He described the power of AA as a place where mutual dependence can be openly expressed and shared, with such dependence placed not on one individual but on an entire group of individuals. Such a group is safer to lean on than any one person, especially among a group of people who have often suffered significant ruptures in their connections with others.

It will be most useful to keep the concepts of this chapter in mind while reading Chapter Three. Reading the steps and learning the dynamics of the 12-step program can be a dry and disembodied experience when approached out of context. This perspective will help illuminate the mechanics of the program and convey it as the dynamic and pragmatic program that it is.

Chapter 3

What Happens in AA?

AA's Twelve Steps are a group of principles, spiritual in their nature, which, if practiced as a way of life, can expel the obsession to drink and enable the sufferer to become happily and usefully whole.

AA's Twelve Traditions apply to the life of the Fellowship itself. They outline the means by which AA maintains its unity and relates itself to the world about it, the way it lives and grows.

—Bill Wilson

COMPARED TO DESCRIBING THE PHILOSOPHICAL foundation of AA, it is relatively easy to describe the elements that form the scaffolding of AA. As noted earlier, there is no substitute for attending an AA meeting personally. However, all too many visitors, and AA members themselves, report some confusion on attending their first meeting. The jargon, the use of shorthand, and the aphorisms can conspire to bewilder a newcomer. This description of the basic building blocks of the AA program is intended to orient you to these pieces, whether it is to relate to your client's experience and reports, or for you to make sense of your own visit.

Learning to speak the language of recovery is the basic aim of this entire book. Your familiarity with this language, and with the worldview that lies beneath it, will be central to your ability to connect with and help guide your clients in their own program. This is the most basic place to begin to learn this language.

The Steps

The 12 steps themselves are the backbone of the program. I list each of the steps and give a brief interpretation that may be useful in explaining this to you, and, by extension, to your client.

Reading the steps without a proper introduction or context can be a dry, academic experience. I encourage you to keep in mind the broader concepts outlined in Chapter Two to help place the meaning of the steps in a context and to give them life.

In working with clients in 12-step recovery, it is important to be conversant with the steps, their meanings, and their implications. The degree to which you acquaint yourself with these steps will affect how closely you can relate to your clients, and how much they will be willing to trust that you understand the process and their situations. It is entirely possible to work within this framework with a superficial understanding of the steps, but it will limit you. It may not be necessary to learn the steps intimately, but some understanding is necessary to be able to comfortably speak the language.

I referred a cocaine-abusing client for a psychiatric evaluation with a colleague of mine who is known universally for his diagnostic and clinical acumen—everyone returned impressed with his quick and sure grasp of their dynamics. This client, however, was not very impressed with him. I received the psychiatrist's report a day or so later and was surprised to find reference to referring the patient to a "7-step program." Apparently, his knowledge base did not include the recovery program, and this clearly was not lost on my patient.

The steps were not a part of the TSF until the publication of *Alcoholics Anonymous* in 1939. They were further elaborated upon in the volume *Twelve Steps and Twelve Traditions* (Alcoholics Anonymous, 1989, aka Twelve and Twelve) originally published in 1952. Although they had some origins in the Oxford Group, they remain the core of the fellowship.

It is also pointed out that the steps are suggestions, not mandates. The program is one of attraction, not coercion. First of all, Bill recognized that alcoholics generally do not respond well to pressure. Second, this is a more realistic position—after all, how does one force another to take such steps? This becomes a factor in such situations as court-mandated attendance at AA or random assignment in research; the value of the program in such situations is highly compromised. The newcomer in AA is frequently reminded that there is no requirement or timetable for following the steps.

Why engage in these steps when sobriety, the ostensible goal of this endeavor, has been achieved? Within AA the answer is that the drinking reflects this underlying self-centered nature of the alcoholic. An alternative, more psychologically minded explanation is that the behaviors of the alcoholic and addict are not isolated from the rest of his or her life, but are embedded within it the way a single thread is embedded in a piece of cloth. Removing the drinking itself does not change the behavior that has been built up around the drinking and drugging, and which supports that behavior. Furthermore, awareness of one's personal areas of weakness provides a measure of insulation against the internal cues for relapse, including all sorts of feelings and beliefs. This is useful whether one views the drugging behavior as the cause of the other behaviors or vice versa. The steps are seen as a program for a healthy lifestyle, one which supports sobriety.

Step 1

> We admitted we were powerless over alcohol—that our lives had become unmanageable.

This is the most basic, and, in the opinion of many, the most important step of all. This is the step that moves a person from the precontemplative stage to the contemplative stage (Prochaska, et al., 1992). At its simplest level, this step acknowledges the existence of a problem and the nature of that problem. At a deeper level, this step suggests profound insights about the nature of the alcoholic and of alcoholism, as well as the human condition.

Although questions of why this powerlessness exists are common, they are best either deferred or given a quick and simple explanation. This line of questioning can all too easily lead to a long session of intellectualization and distraction. The essence of the 1st Step is in the personal experience of its truth, in the self-diagnosis of the client. It is relatively straightforward to discern the powerlessness in a person who spends his entire paycheck on cocaine, or who steps out for an hour for a few beers only to return home at midnight stone drunk.

A traditional interpretation is suggested by Dr. Silkworth in "The Doctor's Opinion" in the Big Book (Alcoholics Anonymous, 2001), and is commonly heard in the rooms. This sees alcoholism as an allergy of the body and a compulsion of the mind. This is the simple formula that has served a majority of clients well, but which may be insufficient for some.

One interpretation that is useful for both clinicians and clients is suggested by Rogers, McMillin, and Hill (1990). The "powerlessness" of this step refers to the core biological transformations that establish the diagnosis—physical dependence, elevated tolerance, and loss of control. (*The Diagnostic and Statistical Manual* of the American Psychiatric Association, 2005, lists seven criteria for substance dependence and it is quite easy to cluster them into these three factors.) These are factors that are primarily biologically driven, and which are not highly amenable to self-control or willpower. *Unmanageable* refers to the consequences—social, biological, psychological, legal, and so on—that result from the inability to control one's substance use (i.e., the power-lessness). Although it is the unmanageability that usually attracts attention and concern, it is the powerlessness that forms the essence of the disease.

> A client sought treatment as a condition of his DUI arrest—his third, as he eventually revealed. This strongly implied that he would be facing some amount of time in jail. As he was discussing his situation, he wryly said, "You know, I really like drinking. I just hate the *consequences* of drinking."

For many people, *powerlessness* refers specifically to the lack of control over the substance consumption. It has often been noted that this is the only step that actually makes reference to substance use; all the subsequent steps refer to the process of living a recovering lifestyle. For other people, this step opens the door to a nearly mystical acknowledgment of spiritual surrender, of one's vulnerability in the universe. Powerlessness, along with a faith in a Higher Power (Steps 2 and 3) assumes a far more important meaning in this context. For the purposes of this chapter, and for the newly recovering client, the simpler meaning is the emphasis. The latter meaning is usually only accessed after extended sobriety and involvement with the program, and is discussed in Chapter 6. Occasionally, a newly recovering person will have a spiritual insight into this larger meaning. It is most useful to refer back to the simpler meaning, while acknowledging that the larger meaning is relevant and valid. In the early stages of recovery, sobriety is paramount (Brown, 1985) and the clinician must be as careful as the client to "keep it simple."

Most addiction programs feature a version of a "1st Step Prep," a worksheet that leads the client through a detailed listing of the damage caused by his or her addiction. Similar 1st Step workbooks are also available commercially. This can be a powerful tool to help focus the client's attention on the extent and consequences of his or her substance use, of the unmanageability of the disease. These can also have an unintended side effect of increasing the degree of guilt and shame experienced by the newly recovering addict, effects that frequently serve to deter them from treatment and from exploring these issues any further. It is suggested that the use of such a 1st Step Prep be incorporated carefully into a client's treatment program, and that it be directly related to understanding the implications of this tool for making the 1st Step a personal reality. Such an exercise is designed to stimulate thought and discussion, not to be an end in itself.

The importance of this step in the TSF goes beyond simply demonstrating evidence of one's loss of control over substance use. For Bill W., the basic starting point of the process was "ego deflation at depth." He considered this the precondition for change. Without a sense of desperation, the suffering alcoholic would not be motivated to grasp for help, would continue to struggle to control the addiction by willpower, control strategies (switching from liquor to wine, buying smaller quantities, etc.), use of defense mechanisms, and denial. Without this sense of hitting bottom, the conditions for spiritual conversion would not be in place.

A quick perusal of the Big Book reveals that the stories of individual recovery, which form the bulk of the book, are divided into sections, including "They Stopped in Time" and "They Nearly Lost All." Bill came to realize that it was in fact possible to arrest the progression of the disease prior to the total disintegration that characterized the "Pioneers of AA." This is possible by recognition that one's illness is the same as that of those with end-stage alcoholism, but at an earlier stage. The end-stage drinkers go through the same stage that these "high-bottom" drunks are currently experiencing. It is through the recognition of this fact that some are able to "stop in time." Furthermore, Bill recognized that not all spiritual conversions were as sudden and dramatic as his—more people came to this point through a gradual process of reflection and awakening.

Step 2

Came to believe that a Power greater than ourselves could restore us to sanity.

The 2nd Step provides the answer to the desperation expressed in the 1st Step. In this step we find a glimmer of hope that an answer exists to the powerlessness and unmanageability, to the sense of defeat that is the essence of the 1st Step. Belief implies hope. By believing that there is a way out, a light, however faint, appears at the end of the tunnel. The use of the phrase "came to believe" acknowledges that for most individuals it is a gradual process, not the sudden transformation that Bill experienced.

One subtle sign of hope is found in the use of the words *us* and *ourselves*. At the very least, the addict reading these lines learns that he or she is not alone in the struggle to overcome this affliction. This is the introduction of the element of fellowship, which is central to the workings of the TSF—people cannot cure themselves alone, but together there is a chance of salvation.

More significant, albeit more problematic for some, is the introduction of the notion of a "Power greater than ourselves." The notion of a Higher Power (sometimes shortened to "HP") becomes central to the working of the fellowship and to the journey of the individual in recovery. The frequent resistance to this concept, with its overtones of organized religion, is a second major obstacle to overcome, and may become a significant therapeutic issue.

Clearly, Bill had in mind a genuine spiritual conversion when he developed the program. However, recall that he was an agnostic when he met with Ebby and that his own resistance was defused by Ebby's suggestion that he could adopt any notion of a Higher Power that he felt comfortable with. This suggestion has opened the door to many in the TSF who might have had a major obstacle with a more traditional conceptualization of God.

The simplest formulation, one suggested by Bill in *Twelve Steps and Twelve Traditions* (Alcoholics Anonymous, 1989), is that the prospective member come to view the group of AA itself as his or her Higher Power. Rather than relying on one's own instincts and preferences, one can use the program for guidance. This reliance can take many forms, including perusal of program literature, listening to speakers at a meeting, or a personal relationship with a sponsor. The important thing is to seek guidance from outside oneself. In this formulation, "GOD" becomes "Group Of Drunks" or "Good Orderly Direction."

Gorski (1989) presented a hierarchy of concepts of a Higher Power, ranging from inanimate objects to another human being to a group of people to a "supernatural Higher Power." Any of these can work (although he is disparaging of those who pray to a Coca-Cola bottle) as long as one can believe in the power of that HP to provide the help that is needed.

For many, the journey to find a Higher Power is difficult, especially if they have had difficulties with formal religious belief and practices in the past. It becomes easy to seize on this possibly controversial phrase to reject the entire program if one is looking to do so. For such people, the idea that the group of AA or NA can provide support and guidance to overcome one's own self-reliance is far more palatable than the supernatural notion. This belief can serve as a transitional phase, as a more traditional belief system comes into place. For others, this belief in the good faith of others is sufficient to maintain sobriety on an ongoing basis.

At this point, it is probably more important to recognize and acknowledge the need for external help than it is to struggle to define or debate the concept of a Higher Power. This can easily become a trap for those who use intellectualization as a defense mechanism.

> One young man with a cocaine problem was describing to the group his need for guidance from the group and from the fellowship in general. "If I listened to myself, I'd be out doing cocaine right now." His seeking help from the group was a form of accepting a higher power.

For Bill (Alcoholics Anonymous, 1989), another function of this step is as an antidote to the ego-inflated pride of the alcoholic. In his view, one of the primary sources of the problem of the alcoholic personality is in its infantile self-centeredness, in seeing itself as the center of the universe. By recognizing a Higher Power, one takes the first steps toward a more humble stance toward life and toward one's own disease.

The final controversy in Step 2 is in the use of the phrase "restore us to sanity." Is the alcoholic mentally ill? If so, what is the nature of this illness? For most addicts and alcoholics, the absurdity of their situation is no secret—they are compelled to continue self-destructive and unsatisfying behaviors even while recognizing that these are not what they wish to do (recall the concept of powerlessness). What could be more insane than continuing to inject oneself with poison? The use of defense mechanisms, denial, and distorted thinking are all evidence of an irrational mind-set.

However, this can be a focal type of insanity. This insanity primarily pertains to the addict's relationship to the drug of choice and to the ancillary behaviors. Most alcoholics and addicts encounter moments of violating one or more of their "I never" rules: I never steal from my family, never lie, never cheat. As these personal mores are violated, one can easily view this as a clear form of insanity. In other ways, alcoholics and addicts may be able to function normally and think rationally; however, in areas that are directly or indirectly connected to their addiction, their thinking is dangerously skewed.

For the stubborn among us, who have difficulty conceiving of or accepting the notion of a power greater than ourselves, it may help to point out that drugs and alcohol themselves are more powerful than we are. A quick detour back to the 1st Step may be in order.

Finally, it has been noted that this step uses the word could. Belief alone will not produce adequate results. This belief must be followed by action. The next step requires an active commitment, if not overt action.

Step 3

Made a decision to turn our will and our lives over to the care of God *as we understood him.*

Whereas the 1st Step asks for an admission of defeat and the 2nd Step requires a belief in a Higher Power, this step asks the member to make a decision and take a more active stance toward recovery.

The "Twelve and Twelve" (Alcoholics Anonymous, 1989) describes this step as opening a door for recovery, with the key being willingness. Here, one of the paradoxes of the program is described—that as one becomes more willing to depend upon a Higher Power, a greater sense of independence is fostered. As AA members come to accept a sense of limitation and external guidance, they actually feel freer.

> A patient was describing a sense of peacefulness and serenity she experienced as she worked on the issue of surrendering to a Higher Power. "It really makes no sense, but it seems to be true," she said, as much to herself as to me.

Many people, especially those raised in Western culture, find the notion of surrendering one's will to be repugnant, with overtones of cultishness and fascism. It is difficult to explicate this paradox to the uninitiated. However, it becomes more palatable to present the failure of one's own self-reliance as evidence of the poor outcome of "self-will run riot." Why not try some external direction?

Accepting external help (even in the form of a sponsor, or accepting guidance from the AA group) may also recapitulate infantile fears of inferiority and impotent dependency. For some AA members, the act of asking for a sponsor is felt as a humiliating act of self-rejection and is a significant stumbling point. It is no wonder that Bill felt that the best stance from which to accept this program was one of complete demoralized defeat.

A distinction that some find helpful is that the notion of belief in a spiritualized Higher Power is useful in a more generalized way, in generating hope and mobilizing courage. Individual AA members may be more helpful in providing specific advice and techniques.

Harry Tiebout, an early psychiatric supporter of AA, wrote a series of excellent articles describing the psychodynamics of recovery (1949, 1953). He described the difference between compliance and surrender as a key to understanding the psychological changes necessary for true recovery to take place. Simple compliance with the 12-step program is a necessary stage for most AAs to go through, but does not constitute the full acceptance of the nature of the disease and the ongoing need for support and may, in fact, represent a resistance to full surrender. Surrender, however, refers to the state of complete acceptance of the program, including the surrender of one's will to a Higher Power. This is the spiritual state of acceptance that helps the recovering addict achieve a state of calmness and peace, and which indicates the dropping of resistance to the program and to recovery.

Step 4

Made a searching and fearless moral inventory of ourselves.

This step comes closer to more traditional ideas about psychological change. It sounds a lot like journaling or doing insight work. It is indeed similar in some ways but is more rigorously structured than such work implies (although no formal structure is prescribed or required).

In the Big Book (Alcoholics Anonymous, 2001), Bill describes the 4th Step as a kind of "personal housecleaning." He likens this process to a taking business inventory—a chance to get rid of "damaged or unsalable goods." He provides a suggested method for compiling the inventory, starting with a list of "resentments," which he regards as the most significant offender. Bill describes a simple method of listing in three columns (a) the person the resentment is directed at, (b) the cause of the resentment, and (c) the life area affected. For example, he lists a resentment at "Mr. Brown" for "his attention to my wife," affecting "sex relations and self-esteem." He suggests that we examine the areas affected in the categories of self-esteem, security, ambitions, and personal or sex relations.

Although not strictly required, the universal prescription is that this inventory be written out, be put in black and white on paper. This is a way of making the list concrete and real. It allows us to examine the list more dispassionately and carefully than if it was purely a mental exercise.

Bill suggests two strategies for dealing with the list of resentments. First, it is helpful to view the transgressors as spiritually sick themselves and deserving of sympathy. Second, it is useful to examine the list for ways in which we made mistakes contributing to these situations. Our own role in creating these problems is central to taking responsibility for their resolution.

Most feel that it is not usually necessary to list every instance of every kind of transgression to put together a personal inventory. What is important is to enumerate the kinds of character defects that can hamper one's personal growth and recovery. Remember that the goals of recovery, in addition to abstinence from substances, are personal change, honesty, and humility as well as spiritual contact with one's Higher Power. It may be more relevant to list "I have been unfaithful to my wife" than to list every instance of that problem. Others feel, however, that a more exhaustive list is more useful at identifying the relevant patterns and feelings.

Another facet of the inventory is that it is also important to list positive attributes. In addition to the surplus and damaged inventory, a shopkeeper will list all salable and positive goods as well. Similarly, a moral inventory lists strengths, skills, and other positive attributes in addition to the negative traits usually associated with this step. This is extremely useful to point out to a person contemplating beginning an inventory, as the prospect of confronting nothing but negative attributes can be quite intimidating.

Don't forget that this step is rarely taken in isolation. Usually, Step 4 is done in consultation with a sponsor or some other person who has done this before. This person can help your client decide what level of specificity or generality is appropriate. This person can also help your client decide what elements to include and what may be irrelevant issues. The rule of thumb, however, is that more is better than less—being too complete provides a better outcome than glossing over potentially difficult areas.

As a mental health professional, you may be asked to provide input into the process or content of your client's inventory. It may be entirely appropriate for you to provide some suggestions and to give some feedback, as you may have a great deal of insight into the client's significant issues. However, unless you have significant experience with this step it is most helpful to avoid being the primary person guiding the client through this process. Encouraging him or her to solicit guidance from a sponsor or another person who is in the fellowship will provide more effective feedback and will also serve to help your client bond more closely with others in the program.

Step 5

> Admitted to God, to ourselves, and to another human being the exact nature of our wrongs.

The 5th Step takes the 4th Step and moves it to a higher level (Alcoholics Anonymous, 1989). It is agreed by all parties, including in the Big Book itself, that the hardest part of this step is the aspect of disclosing this inventory to another human being. Having gone through the process of rigorous self-examination, what is the purpose and benefit of such a difficult disclosure?

Remember that the ultimate goal of the steps overall is to create a sense of spiritual openness, of spiritual surrender. A chief element in such a surrender is creating a sense of humility, in defeating the infantile ego. By sharing such sensitive information with another human being, a sense of humility (not a sense of failure) is fostered. While Step 4 is largely theoretical, Step 5 actualizes the potential inherent in creating such an inventory.

A more conventional reason for this disclosure is that sharing this material helps free the client from it. Sharing with another, and having that person respond nonjudgmentally, provides a tremendous relief. The "corrective emotional experience" is utilized in this way to help the client feel accepted as mirrored by another, and helps to relieve old wounds. The accepting reaction of the listener helps to begin the process of self-acceptance and self-forgiveness. As we share the inventory with another, it ceases to have the same power over us.

Furthermore, by sharing with another, the client breaks through the isolation that is usually quite crippling in the addictive process. By sharing with another member of the group, a bond with the group is tentatively established, or is strengthened. This step helps to rid the client of his or her "anxious apartness" (Alcoholics Anonymous, 1989, p. 56).

Be aware that the process of completing the 5th Step is not a one-way street. As your client shares his or her inventory with a trusted person in the program, it often prompts an exchange of stories, with the sponsor relating the client's disclosures to his or her own experience. This will help demystify the process and normalize both the process of sharing this information and the content of the disclosures. It is a profound relief to share some deeply held experience, only to have listeners reveal that they too have had similar experiences.

Repeatedly, the new AA member is reminded to choose a person he or she trusts and feels comfortable with to work the 5th Step. This would appear to be obvious and yet at times people will choose someone who appears knowledgeable and experienced in the program at the expense of a sense of personal trust and comfort. Some sober thought should go into the choice of a person with whom to share this material.

Occasionally a therapist may be asked to hear a 5th Step, and at times this may be appropriate. There may be no other person the client feels comfortable with, or there may be concerns about confidentiality with members of the fellowship, especially if the client is relatively new or has had issues with betrayal and violations of trust in the past. However, it is usually preferable to direct your client back into the fellowship for this task. Apart from creating a dual relationship with the client, it is important that the client's recovery issues be directed back into the dependency-tolerant fellowship of AA or NA. In the long run, our goal is to facilitate the client's engagement in the fellowship.

Many people will choose a member of the clergy to work the 5th Step with. There are several reasons why this may be beneficial. First is the familiarity that many clients have with the traditional role of clergy in hearing confession or other types of personal disclosure. However, another reason why a clergyperson may be indicated is when there are disclosures of a criminal nature. There are real limits to the confidentiality that a therapist can promise to a client, whereas the confidentiality of a clergy member is more durable and more legally impenetrable than that of a therapist or a sponsor in AA. While this may not be an everyday concern, the increased confidentiality offered by the clergy may be a comfort even when there are no legal issues at stake.

In a clinic I worked in, one of the counselors was also a lay pastor. He dressed in street clothes most of the time. However, on some occasions, he wore his clerical collar to work. It turned out that these were the days when he was working with a client (either his own, or another therapist's) on a 5th Step.

For the person who may be reluctant to burden another with this task, it is helpful to point out that there is benefit to listeners as well. First, they get to reexperience the process and are free to share some relevant experiences of their own. Second, it is part of the basic premise of the program that helping others is central to the recovery process. While a person shares a 5th Step with someone, listeners are working their own 12th Step.

Step 6

Were entirely ready to have God remove all these defects of character.

Steps 6 and 7 form a unit in a way that is parallel to Steps 4 and 5. Step 6 asks clients to become more aware of their personal character defects and become willing to give them up. This is the logical follow-up to the preceding two steps, which heightened one's awareness of areas that were problematic and needed change, but which did nothing to actually change them. This step is a preliminary step in readying oneself to make changes in these areas.

Initially, Steps 6 and 7 may seem deceptively simple. They have been referred to as "the forgotten steps" (Hazelden Foundation, 1987). However, as a key to changing the behaviors and attitudes identified in Steps 4 and 5, they are a critical stage in the entire program.

Step 6 introduces the phrase "defects of character," which requires some comment. In the old days, these character defects were seen as the underlying psychodynamics that caused the addiction. Remember that as recently as in *DSM-II*, alcoholism and addiction were listed as personality disorders (American Psychiatric Association, 1968). This is the psychological model of addiction that is indeed implicit in some of Bill Wilson's writings. However, more recent conceptualizations of addiction suggest that these well-known addictive character traits are more likely the results of addiction than its cause. In either event, the kind of thinking, scheming, denial, defense mechanisms, and such that usually accompany the addiction are genuine impediments to recovery and are an appropriate target for change.

As with several other areas in the TSF, passivity is not called for in this step. Preparing and reflection may sound like passive stances, but in fact, what is required here is an active contemplation of the need for change and an imagining of what life will be like without these character defects. The Twelve and Twelve (Alcoholics Anonymous, 1989) emphasizes how difficult it is to relinquish some personal defects—"we exult in some of our defects" (p. 66). Furthermore, many of these defects are pleasurable in a variety of ways. Thinking through how different life will be without these traits is an exercise in both honesty and open-mindedness.

One of the primary obstacles to successful change in the TSF is shame. Many people enter the fellowship with a tremendous degree of self-criticism and shame about their behaviors in their addiction. This is a direct problem in that it makes such contemplation difficult and avoidance easy. Working through such shame is like working through any other form of resistance—it requires ongoing exposure and insight. In this context, the disease concept of addiction must be invoked and explained to defuse the negative self-attributions that are common to newly recovering addicts. Step 6 is an invitation to accept oneself as is, without the automatic self-criticisms, shame, and guilt that have usually accompanied them.

The Twelve and Twelve also cautions against the reader interpreting this step as a call for perfection. The author suggests using this step as a statement of an ideal, not a practical goal. A popular TSF aphorism calls for "progress, not perfection."

Gorski (1989) sees this step as asking God for the courage and persistence to make the changes that are necessary. However, it is up to each individual to actually make those changes, with the help and guidance of the program and one's Higher Power.

Step 7

Humbly asked Him to remove our shortcomings.

In this step the reference to God is understood to refer to the same Higher Power defined in Steps 2 and 3. However, all sources make it clear that God or the HP does not perform miracles of change. In a more explicit sense, the intent here is for the client to reach out to others in the program and, through contacts with other recovering addicts and alcoholics, to help repair negative interpersonal relations and negative personal behaviors. The program, including the Higher Power, works through its members.

"Removing our shortcomings" is another way of referring to exposing the underlying character and working to build and develop that character. This step implicitly involves developing a set of values and priorities that will guide the rest of the recovery program.

The role of humility, introduced in this step, is a key to much of the working of the program. This quality of humility can be detected in

> A story often told in AA concerns a drowning man who prays to God for rescue. A helicopter comes to him and drops a line. The man refuses, saying, "I have faith in God to save me." A man in a rowboat approaches and offers to pull him in. "No," says the drowning man, "God will save me." A passerby throws a lifesaver to him, which the man declines again. Finally, of course, the man drowns. He gets to heaven and approaches God with anger. "After all these years of devotion, I prayed to you in my hour of need and you didn't come to rescue me!" "What did you expect?" God replies. "I sent a helicopter, a rowboat, and a lifesaver!"

persons who have worked the program for a period of time and have made appropriate changes in their lives. Humility, seen as self-acceptance, recognition of one's limitations, one's sense of connectedness and interdependence with others, is a positive attribute, not a defect. Humility is an attitude of acceptance of one's humanity.

The Twelve and Twelve identifies fear as the source of all character defects. By assuming an attitude of humility, we disarm fear at its basic level. We have nothing to fear if we are fully self-accepting. Our true ego stays intact even if under external attack.

Asking for help, whether of God or of a fellow AA, is easily construed as a humiliating action. In our society, dependence is seen as the opposite of self-reliance, an implicit core social value. Asking for help is actually a further act of spiritual surrender, and a reflection of a more accepting state of mind, an attitude of recovery-mindedness.

Both Steps 6 and 7 have another aspect: renewing one's relationship to one's Higher Power. This is a theme that reverberates throughout the steps and should not be dismissed or neglected. Whether the HP is construed as a supernatural power or as the "Good Orderly Direction" of one's fellow group members, it is a basic element of the entire program.

Step 8

> Made a list of all persons we had harmed, and become willing to
> make amends to them all.

The 8th and 9th Steps have become familiar to many of us, in that these
steps are more visible to outsiders. They are also easy to parody—an
episode of *Seinfeld* had George demanding a 9th Step apology from a
newly recovering friend. "The 9th Step!" he fumed. "That's the most
important one!"

In one view, the first three steps involve getting right with God,
Steps 4 through 7 involve getting right with ourselves, and Steps 8
through 12 involve getting right with others. While straightforward, this
analysis bypasses the point that all these steps have the benefit of getting
right with ourselves. In working Steps 8 and 9, there is a benefit to the
recipient of the amends, but the far greater benefit comes to the person
who is working the steps.

Again, note that for Bill, restoring relations with others had the
effect of renewing our relationship with our fellow man and worked
against the egocentricity that he felt was at the core of alcoholism.

As with Step 4, it helps to review this list with a sponsor or another
trusted guide. Here, a therapist can be helpful in assessing where harm
has been done.

The Twelve and Twelve reminds us that it is important to be thorough in compiling this list, even if amends and restitution are not to be
made in Step 9. Since the primary benefit of this step is for the person
making it, the fact that an amend is not possible does not eliminate the
need to account for and acknowledge the wrong that has been done.

Step 9

> Made direct amends to such people wherever possible, except when
> to do so would injure them or others.

The Twelve and Twelve states that Step 9 calls for "good judgment, a
careful sense of timing, courage and prudence" (Alcoholics Anonymous,
1989, p. 83). It suggests that we distinguish between those to whom an

immediate response is called for, those for whom a delayed or partial response is indicated, and those for whom no amends are possible or appropriate.

The attitude of the person performing this step is part of what distinguishes such apologies from those offered in a state of hangover the morning after.

Sometimes a general admission of acknowledgment of injury is sufficient. At other times, more specific amends may be necessary. This process may occur rapidly, in a desire to clear the slate, or it may take time. As memory and cognition improve with extended sobriety, additional steps may be necessary later on.

The question of avoiding making amends for fear of creating further injury is a thorny one. In some cases it is obvious that the destructiveness of an apology or the revelation of some past misbehavior outweighs the benefit to the client. At other times, it may be a more difficult judgment call. However, we are cautioned to be careful not to use this clause as a means of avoiding dealing with real injuries that require, and can bear, an apology or an amend. "Let's not talk prudence while practicing evasion" (Alcoholics Anonymous, 1989, p. 85).

Another distinction is that making such amends is necessary for the personal growth of the client. The recipient of the amend or apology may not be receptive. Generally, this does not absolve the client of the responsibility to make the apology, however. Our goal is not to receive forgiveness, but to clean our own slate of unfinished business.

In cases where amends are not possible or appropriate, the important task is the willingness to do so. Again, this is a question of attitude and outlook, and sometimes the best we can do is to make some other effort in that direction. It may not be appropriate to reveal an extramarital affair if it may break up a current marriage just to ease one's conscience; in such a case, a substitute amend may have to be performed.

As usual, the role of a sponsor or spiritual advisor is important in helping to resolve some of the ambiguities of this task. There are many situations in which a clear answer is not available, and any answer at all will be difficult.

Step 10

> Continued to take personal inventory and when we were wrong promptly admitted it.

Step 10 is the ongoing application of Steps 8 and 9. Rather than needing to excavate old damages and rid ourselves of them, here we are trying to prevent the accumulation of new resentments and injuries, the "emotional hangover."

> I was describing this step to a client new to the program. He listened, looked puzzled, and said, "That's a step in AA? That's just good manners."

Maintaining an ongoing awareness of one's impact on others is one way to keep the slate clean. It is suggested that AA members review their day each evening for any signs of unfinished business, both with others and within themselves. This calls for a classic combination of honesty and humility. While some pieces may be obvious, others may be hidden under rationalizations and other defensive maneuvers. For some people, a printed list of reminders is useful in reviewing the day. Similarly, beginning each day with a review of the day to come can help prevent problems before they begin.

A special consideration is made for issues of anger and resentment. Generally, these are seen as luxuries, which are damaging to people in general but especially risky indulgences for recovering addicts. "Resentment is the number one offender" (Alcoholics Anonymous, 2001).

Step 11

> Sought through prayer and meditation to improve our conscious contact with God *as we understood Him*, praying only for knowledge of His will for us and the power to carry that out.

It is clear from reading the Twelve and Twelve that the conception of meditation offered in this step is not the caricatured lotus position, nor any form of esoteric mysticism. Although there is certainly room for a more in-depth form of meditation, what Bill had in mind is more of a clear-minded self-reflection.

In terms of prayer, although a more traditional sense of prayer is described, the purpose is also portrayed as prayer to one's Higher Power for a sense of direction. The prayer "God's will, not mine, be done" is frequently added to the Serenity Prayer at the conclusion of 12-step meetings, and reflects a move away from the egocentric position of the active alcoholic or addict.

The Serenity Prayer, which has been appropriated almost universally in the TSF, provides a great point of entry into the discussion of prayer.

> *God Grant Me*
> *The serenity to accept the things I cannot change*
> *The courage to change the things I can*
> *And the wisdom to know the difference.*

Finally, one of the great rewards of prayer and meditation is in developing a sense of belonging, which also combats, in a different way, the isolation and egocentricity of the typical active alcoholic or addict.

Step 12

> Having had a spiritual awakening as the result of these Steps, we tried to carry this message to alcoholics, and to practice these principles in all our affairs.

In some ways, the 12th Step is the essence of the entire program. The notion of service inherited from the Oxford Group was the founding principle that brought Bill Wilson and Dr. Bob together—Bill's need to reach out to another alcoholic was what kept him sober, not the other way around. Recall that in his early sobriety, Bill tried to save one hopeless drunk after another, but the only one who really benefited from this effort was Bill himself.

There are any number of ways in which such service is provided. At a mundane level, some AA members make commitments to help out at meetings by arriving early to set up the chairs or make coffee; others agree to help clean up afterward. Staying later to provide support and encouragement to a newcomer is another highly valued form of service. Offering to chair a meeting (often for a set period of time, such as 6 months) is also an important way to provide service. It is also helpful to participate on organizational committees, such as the H&I Committee (Hospitals and Institutions), which brings AA meetings and speakers to hospitals, rehab centers, and prisons.

Another significant way to work the 12th Step is to share one's own story by being a speaker at a meeting. Often this is done at an anniversary of one's sobriety, such as a 1-year mark. It may not be a good idea to offer to do this too soon, but there are always exceptions, and sometimes this is a good way to firm up one's own dedication to sobriety. Often, meeting chairpersons are responsible for arranging to bring speakers for the meetings, and typically they may ask a friend, or someone they are sponsoring to tell the story.

At times, AA members may be asked to make a 12th Step call. This involves two or more AA members going to visit an active alcoholic to convey the hopeful message of the program to him or her. This is not done in a proselytizing or coercive fashion; the callers merely present their own stories of recovery and offer themselves as supports for the candidate.

The original 12th Step call was performed by Bill and Dr. Bob on an unsuspecting alcoholic (Bill D.) hospitalized and in restraints for his drinking problem. The two founders sought him out as a kind of experiment with their newly hatched ideas about a spiritual recovery for alcoholics. You can read Bill D.'s narrative in the Big Book, under the heading "Alcoholics Anonymous Number Three." He provides an excellent picture of what the experience is like.

> After AA # 3's wife had described the two men who wanted to talk to him to help themselves stay sober, Bill D. recalls "I felt as if I would be a real stinker if I did not listen to a couple of fellows for a short time, if that would cure *them*." He recalls their "sales pitch": "It's none of our business about your drinking . . . but we have a program whereby we

think we can stay sober. Part of that program is that we take it to someone else, that needs it and wants it. Now if you don't want it, we'll not take up your time, and we'll be going and looking for someone else." (Alcoholics Anonymous, 2001, pp. 185–186)

Newly sober members should never participate in a 12th Step call, and AA members should never do this alone. It is more appropriate for newcomers to offer service by such things as making coffee, distributing the literature, and so forth.

The Traditions

The early members of AA developed a set of 12 Traditions that concern the organization and procedures of the fellowship. Some say that these were put in place to curb the egos of the founders (especially Bill Wilson), and others believe that the founders themselves put these in place to put checks on themselves. In the traditions we find an outline for the functioning of a decentralized, anarchic organization. I will review the 12 traditions of Alcoholics Anonymous, which forms a model for similar traditions in other fellowships.

Tradition 1

> Our common welfare should come first; personal recovery depends upon A.A. unity.

There is a bit of paradox in this step: the program is about personal recovery first and foremost, but this individual recovery depends on group unity, even in such a loose fashion as is found in AA. In a sense, this tradition is a blend of Steps 1 and 12, and presents a possibility of some degree of conflict. In practice, however, this rarely occurs. On some occasions a member may arrive for a meeting intoxicated and rowdy, threatening to disrupt the meeting for the rest of the group. Usually, this person is graciously escorted to a back room by a few other group members, counseled that his behavior is not acceptable or appropriate, and reminded to "keep coming back." There is no mechanism or authority to expel a member from AA, and in fact, there are numerous instances of members attending meetings intoxicated for years before they came around.

> Although it was not an AA meeting, I once ran a group where everything went wrong. Underestimating how drunk they were, I erroneously allowed two intoxicated members into the group, who then dominated the meeting with drunken antics, apparently attempting to outdo each other. I kept thinking that I could handle the situation, even as it got worse and worse. However unproductive this group was for the other members (not to mention the two drunk guys), I learned a valuable lesson. At the end of the group, one group member, a man with several years' sobriety in AA, thanked the two drunk men for coming to group: "I know you must really want sobriety if you came here, and just seeing you in that state reminds me of where I was 5 years ago. Thanks to you, I know I won't drink tonight." A second lesson occurred after the group when I had to do my own soul-searching for why I thought I could violate one of the primary rules: don't let intoxicated members into an active treatment group. Apparently my own ego had taken charge of my decision-making abilities that night. It brought home the meaning of the aphorism, "principles over personalities."

Tradition 2

> For our group purpose there is but one ultimate authority—a loving God as He may express Himself in our group conscience. Our leaders are but trusted servants; they do not govern.

It is often surprising to newcomers to learn that there is no central authority in AA, like there is in other large organizations. There is a general service organization, located in New York City, which provides coordination and service, especially in the area of publishing and distributing literature. However, there is no authority in this office. Nobody dictates AA policy (apart from the traditions, there is none) or sends out

AA's position on issues. The most typical communication from this office is simply, "AA takes no position on outside matters."

The chair of a meeting (a person will often agree to chair a certain meeting for a few months) has responsibilities—arranging a speaker for speaker meetings, making sure that the coffee makers have their supplies, and so on, but little in the way of power or authority. What power they have is confined to what happens during the meeting itself—whether to cut off a long-winded speaker, who to choose to speak next, or whether to ask an obviously inebriated member to meet outside with a few other meeting-goers.

Similarly, committees exist for a variety of purposes but they answer to the group, not dictate to the group. The notion of group conscience is taken quite literally and seriously in this program.

Tradition 3

The only requirement for AA membership is a desire to stop drinking.

According to Kurtz (1989) the original versions of this tradition called for an honest or sincere desire to stop drinking. This was dropped in 1949, after it was recognized that the depth of a newcomer's sincerity or honesty was not obvious to anyone else, and should not be an obstacle for membership in any event.

There are two significant corollaries to this tradition. One is that the fellowship is a program of attraction. Nobody can approve or reject a member. One becomes a member simply by saying so. The second is that a desire to stop drinking does not preclude a coexisting desire to keep drinking. As long as people want to stop drinking they are welcome at an AA meeting, and the evidence of such a desire is indicated by their presence at an AA meeting.

Tradition 4

Each group should be autonomous except in matters affecting other groups or AA as a whole.

Although the central office of AA (and regional offices) keeps an official list of AA meetings, this is not for any other purpose than guaranteeing accessibility. If someone calls that office looking for a meeting that night in a certain city or neighborhood, that information is readily available. In fact, it is now usually available online as well. Any group of alcoholics (or, respectively of addicts or overeaters) can establish a new AA/NA/Overeaters Anonymous group and are free to register with the central office. They can derive their own practices, traditions, and legacy, as long as these are consistent with the traditions of AA.

This may present a conflict in the area of certain specialty meetings, such as women- or men-only meetings, meetings for gay or lesbian members, meetings for lawyers or medical professionals, and so on. Because of Tradition 3 (and after great debate over the years), such a limitation on membership is not according to AA rules. There appear to be two ways of resolving this dilemma. One way is to list the meeting with the central office and welcome others if they show up, with the meeting's focus being merely an unofficial designation. Another way is to keep the meeting off the books. One thing is clear—if the meeting is listed in an official meeting list (published by regional central offices), any alcoholic is welcome to attend.

Tradition 5

> Each group has but one primary purpose—to carry its message to the alcoholic who still suffers.

The limited focus of AA has been criticized, but it is really the source of its power. AA has endured for over 70 years as of this writing, and one of the reasons for this longevity is that it has not wavered from its original and only purpose.

To outsiders, AA's exclusive focus on alcoholism can be quite puzzling. If "a drug is a drug," why not open up AA to include persons with other drug dependencies? Why is there a tendency (not universally, but generally true) for AA meetings to discourage or openly ban discussion of other drug problems?

This question was addressed early on, in a pamphlet titled "Problems Other Than Alcohol," (alcoholics Anonymous, 1958) in which the writer (presumably Bill Wilson) defended the focus on alcohol as necessary to avoid diluting the focus of the fellowship. He encouraged persons with other problems to form their own associations. In this spirit, other fellowships such as NA, Cocaine Anonymous, and several others were formed. After a great deal of internal debate I have come to recognize the wisdom and value of this self-imposed limitation.

In my area some meetings are known to be more traditional and others more open minded in their acceptance of those with other problems. However, generally speaking, people with drug problems who attend an AA meeting are advised to limit their comments to those pertaining to their problems with alcohol, or to phrase their comments quite generally.

Tradition 6

> An AA group ought never endorse, finance, or lend the AA name to any related facility or outside enterprise, lest problems of money, property, and prestige divert us from our primary purpose.

Early on in the history of AA, Bill Wilson was given a chance to operate a ward according to AA principles in Towns Hospital (where he had achieved his sobriety). Apart from giving himself financial security, it was a tremendous marketing coup, giving AA exposure and legitimacy. However, the group conscience spoke up (Tradition 2) and cautioned Bill strongly against taking this position, in that it could corrupt the purity of the mission (Tradition 5). Reluctantly, Bill conceded the point and refused the job (White, 1998).

This has become quite sticky in the case of treatment facilities that employ recovering addicts as counselors and that rely on the TSF as the basis of their treatment programs. It is terribly important to draw several distinctions in these situations. First, AA or NA members who work in such a facility do not do so in their role as AA or NA members. Their AA experiences may certainly have molded their views of addiction and recovery, and may in fact be powerful in working with other newly recovering addicts, but in their employed role they do not in any way represent or embody AA. Similarly, the programs themselves will often announce that their treatment is based on 12-step principles and that regular AA or NA meetings are offered, but this does not imply any endorsement from these programs. Any meetings that occur on the site of a treatment facility are conducted by outside AA or NA members who volunteer to come in as part of the H&I Committee. The meetings themselves are independent of the facility.

Tradition 7

> Every AA group ought to be fully self-supporting, declining outside contributions.

As AA evolved, Bill and Dr. Bob sought ways to provide for financial security for themselves and for the program. In 1938 they approached John D. Rockefeller Jr., then the world's richest man, and one known for philanthropic contributions. Although he was interested in their work, he recognized that AA must be self-supporting to stay true to its purpose, and that finances could ruin the good work that had been done. He did provide a small donation to help Bill and Dr. Bob support themselves (they were both working almost full time to the development of the program, and Bill and Lois had been staying with friends for much of the early years) and helped with some publicity. However, following a period of bitter disappointment, they both recognized that external financial support could ruin the purity of their mission.

Tradition 8

> Alcoholics Anonymous should remain forever nonprofessional, but our service centers may employ special workers.

As stated in Twelve and Twelve, "money and spirituality do not mix" (Alcoholics Anonymous, 1989, p. 166). This tradition covers the more limited experience of hiring people to do work for AA, the converse of the situation addressed in earlier traditions. Early on, much of the work of the program was done by volunteers, who answered phones, cleaned the clubhouses, and so on. As the program grew, it became necessary to hire outsiders who were more reliable and skilled than members. Although this generated controversy (although not as much as AAs who were hired in the field and accused of "selling the 12th Step") it seems fairly commonplace now to find a hired manager or cleaning service in AA offices and clubhouses.

Tradition 9

> AA, as such, ought never be organized; but we may create service boards or committees directly responsible to those they serve.

As noted earlier, there are committees within AA that provide certain services to the membership as a whole. The guiding principle is to structure the fellowship as minimally as possible to allow it to function in its mission of helping alcoholics to recover. A committee or board within AA does not govern. It can provide suggestions and recommendations that the membership can then accept or reject.

It is extremely difficult to comprehend that an organization with so many members, such widespread influence, and so much success can function in such an anarchic and unorganized fashion. And yet it does.

Tradition 10

> Alcoholics Anonymous has no opinion on outside issues; hence the AA name ought never be drawn into public controversy.

As noted in Traditions 5 and 6, AA is focused on its primary purpose and avoids getting involved in other issues, even those that have some peripheral impact on alcoholics, for example, legislation seeking to expand access to treatment. While this certainly would affect alcoholics and addicts, AA will not lend its name to such programs. In similar fashion, no individual group (or member) can speak for AA. In some cases, advocacy groups have emerged to carry this campaign on, which are independent of AA, NA, and other such fellowships. PRO-ACT is such a group, which advocates for parity in, and normalization of, treatment of addicts in much the same way that the National Alliance on Mental Illness advocates for the rights of the mentally ill.

Tradition 11

> Our public relations policy is based on attraction rather than promotion; we need always maintain personal anonymity at the level of press, radio, and films.

We have become used to celebrities touting their enrollment in rehab programs and their membership in various TSFs. Some have even defended such disclosures in the hopes that their exposure will encourage others to face their own addictions. Others in recovery have seen such disclosures as violations of the 11th Tradition.

Over time, an elaborate tap dance has evolved in which people in recovery may disclose their attendance at a rehab, may refer to "getting help," or use a variety of code words for membership in a TSF without actually mentioning the fellowship itself. It may seem like splitting hairs, or euphemistic language out of *1984*, and there certainly is some truth to that observation. However, the general principle that the TSFs are programs of attraction, not promotion, is important. There is no proselytizing, no missionary work, no attempts to recruit members. What little effort takes place in this area is subsumed under the 12th Step. Members may make 12th Step calls when asked, may provide an informational speaker at a school, or may set up a booth to distribute literature at a psychiatric or psychological convention. The tradition of using one's first name and last initial has evolved to allow such communication to take place and has even extended to book authorship.

Tradition 12

> Anonymity is the spiritual foundation of all our traditions, ever reminding us to place principles before personalities.

Anonymity, so important to the program that it is part of the name of the organization, has two purposes. The first is the protection of the membership. Although now it is commonplace, or at times even fashionable, to declare oneself a recovering addict or alcoholic, in the early days addiction was one of the more taboo disorders imaginable. An early publicity photo of an AA meeting shows the members sitting in Lone Ranger–style masks (White, 1998). This was not an admission that one was likely to make with friends, much less in public.

The deeper meaning of anonymity is a spiritual one. It is yet another way of keeping one's ego in check. In particular, it seems to have taken this aspect on as a way of keeping Bill Wilson's ego in check, as his tendency toward grandiosity was legendary. (At one point, he made a suggestion that the movement be called The Bill Wilson Movement; needless to say, this was summarily rejected.) Seen in this light, anonymity provides a check against the natural tendency to seek acknowledgment for one's efforts and helps ground members in a sense of humility.

The Meeting

At its base, the core of the TSF is the meeting. Although some might argue that the steps and traditions are more important than meetings in preserving the intent and spirit of AA, the meeting is the place to begin to observe AA in action. There were AA meetings before there were steps, traditions, or even the Big Book. An AA meeting has been described as "any two alcoholics and a coffeepot." The original AA meeting, between Bill W. and Dr. Bob, occurred without any prior agenda and lasted 6 hours. Most meetings nowadays are more structured and focused, but there remains a great deal of variation in how meetings are conducted and construed. Some meetings may include 100 or more members; others may be two AAs talking on the phone. There are even meetings that occur in cyberspace. The steps cannot exist without some form of meeting, even if it is in the form of a letter or e-mail—usually, they are found in meeting rooms in schools and church basements.

As noted earlier, one of the facts that is difficult to grasp in AA is that there is no central organization. Each meeting is a free-standing entity and is entitled to set up its own protocols and establish its own culture. Tradition and custom have instilled some uniformity of practice across the program but there are still considerable differences between meetings and between regions of the country.

One thing that is clearly articulated in the traditions is that any meeting is open to any person seeking help with alcoholism. Over time, various specialty groups have emerged within the TSF for medical professionals, lawyers, women, men, persons with HIV, gay (men, women, or both), and so on. These are set up to provide a greater sense of anonymity, familiarity, and comfort to the members. However, at root, all are AA meetings and any alcoholic can attend.

Some meetings are designated as open meetings, referring to the general public. At such a meeting, in addition to the alcoholic member-ship, anyone with an interest or curiosity about the program is welcome to attend. Closed meetings are open only to alcoholics themselves. At some meetings, these distinctions become blurred, and at any rate, it is irrelevant to the alcoholic or addicted client, who is, of course, welcome at any of them.

The focus in AA is exclusively on alcoholism. As noted in the discussion of Tradition 5, outsiders and newcomers often find this difficult to understand—it is often assumed that any and all addictive behaviors, especially drug addictions, should be fair topics for discussion in AA. Indeed, some AA meetings have a higher degree of openness to other addictive issues (one meeting near my home is called Openminders for just this reason). Other meetings, however, hew to the more traditional perspective that AA is only about alcoholism.

In contrast, NA meetings are more open to discussions about any substance abuse, including alcohol. The philosophy there appears to be "a drug is a drug."

In the early days, Bill Wilson struggled with this. His primary motive in restricting the focus was a fear of diluting the power of the program if too many other perspectives were included. He encouraged others to establish parallel organizations. Starting with NA in 1950, we have come to see an explosion of groups based on the original 12-step model, including Overeaters Anonymous, Gamblers Anonymous, Sex Addicts Anonymous, and Emotions Anonymous.

What Happens in AA?

It is helpful in your practice to come to understand the local differences between groups in order to match your client with a compatible group. In my area, I am aware of which AA meetings are more receptive to those with multiple addictions. Many times, meetings are chosen on the basis of demographic or geographic interest.

In the case of clients with multiple addictions who choose to attend AA, generally the practice is to attend the program but only speak of alcoholism issues. This is more awkward when the alcoholism is seen merely as a peripheral issue to another more pressing addiction (such as cocaine), but frequently relevant perspectives can be gained by speaking of one's alcohol use, or by simply listening and applying the message to one's own unique situation.

Of course, in such cases it is always possible, and indeed appropriate, to attend a meeting for one's specific addiction, whether that meeting is Cocaine Anonymous, Pill Addicts Anonymous, or NA. However, many people feel compatibility in one group or another because of demographic factors and prefer to attend those. Also, in most areas, AA is far more ubiquitous than meetings for other addictions.

A young black man, serious about his recovery from his cocaine addiction, had difficulty finding a meeting that he felt compatible with. Apparently, the NA and Cocaine Anonymous meetings he attended had too much of a "street culture" and prompted some thoughts about using. One week he arrived at therapy openly relieved that he'd finally found a meeting where he fit in and where he felt welcomed. It turned out that he had stumbled on an AA meeting in South Philadelphia where the members were predominantly older Italian males. "They're a bunch of old winos," he told me, "but they don't care that my drug of choice was cocaine." They referred to him as "the kid" with a great deal of affection and respect for his obvious motivation.

Apart from the specific focus of the meeting, compatibility with specific meetings is critical. Some meetings have different flavors and cater to different people. Even clubhouses (dedicated spaces rented by AA where meetings are held all day, and where people can often be found between meetings) have different atmospheres at different meetings.

> I was working with a mild-mannered middle-aged woman who was quite nervous about attending AA at all. I realized that I had a very seasoned AA in my waiting room, so I went out and asked him for an appropriate meeting for a timid female newcomer. I came back with a recommendation for the woman, who agreed to attend. The next week she came back in a state of shock. Apparently, the chairperson of the meeting, identifying her as a newcomer, had immediately approached her and insisted that she tell her name and reason for attending. She had been mortified. As it happened, the same person was in the waiting room, so I told him what had happened and asked him for a second opinion. "Well, Charlie [the chairperson of the meeting in question] can rub a lot of people the wrong way. If she hated that, then she'll love Sunday at 10AM at Chestnut Hill." I persuaded her to try again, and, to her credit, she was willing to go. This time she returned ecstatic—this was a quiet, contemplative meeting, where all the introductions had been on an individual, personal basis, and which she found extremely rewarding.

There are several different formats for meetings, which are invariably included in meeting lists.

A speaker meeting features an AA member who tells his or her story. The format of the personal story (sometimes called a "qualification," or a "drunkalogue" if it meanders too much through war stories of addiction, neglecting to focus on recovery) generally follows a simple outline:

- What it was like
- What happened
- What it is like now

After the speaker completes the story (and sometimes after a brief smoke or coffee break) there is often time for personal sharing, often responses to the speaker's story. The expectation is that comments about the speaker's story and messages are to be related to something in one's own experience. Criticism of the speaker is rarely, if ever, offered, although sometimes a responder might say, "My experience was quite different."

A discussion meeting focuses on a specific topic. The chairperson typically chooses a specific area to focus on and may begin with comments on it. A sample topic might be humility or handling shame. Comments are generally made on the general theme that was presented; however, a person who has a pressing issue on an unrelated topic is certainly welcome to share that as well.

Step meetings generally begin with a reading of a chapter from the Twelve and Twelve (Alcoholics Anonymous, 1989) concerning one of the steps (usually, such meetings will continually rotate through each of the 12 steps on a weekly basis). Members may then share how they each interpret the step or how it has relevance for their lives. Similarly, a tradition meeting will discuss one of the 12 traditions in the same fashion. A Big Book includes a reading of one of the personal stories found in the Big Book and sharing based on relating that story to one's own experience.

Although beginner meetings are oriented to the newcomer, there is a lot of variation in how they are structured. Some are little more than regular discussion or speaker meetings in which newcomers are welcomed. Others provide a more organized presentation of the AA program. Still others (like the one mentioned earlier) provide a more formal setting to introduce new members and have them become known to the group, and vice versa.

AA meetings rely on members sharing personal experiences. Some meetings have a time limit, while others are fairly open ended. Generally there is a sense that one should share constructively and not hog the time. The chair can intervene if a speaker is becoming too tiresome or tangential, but this is relatively uncommon.

It is often a surprise to a person who is used to a traditional Yalom-like treatment group to observe that cross-talk is not usually allowed in a TSF meeting. This allows personal sharing without fear of contradiction or negative feedback. Each person's comments stand independently and are received openly by the group. Occasionally a person sharing will make reference to a previous sharer, but usually this is merely a jumping-off point for the person's thoughts. Quite frequently people will approach someone after the meeting ends to comment on the contribution or to offer support. This is perfectly acceptable and is usually welcomed. Newcomers especially, when sharing, will value having someone come up afterward to say that they appreciated what they had to say or how it had helped them. The TSF is that rare setting in which a seasoned member can appreciate and benefit from what a newcomer has to say.

Sponsorship

Sponsorship is a key ingredient in the process and a significant hurdle for many beginners. To a mental health professional it is easy to assume that a sponsor is like a junior therapist and is there to help the member with all sorts of life problems. In some cases this does happen, but this is not the ideal, nor is it a very good idea.

A sponsor is a more senior member of AA who provides guidance on working the steps. Nothing more, nothing less. It is true that working the steps can lead one far from what is written in the Big Book, but the basic process of sponsorship is quite simple.

At some meetings (often at beginner meetings) the chairperson may ask anyone looking for a sponsor to raise their hands. At other meetings, a list of names of potential sponsors is circulated or posted. Most often, however, it is up to new members to raise their hands and simply state that they are new to the program and are looking for a sponsor. Almost invariably, there will be a response from others, either in the form of a piece of paper with a name and phone number, or by contact at the end of the meeting.

Newcomers can ask for a temporary sponsor, someone to help them through the early days until a more permanent sponsor can be chosen. This is not considered a second fiddle position, and the member's choice to switch sponsors later on is not usually taken personally (and sometimes a temporary sponsor can become a permanent sponsor and life-long friend). On the other hand, some view the idea of temporary sponsors as suitable for those looking for temporary sobriety.

The choice of a sponsor is a serious matter in which there is a great deal of individual variation. Some sponsors are more involved, calling their "sponsees" regularly and giving tasks on an ongoing basis. Others are more reserved and standoffish, making themselves available, but placing the burden of contact on the sponsee. Neither of these is the best way to be a sponsor. Each person has different needs—while one person may feel invaded by a more aggressive sponsor, another may know that he or she needs help to stay accountable. Others may find that a more distant style allows them to proceed at their own pace and may value the respect for their individuality that this stance demonstrates. It may also be that an AA member's needs change over time. A person with a need for a more active sponsor in the early days may find that a more contemplative person is appropriate later on.

The difficulty, of course, is in being honest with oneself about those needs. It is not uncommon for those with ambivalence about the program to choose laissez-faire persons as their sponsors, in that it allows them freedom to goof off and not work seriously on their goals. It can then become convenient to blame the sponsor's stance for the member's failure to engage in the program. Conversely, someone may choose a more aggressive sponsor out of masochistic needs and set up a negative cycle of guilt and punishment that does little to bring the client toward serenity.

It is also helpful to look at the length of a sponsor's sobriety. The sponsor should have at least a year of sobriety, and preferably more than that. Some have said that the sponsor should have less than 10 years sobriety, so that they can remember what it was like to not be sober, but this is not universally prescribed. It is also helpful to know if this person is already sponsoring several others. This could indicate that the sponsor is taking on too many people for narcissistic purposes, or may not have enough time to give to each one. Finally, it is most important to look at the quality of potential sponsors' recovery. Are they working a program that you would like to emulate? Are they enjoying their sobriety and their life? Are other aspects of their life in order; do they have balance? This may be the most critical factor in such a choice.

Interestingly, sponsorship is not defined in the Big Book, or in the Twelve and Twelve; both books make only passing reference to "spiritual advisors." The practice arose early in the history of AA, probably in the Cleveland group (Kurtz, 1989) and became codified in a later pamphlet. Some see the introduction of sponsorship as one of the early AA experiments that became part of the program simply because it worked (White, 1998).

Although it may be redundant, it is important to state what a sponsor is not. A sponsor is not a teacher or guru, other than as a guide to the process of working the steps. The sponsor is not a therapist, and is not skilled to address all the many life problems that newcomers bring into the program. The sponsor is not a job coach, a check-cashing agency, or a referral service. A sponsor may fulfill any or all of these roles over time, but this is not the primary mission, and these are incidental tasks. The sponsor is simply there to share his or her experience as a guide to helping the sponsee work the steps. Yet this relationship can assume a profound place in both lives.

Obviously, this is a position that is easy to abuse, and there are all sorts of stories of sponsors who fail in this role, in all sorts of ways. There is little in the way of a self-correcting mechanism in the fellowship for such abuses. The sponsee must find a way to check his or her experience with other AAs and can be encouraged by others to confront the sponsor or terminate the relationship.

As a means to minimize certain obvious abuses and to keep things simple, sponsors are always encouraged to be of the same sex as the sponsee. Cross-gender sponsorship (except in gay meetings) is frowned upon, and is invariably a recipe for disaster. (Seduction of attractive and vulnerable newcomers, usually female, is often referred to as the "13th Step" and is, of course, discouraged and viewed negatively.)

Do not forget that the sponsor also derives benefit from this relationship, and not in the sense of ego satisfaction. The 12th Step calls for helping others and is at the core of the fellowship, in the experience of Bill and Dr. Bob. The sponsor's role in helping the newcomer is at least as important as the newcomer's need for spiritual and program guidance. Being a sponsor is part of working a program.

Aphorisms

Over the years, the TSF has developed an entire lexicon of aphorisms that are both useful and readily lend themselves to parody. Anyone with more than a passing acquaintance with AA can tell you about encountering members (stereotypically crusty old drunks) who speak almost exclusively in aphorisms, and for whom these sayings have become an entire vocabulary.

This is unfortunate, because many of these sayings are like bite-size pieces of recovery wisdom. The slogans may serve to cue recall of larger points of the program (McCrady, 1994). For a newly sober addict, they are easy to remember and may be all of the literature that a person can absorb. In this role, they are often crucial for sobriety as well as personal growth.

- One day at a time: Reminds the recovering addict that sobriety is a daily renewal and that worrying about sobriety over a lifetime is a meaningless and intimidating task.

> An undoubtedly apocryphal AA story has a newly sober young man talking to an old timer and marveling at the older man's length of sobriety. "It must be amazing to be sober for 25 years like you." The old man replied, "What time did you get up this morning?" The newcomer, puzzled, replied, "About 8AM. Why?" The old timer replied, "Well, today I got up at 9. Today you've been sober longer than I have."

- Easy does it: Encourages the recovering person not to get too upset by life's ups and downs. Taking life's struggles in stride is a key skill in remaining sober.
- First things first: Specifically, a reminder that sobriety is the most important task for a recovering addict, and that this must take

priority over all other considerations. More generally, this refers to the need to prioritize needs and to take it easy.

- Life on life's terms: The addict, long used to wanting to have things his or her own way, must come to understand that this is not always possible. The ability to accept life on life's terms is contrasted with the desire to have life on one's own terms. This is related to the surrender experienced in the early steps of the program.
- Let go and let God: "Letting go" can refer to old grievances, old wounds, and to the egocentric view that goes with most addictive lifestyles. "Letting God" means accepting the role of the Higher Power in guiding your life.
- Keep it green: Do not become complacent in your recovery—keep it fresh. It is not uncommon to hear stories of formerly destitute addicts, now stable and successful, who continue to attend meetings in homeless shelters or in detox centers to "keep it green" for themselves, as well as to provide a sense of hope for those in the early stages of recovery.
- Keep it simple: This was a favorite phrase of Dr. Bob's. For him, it was a caution (perhaps primarily directed to Bill) to avoid making the program too complex and too esoteric for the average drunk to comprehend. It can also refer to individual people's recoveries—remember that sobriety is the key to all other personal growth. When in doubt, what actions support your sobriety?
- Principles over personalities: The principles of the program are what guides actions and what sustains the program in general. This notion has led to the traditions of the program, a simple codification of its basic premises; this phrase itself derives from the Twelfth Tradition. The TSF is most definitely not a cult of personality; in fact, it may be that downplaying the personalities of the founders has allowed it to flourish where many other recovery programs have floundered (White, 1998). It is important, especially in moments of conflict, to separate the message from the messenger.

- Progress, not perfection: Recovery is a journey that is never completed. This is a reflection of our recognition that we are not God (Kurtz, 1989), as reflected in the famous phrase from the Big Book, "First, we had to quit playing God" (Alcoholics Anonymous, 2001). Allowing ourselves to be imperfect frees us from our lust for perfection and the inevitable sense of failure that this generates. However, we must remain focused on making progress in our own personal growth.

90/90 and 20/20

The admonition that a member attend 90 meetings in 90 days is widely known and is often seen as a requirement for membership. In fact, this prescription has evolved gradually and is not really part of the primary literature of AA. However, the practice of immersing oneself in the program has a great deal of value, whether done at the beginning of one's affiliation or later on. I have known alcoholics who dabbled in the program for extended periods of time before taking on what seems like a tremendous commitment—invariably this has deepened their involvement in their recovery and their investment in the program. Conversely, I have known some people who have taken on a commitment of 180 meetings in 90 days. For those with less structured lives, this can provide social and organizational benefits in addition to the specific recovery lessons learned.

A less well-known admonition is "20 and 20," referring to a practice of arriving 20 minutes early for the meeting and staying 20 minutes after the meeting. Some people will show up exactly at the start time for the meeting, and leave immediately after it ends. While sometimes this is necessary in a busy life, more often this reflects a fear of getting involved or a sense of social awkwardness. Arriving early and, more particularly, staying late allows a more informal connection with others in the meeting. Often enough, such connections can be more powerful and meaningful than the actual content of the meeting itself.

Social Recovery

Many people attend AA and pay scant attention to the steps and other aspects of the program. Indeed, one of the real benefits of the program is the substitution of a healthy, sober outlet for the social contacts of the addictive lifestyle. For some of these people this represents a transitional stage—they are testing the waters about their involvement in this group. Perhaps the spirituality of the program puts them off, or they may be alienated by some of the lingo they hear. Some of this group will deepen their involvement eventually, and others drift off, either back to their addiction or to find some other form of support. However, many maintain sobriety purely by social recovery—ignoring the spiritual component of the program, but becoming involved in the social support of the recovering community. While some may view this as a more superficial recovery, there is no question that it provides sufficient support for many to maintain more long-standing recovery.

> An acquaintance of mine had a drinking problem and I heard through the grapevine that he had joined AA and was sober. I ran into him at a social function and of course we discussed his involvement. "I don't believe any of that spiritual stuff. I know I used to spend all afternoon hanging around in a bar with a bunch of guys, and now I still need a bunch of guys to hang around with. It's just a sober bunch of guys." As of this writing, he has been sober about 3 years and has truly restored some sanity and stability to his life. He has custody of his children, has found a career, and has maintained employment.

Working the Program

Paying attention to the language that your clients use to describe their contact with the program can reveal a great deal about their involvement. It is clear from the discussion of the steps that a passive approach will not work, and active language is more reflective of an active stance than passive language. I am always gratified to hear clients describe themselves as "working the program" rather than "going to meetings," even if going to meetings is one of the key ingredients in working the program. Of course, in the beginning any involvement is positive and attending meetings is all that you can expect. As the person progresses, you can often pick up a shift in the language used, and the way the program is portrayed.

There are other ways to gauge the degree of your clients' involvement in the program. One significant milestone is the acquisition of a sponsor, even a temporary sponsor. In the "good old days" of inpatient rehab, patients were usually given a pass of several hours to go home, locate a meeting, and secure a temporary sponsor, so that they would have a place to go and a contact to make upon discharge. Some people have great difficulty securing a sponsor, often reflecting a difficulty in asking for help or a sense of humiliation in needing to do so. This becomes a relevant issue for outside therapy.

Another measure of involvement is in the assumption of some commitments or responsibilities. It is never too early to take on some minor commitment, such as arriving early at a meeting to make coffee or sweeping up afterward. Participating on committees is another way to provide service, although usually this is more appropriate further along.

Two more advanced modes of involvement include agreeing to chair a meeting and telling one's story. While chairing is usually done after a period of sobriety is established, people can tell the story of their addiction as early as 30 days into sobriety. While this is not for everyone, it can be a profound experience to describe one's progression into and recovery from addiction to a roomful of other recovering addicts. In terms of the steps, this act works several steps at one time, including the 1st (reaffirming one's powerlessness over substance use) and the 12th (bringing the message to other addicts and alcoholics). Furthermore, this act bonds one to the group in a way that has few other equivalents.

Finally, another way of gauging the client's involvement is listening for increased social contact within the program. As noted several times, the program extends beyond the meetings, and it is almost traditional for a meeting to evolve into going for coffee afterward. As opposed to traditional dynamic therapy groups, social contact between group members is encouraged and welcomed. Some clubhouses and meetings sponsor structured social events, including picnics, dances, and fishing trips. More informally, recovering members get together for social events much as everyone else does, but the opportunity to socialize without mind-altering substances is a relief for most newcomers. It is not necessary for a newcomer to watch the Super Bowl alone with white knuckles; it is virtually guaranteed that there will be a group getting together at someone's home to watch the game and drink nonalcoholic beverages. Within Gamblers Anonymous, a morning meeting often turns into an all-day family affair, with spouses and kids joining the members after the meetings for lunch and some other activity, such as bowling or touch football.

If your client is mentioning that he met someone at a meeting that he feels compatible with, it is likely that they will get together for some social contact, and this is highly encouraged. Lasting sober friendships can emerge from such contacts and help the newcomer feel part of a valid social network.

Literature

Over the years a bounty of literature has accumulated that supports and conveys the TSF. Some of this literature is official; that is, it is approved by the general services organization of AA or one of the other TSFs. There is also a wide variety of other literature published by independent parties, which interprets, expands, or dissects one aspect of the program or another. A publisher such as Hazelden (www.hazelden.org) provides an extensive catalog of literature published by Hazelden itself, by the fellowships, or by independent parties.

However, the emphasis here is on the literature directly published by the fellowships themselves, especially the more extensive body of work developed by AA, which is, of course, the longest-lived of all the TSFs. Beginning with the Big Book itself (Alcoholics Anonymous, 2001, original edition published in 1939), a body of work has developed that has formed a framework of 12-step knowledge. This body includes several books about the fellowship and its history, basic skills for sober living, a variety of pamphlets on specialized topics, and a magazine of AA experience and wisdom.

The Big Book (Alcoholics Anonymous, 2001), often referred to as the basic text of AA, comprises two basic sections. The first consists of 11 chapters, a chapter titled "The Doctor's Opinion," and forewords to each of the four editions. "The Doctor's Opinion" consists largely of Dr. Silkworth's opinions about alcoholism, and his theory of alcoholism as an allergy combined with a compulsion, which underlies the AA view of the disease. This section has remained virtually unchanged since the first edition. ("The Doctor's Opinion" was moved from the numbered pages to the front matter pages, marked by roman numerals, after the first edition. Some have noted that by making this move, the editors have made a mistake, in that eager newcomers may choose to skip this important chapter.) The second section consists entirely of personal stories of AA members. In the first edition (a reproduction of which is available from the Anonymous Press at anonpress.org) 29 stories of the early members were included, including the stories of Dr. Bob himself. Later editions have changed the stories to reflect the changing demographics of the fellowship. Sections titled "They Stopped in Time" and "They Nearly Lost All" were added to reflect the growing realization that, for some members, it was not necessary to hit bottom to fully engage in the fellowship.

Many newcomers to AA, myself included, have been advised to read Chapter 5 first as an excellent introduction to the workings of the program and the fellowship. This brief chapter, "How It Works," provides an introduction to the fellowship and the steps. However, as I have worked with the program, I have become more impressed with the need for newcomers to read the book in sequence, beginning with "The Doctor's Opinion." Especially for the potential member, this sequence has the benefit of explaining the disease first and promoting a powerful identification with the fellowship. Just as it is less productive to offer an active intervention to someone in a precontemplative stage of change (Prochaska et al., 1992), the specifics of "How It Works" can potentially be lost on a person who is not yet convinced that this material is personally relevant.

In addition to the Big Book, another essential volume in the TSF is the Twelve and Twelve, formally titled, *Twelve Steps and Twelve*

Traditions (Alcoholics Anonymous, 1989, originally published in 1952). This is a series of essays on each of the steps and traditions, written by Bill W. Much of our knowledge of the meaning and implication of the program of AA is derived from this volume.

Less cited, but equally important, is a thin volume titled *Living Sober* (Alcoholics Anonymous, 1975). This book consists of common lessons and tips for sober living from the experience of AA members themselves. While many of these tips are common sense (e.g., empty the house of alcohol), they form a great set of guidelines for sober living.

Later on, a sense of perspective came to the early members, and a series of books documenting the history of the fellowship was produced. The most important of these was *AA Comes of Age*, which outlines much of the early history, and whose title reflects the sense of maturity that the early members were experiencing. Biographies of the founders were also written (*Pass It On*, a biography of Bill Wilson, and *Dr. Bob and the Good Old Timers*, of Dr. Bob Smith), which detail the precarious state of the fellowship in the early days. Subsequent biographies of Bill Wilson (e.g., Cheever, 2004) present less sanitized views of the founder and also take advantage of more recent historical findings.

Bill continued to write prolifically, for the AA newsletter (*The Grapevine*) and in other contexts, and some of these writings have been collected and published in anthology format (Alcoholics Anonymous, 1967). In an attempt to reach diverse populations, the fellowship has also published numerous pamphlets on specific topics. Some are aimed at young people, older people, or incarcerated people ("It Sure Beats Sitting in a Cell"), and there are comic books for those who are unable to read. There are pamphlets on topics of interest to members: "What Is Sponsorship?" "Drugs Other Than Alcohol"; and prospective members: "Is AA for You?" "44 Questions." There are also pamphlets written for professionals allied with the fellowship ("About AA: A Newsletter for Professionals," "Let's Be Friendly With Our Friends").

In keeping with the times, AA now has a Web site (http://www.alcoholics-anonymous.org/) on which one can read anything from the Big Book to a pamphlet, and can help viewers find an AA meeting in their location. I recently used the Internet to locate a meeting for a client who was returning to his native Greece.

Narcotics Anonymous World Services (1988) incorporates aspects of the Big Book and the Twelve and Twelve for the NA fellowship. This book includes discussions of the workings of the fellowship, the steps (overtly adopted from AA), and stories from the membership. NA also publishes a very accessible step workbook, which can be useful to members from other fellowships as well.

For lone or international (e.g., seagoing) members of AA (numbering 292 based on the recent member survey) the literature serves as their sole connection with the fellowship. Reading a life story in the Big Book can serve as a surrogate for a speaker meeting, and reviews the "experience, hope, and strength" conveyed in a more typical meeting. For most other people, the literature provides a source of inspiration and direction in working the program.

Chapter 4

Defining the Goals of Treatment
and a Therapeutic Stance

Such privileged communications have priceless advantages. We find in them the perfect opportunity to be as honest as we know how to be. We do not have to think of the possibility of damage to other people, nor need we fear ridicule or condemnation. Here, too, we have the best possible chance of spotting self deception.

—Bill Wilson, 1961

Goals of Treatment

THE THERAPIST'S USE OF THE TSF IN THERAPY must be viewed in the context of a larger set of goals in the treatment of addictions. Too often a casual referral by a therapist to AA is not part of a coherent plan for the client's recovery. Such a referral may not be followed up properly, may be made without reasonable preparation of the patient, or may be done without an adequate conceptualization in the mind of the clinician.

This is a problem not only with individual therapists, but with addictions treatment programs as well. Many programs define their goals and procedures extremely vaguely in their policy and procedure manuals, and offer generic descriptions of what they do. Even a phrase like, "We base our approach on the TSF philosophy" does little to describe what actually goes on in such a rehab, or what modalities or techniques the clinicians employ. Developing a clear and consistent philosophy of treatment will be extraordinarily important in ensuring that treatment is focused and effective, and not just a "throw it against the wall and see what sticks" approach.

The model I employ owes a tremendous debt to the chronic disease model of Rogers and McMillin (1989). Their explicit delineation of treatment goals was the first clarity I experienced in my own development in the addictions treatment field, and was the beginning of my understanding of the disease concept and its value. It marked the beginning of my treating addictions as a primary entity and a step away from the vague, psychologically-based treatment I had been practicing. Although the ideas gleaned from their work have undergone significant changes, a reader of their work will clearly recognize their influence in the ideas that follow.

The overarching goal of the therapist in working with patients in the TSF model is to help the client achieve sobriety and to assist in removing the roadblocks to full engagement in the TSF. Under this general heading, I propose four further specific goals of treatment. These goals are subject to infinite individualization. However, they are broad enough to include the vast majority of clients suffering from addictive diseases. Each of these goals, furthermore, suggests a specific intervention or interventions. The specific goals for patients are:

1. Learn about the addiction
2. Self-diagnosis
3. Learn sobriety skills
4. Accept personal responsibility for recovery

The first goal—learn about the addiction—is critical on a number of levels. By providing a coherent understanding of the addiction (e.g., as provided by Dr. Silkworth in "The Doctor's Opinion" in the Big Book) we transform the nature of the task at hand. Rather than focus on developing willpower or moral fortitude, or on resolving internal conflicts, the client is refocused on coming to terms with a chronic illness. Rather than struggling with other areas of life (perhaps relevant, perhaps not), one's attention can be channeled in a direction that can be more productive for the client.

Another benefit of understanding addiction as a chronic disease is in removing the misguided guilt and shame that accompanies most addicted clients as they enter treatment. By accepting their problem as a disease, much of the burden of self-recrimination can be addressed and eventually released. The phases of such acceptance are not unlike the phases experienced in accepting other chronic conditions, but are exac-

erbated by ongoing public stigma (itself based on misunderstanding of the nature of the illness).

Explanations of phenomena that a client is experiencing, such as post–acute withdrawal (Gorski & Miller, 1986), are often ongoing elements of the therapy. A client experiencing mood swings or sleeplessness in the first few weeks of sobriety can often be comforted by the knowledge that this is a normal, biologically driven rebound phenomenon, which will pass in time.

The second goal—self-diagnosis—takes the first goal and makes it relevant to the client. Rather than helping clients become experts on addictive diseases, it is important that clients become experts on themselves, and their relation to the disease of addiction. Believing that one actually has this disease is a key step in developing the motivation to do something about it. Helping clients absorb factual information about the nature of alcoholism and addiction and apply it to themselves is the second key task of the clinician. Anyone who has worked in the addictions field for any length of time has encountered patients who have been in rehab any number of times, can deliver the treatment lectures as well as any of the staff, can quote chapter and verse of the Big Book, yet still harbor reservations about their own addictive status. This is because they have failed to adequately self-diagnose their illness and have failed to engage in thorough self-reflection. Therapeutic interpretations about self-destructive tendencies and self-sabotage may miss this more simple explanation.

Learning sobriety skills, the third goal, can be divided into three subgoals. The first two are often seen as the domain of relapse prevention programs (Gorski & Miller, 1986; Marlatt & Gordon, 1985), but are here simplified. The first one is to learn to identify and manage internal relapse triggers, or drinking cues. These are easily remembered by the acronym HALT (standing for hungry, angry, lonely, and tired). Although these are usually seen as primary internal relapse triggers, there are, of course, many more specific internal states that may trigger urges to drink or use drugs in specific individuals. A vital therapeutic task is to assist the client in identifying the internal states that may be relevant, and identifying effective coping skills to deal with them or avoid them entirely. (The additional physiological problems created by hunger are too frequently neglected in addictions treatment settings but are quite powerful in their own right. The discussion of this is beyond the scope of this volume, but the reader can consult a good book by Ketcham and Mueller, (1983), for basic advice in this area.)

The second subgoal addresses the avoidance or management of external relapse triggers or cues for using. Anyone with even a passing acquaintance with the TSF will have heard the phrase "people, places, and things," which refers to any person, place, or object that is associated with one's addiction. These are abbreviated as PPT as an easy mnemonic, the external counterpart to HALT.

It is important to emphasize that the problem with these persons and places is not in the person or place itself. The problem is in the classically and operantly conditioned responses that these factors trigger in the client. Assuming that one frequently got high with a certain friend Charlie, the direction to avoid him is not so much out of fear that Charlie will press a beer or joint on the patient (although that could be a concern as well), but that being in the presence of Charlie will trigger an urge to use in the patient, regardless of Charlie's actual behavior. This is, in essence, no different than a person feeling hunger pangs when he walks by a favorite restaurant or smells cooking coming from downstairs.

Avoidance of PPT is the key strategy to deal with these cues and the one most favored in TSF rooms. Some are quite obvious—recovering alcoholics should not hang out in bars, where the cues to drink will likely overwhelm even a firmly committed person. The sights, smells, and sheer camaraderie of such a setting will prove irresistible to most. ("You don't go to a whorehouse to read the newspaper" is how one veteran client once put it, ever so diplomatically, to another group member.) In the early days of sobriety, this is clearly the best and most clear-cut method, and one which should be advocated clearly. Client resistance should be anticipated, whether due to realistic factors or ego factors.

However, this is not always possible, and sometimes attendance at a place that has been associated with one's addiction (or a setting in which alcohol is being served) is unavoidable. Certain work situations, social demands, and unanticipated events may necessitate exposure to drinking environments or to dangerous triggers.

There are two levels of clinical response to this sort of dilemma. The first is to determine if the event is truly unavoidable. As in the Serenity Prayer, the key is in "the wisdom to know the difference." Most addicts find it quite easy to fool themselves, not to mention others, into simply accepting that they just cannot avoid going to a certain social event. Force of habit, if nothing else, can lead to placing oneself in jeopardy of a relapse. It is one short step to relapsing into active addiction, once placed in such a position.

The second level of response is to learn to cope with the temptations that are inevitably around us. Coping with such situations leans on a set of skills that are not necessarily natural but that flow from the principles of the TSF program, especially the principle of mutual support for recovery.

A woman in early recovery was faced with the prospect of attending her sister's wedding, which she knew would eventually turn into a drunken bash. Her group mates suggested that she skip the wedding entirely, given her early stage of sobriety, but this would have created more intrafamilial conflict than it would have resolved and, in any event, was not acceptable to the client. With the consultation of her therapy group and her AA sponsor, she developed a plan. First, she attended an AA meeting prior to the event to get herself into the correct frame of mind. Second, she had an AA buddy accompany her to the wedding for additional support. Third, she attended the ceremony but left the reception relatively early, after greeting all significant family members (so they would remember seeing her there) and before the party got too rowdy. Finally, she and her friend attended an evening AA meeting following the reception. Given all these safeguards, she was able to successfully attend the wedding without drinking and felt a sense of accomplishment.

Such a plan might not please a diehard AA member, given that this was exposing the client to drinking at a relatively vulnerable stage in her recovery. However, this decision was pondered by the client, her therapy group, and her sponsor (and was undoubtedly discussed in an AA meeting or two) and was ultimately her own decision. As much as we like to discourage our clients from playing Russian roulette with their sobriety, this was a calculated risk, entered into with clear and thoughtful preparation, rather than with headstrong abandon. The danger in such a success is in giving the client a false sense of safety and security. Ongoing therapy and AA work was key in helping her to recognize that her success was due to placing extra safeguards in place, not to any renewed ability to resist temptation.

The third subgoal within this heading is the development of some sort of group support for ongoing recovery. Obviously, within the goals of this book, the use of AA, NA, or other relevant TSF is advocated. However, should a client choose some other form of support group (e.g., SMART Recovery, Women for Sobriety, a church group), it can serve some of the same function. From this perspective, the minimum goal of ongoing support is necessary; however, from the perspective of the TSF, these other groups rarely provide the same sort of opportunities for personal growth and are not really addressed in this volume. This subgoal also provides the rationale for this book in general, as there is little to guide a newcomer or a clinician in understanding the workings of the program.

The fourth goal—accepting personal responsibility for one's recovery—may be the most elusive one. As described earlier, accepting that one has a chronic disease carries with it the burden of managing that disease, at the risk of continuing life chaos. Understanding the disease, self-diagnosis, and learning sobriety skills will be useless if one does not come to recognize that there is a responsibility to take charge of that aspect of one's life. While an essential message of the TSF is that one cannot work a recovery program without support, the converse is also true—that nobody is going to do it for you, and that nobody can make you do it.

This goal requires an awareness of one's existential position of aloneness, the need to acknowledge that condition, and then to connect with others around this very position. This carries with it the terrifying awareness that your life is of your making; rather than being an actor in a movie of your life, you are, in fact, the director. Even with the limits imposed by the recognition of one's alcoholism, or other such condition, the way that realization is handled is a matter of action and responsibility. This goal requires an abdication of the infantile position of passivity and the recognition of one's power and finite nature. In the face of such large-scale concerns, it is no wonder that this task is often avoided or is easily relegated to the sidelines.

Each of these four general goals implies a specific clinical intervention to realize it. The first goal, learning about the disease, suggests a didactic, educational mode of interaction. In fact, a great deal of work with addicts and alcoholics in early recovery is exactly of this nature. It has been estimated that 75% of primary treatment of addiction is simply education. It may not feel like classic psychotherapy, but a great deal of benefit is to be gained from simple educational interventions. I have developed a series of 2-minute lectures encapsulating specific bits of information that work toward demystifying and destigmatizing the nature of addiction. While there is undoubtedly an art form in deciding when and how to provide such information (based a great deal on the client's stage of readiness for change), such didactic work is a vital part of the entire clinical process of recovery. As noted by Brown (1985), behavioral change, without insight into the nature of the illness, is likely to be unstable and short lived.

I make a regular practice of providing feedback along these lines in every intake interview I conduct. When done well, this explanation of the disease can create an "Aha!" moment, which can be critical in both explaining clients' behavior to themselves and in piquing their curiosity for more such understanding.

I conducted an intake interview with an older alcoholic man and his wife. He presented with a clear-cut maintenance drinking pattern—he was physically dependent, with a high tolerance level, so he drank daily to avoid withdrawal but rarely got drunk or lost control. I explained the nature of this particular pattern to them, including why it is so hard to come to terms with it, as external consequences can be minimal. As I finished my little lecture, the wife turned to her husband and said, "He understands you better than you understand yourself." Fortunately for all of us, the man laughed and nodded and agreed that my description was indeed accurate.

The second goal, self-diagnosis, is accomplished largely through psychotherapy. The clinician must make use of the knowledge conveyed in the first goal and the data of the client's life to assist the client in making the connections between these two domains. One simple example is the phenomenon of tolerance. While many clients enter treatment with the idea that high tolerance is a sign of their ability to handle alcohol, it can be revelatory to explain that this is, in fact, just the opposite—that the human body is not supposed to handle a case of beer without some dire consequence (such as vomiting or passing out). While the client may debate this point, protests become harder and harder to maintain in the face of increasing evidence of impairment. The acknowledgment "I am an alcoholic" becomes a pivotal point in treatment.

It has been noted that the verbal acceptance of one's condition is only one part of the self-diagnosis process. Behavioral self-diagnosis is the next step in such acceptance: does the client behave as if he believes that he has this disease? Does he follow through on treatment recommendations? Does he demonstrate a respect for the disease? These are simple methods of judging if the self-diagnosis is more than just skin deep.

A man presented for evaluation of his alcoholism in an outpatient program. He verbally described himself as an alcoholic and reported a full picture of symptoms consistent with this diagnosis. He also noted that recently he had been vomiting every morning and that some mornings he thought he saw blood in it. We recommended that he enter detox immediately, given the potential health hazards of this condition. However, to our surprise, he refused admission for several days while he completed a project at work. All our entreaties were to no avail (e.g., "If you had a heart attack, you'd go straight to the hospital and not worry about the project"). After spending a great deal of time and recognizing that we had no leverage, we allowed him to leave, with our 24-hour hotline number. (To the amazement of all, he showed up on Friday, ready for his admission to detox, where he was successfully detoxed from alcohol and subsequently entered outpatient treatment.)

Here is a man who has all the data available, has made a verbal self-diagnosis, but whose behavior strongly suggests that he does not fully grasp the seriousness of his condition. He has failed to internalize his diagnosis.

The process of self-diagnosis may be thought of as an early stage task, relevant primarily in the precontemplative or contemplative stage. However, this is actually more of an ongoing task, often extending further into treatment as more complex recovery tasks are encountered. Just as the 1st Step is one that must be reworked and renewed regularly, this task of self-diagnosis requires ongoing reexamination and reevaluation.

The importance of group work in this goal cannot be overestimated. The power of group feedback to help people grasp the full reality of their condition can be far greater than that of an individual therapist, although the form it takes is often unsophisticated and begets resistance. However, it can be difficult for a client to ignore feedback, as well as similar stories, from peers. The less direct feedback available in the TSF can also be significant in helping people come to terms with their condition.

The process of "comparing-in" becomes relevant here. It is easier for people to make distinctions than to note similarities—it is a basic cognitive operation to see the differences between people rather than the commonalities. It is quite typical for newcomers to AA to think, "I'm not like those people," based primarily on some of the more extreme stories that they might hear at a meeting. By focusing on differentiation, newcomers then easily can "compare-out" and exclude themselves from the relevant contributions. Encouraging clients to compare-in when attending a meeting is vital to approaching the meeting with a more open attitude and can provide a focus for subsequent therapeutic input. Asking clients to identify five things they heard that were relevant to them (or asking them in advance to listen for them) can help clients utilize the meeting more productively and aid in the process of self-diagnosis.

However, even individual clinicians can be instrumental in helping clients grasp the nature of their disease. The finer tuning available in the individual setting, including the use of motivational approaches (Miller & Rollnick, 2002) may be more effective in allowing clients to relax their defenses and let the realizations take hold. Clinicians must find their own comfortable balance between a directive mode and a more nondirective motivational approach.

The third set of goals, learning sobriety skills, is managed by a combination of educational and therapeutic interventions. Some skills are best presented didactically, then processed therapeutically. In other words, a brief presentation of the basic principles of relapse prevention (e.g., internal triggers) can be followed by work on helping clients personalize and identify their own cues. In a group setting, the group can be given a structured task of processing the information; in individual work, this can be done less formally. This work is more appropriate to clients already in the action stage of change.

In this context it is not surprising to learn that role-plays and behavioral rehearsals can be quite useful in preparing clients to deal with such situations in real life. While this can often be done in an individual setting, group work provides a readily adaptable venue in which to practice such sobriety skills.

The preparation of clients for attending a TSF meeting is another important area. I find that some basic orientation is helpful to ease the culture shock that many clients experience on attending their first meeting. Some brief background about the nature of the fellowship, a few words about some of the local customs, and encouragement to linger afterward for some social contact may be all that is necessary. However, be prepared for questions and stories about the person's experience in the meeting. A client who has attended one or two meetings may be more receptive and curious about the customs and traditions of the program.

As noted earlier, the fourth goal, accepting personal responsibility, is the most elusive. This is partly due to the abstract nature of the goal, although the manifestations of such acceptance can be quite concrete. A person who cancels or reschedules his weekly tennis game to attend a favorite meeting is clearly demonstrating personal responsibility. A person who spontaneously goes out and reads a book on recovery is similarly demonstrating initiative to work her program. The absence of such responsibility is often easy to detect as well: skipping meetings, visiting with a friend in a bar, allowing others to smoke pot in one's apartment, or hanging out with old friends who continue to use drugs (even if not in the client's presence).

The primary modality for this goal is individual therapy and working the TSF with a sponsor. This is best thought of as a long-term goal. It is rare that a client understands this immediately, although some do. Accepting personal responsibility is a more gradual process, akin to the process of spiritual experience described in the 12th Step. As noted earlier, this often involves grappling with certain larger existential truths, which can be quite disturbing and thought provoking to the client.

Within therapy, this can also include some didactic elements. I find it helpful to draw a yin-yang symbol on a blackboard or piece of paper. I label one side "disease" and the other side "responsibility." In this manner, I can ensure that these two elements are viewed as inseparable and that the presence of a disease inherently mandates the acceptance of responsibility for managing it. I recall the story of my diabetic friend who took no responsibility for managing his disease, and our declining sympathy for him, despite our awareness of his lacking any sort of blame for contracting his disease. There is no blame or guilt involved in having such a chronic disease—however, managing such a condition is a matter of responsibility, decision, and effort. For a diabetic, this might take the form of self-monitoring of blood sugar levels and diet; for an alcoholic this involves working the 12 steps, avoiding PPT, and managing HALT.

Differences and Similarities in Psychotherapy and Addictions Counseling

The therapist working with an addicted client faces a different set of assumptions and principles, which are based on both stereotype and reality. It is helpful to contrast the following assumptions of psychotherapy and addiction treatment.

The Idea of Cure

Most psychotherapies carry some implicit assumption that the clinician will fix something about the client. Depending on the therapist's theoretical orientation, the therapist may be working to resolve internal conflicts, correct dysfunctional thinking, remove maladaptively conditioned responses, and so on. There is the notion that some aspect of the client is broken and requires repair.

In working with addicted clientele, the primary flaw in the client is unfixable. This flaw is the client's powerlessness over substance use, which is now seen as rooted in brain chemistry. The 12-step view of this is as an "allergy coupled with a compulsion," invoking both physiological and psychological dimensions, but both are seen as inherent in the nature of the alcoholic, and as a given in the scheme of things. While certain other aspects are subject to change (e.g., the client's acceptance of the condition, certain behaviors around the addiction), these are viewed as secondary, and not the primary issue, even if they do comprise a major focus of the clinical work.

Functional Versus Structural Analysis

Most American psychology is built upon the functionalist assumptions of William James, in that the mind is best understood by assessing its adaptations to its environment. The proper question to be asked of an alcoholic is "Why do you drink?" to understand the function of the drinking in his or her life. This is the assumption underpinning the typical psychological approach to addiction—to identify and address the issues underlying the client's use of substances. This is seen in the analytic search to resolve unconscious conflicts and in the cognitive psychologist's attempts to correct cognitions leading to drinking (Beck, Wright, Newman & Liese, 1993). With the emergence of the disease concept of addiction, viewing alcoholism and addiction as primary diseases in their own right, such an analysis appears misplaced.

In addictions counseling, the focus is not on why the addict is using, but on how the addiction works. The relevant issues here are in identifying the specific mechanisms of action of the drug on the system and on the behaviors associated with such use. Understanding patterns of drinking, for example, is more useful in helping a patient than understanding why the patient drinks in the first place. The question of etiology is still a relevant and important question but has less relevance and utility in the clinical setting.

> A group member was expressing the belief that if she could understand the reason why she drank, it would be easier to maintain sobriety. Another group member offered an answer, "Because you're an alcoholic, that's why." This was not half as sarcastic as it sounds on paper.

Something that can be heard in AA meetings, in a variety of forms, is the idea that if you have diarrhea, understanding how you got it will be a lot less useful than finding a bathroom.

Values

Implicit in most therapeutic work is the value of individual autonomy. In most therapies, great emphasis is places on successful individuation and models of psychological health that are based on human family functioning as the prototype of human development. Often, in family therapy, for example, a greater emphasis is placed on the task of individuating from one's family of origin (Haley, 1997; Leupnitz, 1988) than on preserving connections within the family.

In 12-step work, however, a model of interconnectedness influences the picture of mental health and values of recovery. The value of surrender, often invoked in recovery literature (cf. Tiebout, 1949, 1953), and the negative connotation of self-will are evidence that interdependence is more important to the process of recovery than is individual self-determination. The principle involved in this counterintuitive view is directly derived from the spiritual roots of AA, and the emphasis on community found in the Oxford Group. Without the Twelfth Step, invoking the need for recovering individuals to reach out to others suffering from the same disease, the entire fellowship would have ground to a halt after the first generation. More important, however, is the role that reaching out plays for reachers themselves in developing their own spiritual wholeness and in asserting the interconnectedness of all recovering alcoholics. In this context, the First Tradition, that AA unity comes first, also has a spiritual aspect.

Bill Wilson also invoked the model of human development in describing the growth of the fellowship and of the individuals within it.

His choice of the title *AA Comes of Age* (Alcoholics Anonymous, 1990) for his history of the fellowship reveals his concern for maturity, as opposed to infantile self-centeredness. However, his view of maturity is one in which the individual's autonomy is based in a secure foundation of dependence upon his fellowman as well as his Higher Power.

The Healing Process

In psychotherapy, a great deal of energy is invested in the relationship between the client and the therapist. This is most explicitly seen in analytically oriented therapy, in which the relationship itself is seen as the healing mechanism. The idea of transference is central to all psychoanalytic thought, whether as the mechanism for observing cognitive distortions in vivo or in providing a corrective emotional experience. Methods of treatment involve Socratic dialogue as well as more affectively laden interventions; however, the therapeutic relationship is viewed as the central agent for change.

In recovery work, the therapeutic relationship is viewed as secondary. The therapist is more of a coach for the real game, which is the TSF itself. The therapist is adjunctive to the major change agency, which is to be found in both the fellowship and the spiritual connectedness of AA or NA. The dependency that is often fostered and examined in analytic treatment (whether to help the client renounce it or to reexperience it in a healthier context) is, instead, transferred into the fellowship, where, in a more diffuse form, it is fostered and celebrated. This dependence, which is then experienced in a safer context, is reexperienced as one of the elements that render us human and imperfect, therefore serving to bind us together. The healing is to be found, not only in the other members of the fellowship, but in the fellowship itself. For many, this provides a safer setting for dependency than an individual relationship, although it may take some time for this feeling of security to take hold.

Defining a Therapeutic Stance

In general, most of the generic clinical skills of any good practitioner will apply to working with addicted clients (Hubble, Duncan, & Miller,

1999). Developing a positive therapeutic relationship is central to any further work with clients of any diagnostic group. A wide range of approaches may be useful in dealing with this clientele, and much will depend on the profile presented by the client. A few words may be helpful, however, in avoiding some of the more common traps.

Generally, as indicated in the previous section, the individual clinician working with a TSF should regard his or her work as ancillary to the work occurring in the fellowship (Brown, 1985). This requires a shift on the part of most clinicians, both in theoretical orientation and in terms of countertransference issues. Theoretically, the fellowship is seen as the primary agent of change, and the therapist's role as helping to facilitate that engagement. This may result in a premature termination of therapy, as clients feel that they are benefiting more from AA than from the therapy. The clinician must be prepared for this. However, this may not always be premature—it may be appropriate for clients to seek to deepen their involvement in the fellowship, and they may actually be getting more benefit viz-à-viz his recovery than from the individual therapy.

The key to a positive outcome lies in establishing a positive relationship with the client. More appropriate than terminating therapy might be reducing the frequency of sessions so as to maintain some contact as the recovery work progresses. The positive relationship with the therapist will make it more likely that the client will return should there be a relapse, and return without too strong a sense of failure or shame.

In fact, although most 12-step-oriented therapists might not agree, I will work with a client who is not convinced that he needs sobriety and wants to work on moderation goals. In such a case, I am prepared for the moderation goal to be successful or to fail. If it is successful (over a significant period of time, of course), this can be seen as a successful outcome. A client who fails, may then be more receptive to a discussion of sobriety and AA participation; sometimes this takes several cycles of attempt and failure to come to some sort of resolution.

In general, I prefer to remain in a relationship with clients, even if the recovery work is going poorly, rather than to give clients an ultimatum and risk losing them. As long as the client remains engaged in treatment we can continue to explore avenues for recovery in one fashion or another (White & Kurtz, 2006). The clinician should be reminded that the path to recovery is rarely a straight and uninterrupted one; one should anticipate relapses and setbacks—while not welcoming them, it must be recognized that they are common. What is critical from a therapeutic standpoint is to remain present and involved in the life of the client, so that successes and failures can be processed and learned from. I remind clients that every mistake, if it is not fatal, has a lesson in it, and that is the purpose in making them. The real tragedy is in making mistakes and not learning from them.

In this context, it is also important to keep in mind the sacrifices that we are (implicitly at least) asking the client to make. To give up drug and alcohol use is to ask the client to give up a secure and relatively reliable source of relief from daily pressures, and a major reinforcer of the central nervous system. This is no small loss, and one role of the therapist in this situation is to help replace the void created by the absence of the substance. The clinician can be viewed as a transitional object, halfway between the active addiction and the ongoing security of the 12-step program.

> One client, who lived at a distance, had infrequent sessions, but regular e-mail correspondence with me. Although she had been able to resolve her dependence on opiates, she now faced a variety of unpleasant life circumstances, including a difficult marital situation, exacerbated by her husband's drinking. However, one of the most stressful experiences for her was giving up the profound relief offered by her use of opiates. "It's like being kicked out of the Garden of Eden, never to return," she wrote. I recognized that none of the usual bromides would respond to the reality of her loss—she might repair her relationship with her spouse, she might improve other areas of her life, but for her the loss of pleasure associated with her drug of choice was experienced as a loss of cataclysmic proportions.

Of course, there are times when an ultimatum is the only ethical or practical option, but these are usually rare. There are times when a client's behaviors are dangerous enough to warrant a facsimile of the duty to protect. A client sharing needles with other addicts is at risk for contracting or spreading the HIV virus; clients who continue to drink and drive present a risk to themselves as well as to the public. There are less severe cases in which it is clear that the client needs a higher level of intervention and care: a public figure who goes to dangerous areas to cop drugs risks ruin of his career and family; a college girl who prostitutes herself for cocaine risks infection and physical danger. A failure to maintain even a small period of sobriety in spite of good honest effort is also grounds for seeking a higher level of care.

In such cases, a referral to an intensive outpatient program (IOP) or an inpatient level of care is necessary. This is best presented as a requirement for the client's own safety, if not only for the sake of entering a recovering lifestyle. What is important here is that the therapist reassure the client that the therapist is prepared to continue work with the client when this level of care is completed and will be involved during this treatment if possible. It is imperative that this referral is not seen as a rejection or as evidence of a failure. Some people simply need these levels of care and will do better being immersed in the culture of recovery in a rehab or similar therapeutic setting.

In some less severe situations, it may be necessary to refer a patient directly to the 12-step program in the belief that this is vital to the client's recovery. In such cases, I find it useful to direct clients to a specific meeting if possible, or to encourage them to find a friend, relative, or acquaintance who is already in the program (and invariably there is such a person in their life) to accompany them to a meeting or two. I also encourage a certain degree of shopping around in the beginning, although too much of this, or doing it for too long, can delay the establishment of a home group. Finally, I ask clients to pay attention to the other speakers in the meeting. I ask them to approach someone afterward that they felt some similarities to, and find out where that person goes to meetings. This can be an effective way of screening meetings.

Therapists' own ego needs come into play if they view themselves as being relegated to a secondary position. Most of us in the helping professions have a "righting reflex" (Miller & Rollnick, 2002) and, whether we like to admit it or not, derive satisfaction from viewing ourselves as significant agents of change. Acknowledging our secondary role or, even worse, losing our client to a self-help group (and a free one at that) can be deflating, to say the least.

I encourage clinicians to view themselves as part of a treatment system and to view their role as critical to the overall movement of that system. Generally, we only work with a subset of alcoholic and addicted patients—those who have problems in accessing recovery on their own. Many people enter the fellowship with no professional intervention at all. We are coming to learn that many others achieve sobriety without any external help at all—they just stop using, or "mature out" of the addiction. We work with those for whom these avenues of natural recovery have not been accessible, a tough group indeed. Our role in facilitating the process of their engagement in recovery is a crucial task, even if it is a limited one. We, too, must learn the lessons of humility we encourage in our clients.

Another factor influences the level of involvement in working on 12-step goals with the client. Nowinski (2003) refers to the distinction between active and passive facilitation. In passive facilitation, the client's TSF involvement is a secondary issue in the treatment, whereas in active facilitation, the client's TSF participation is a central theme in the therapy. For example, a person already in recovery may seek the assistance of a mental health clinician for other problems, such as depression or marital friction, and the awareness of recovery issues may be a secondary focus of treatment. On the other hand, a client may seek treatment specifically for issues relating to substance use, and our involvement may be more active in invoking the 12-step program.

A final issue in defining a therapeutic stance concerns the proper place of clinical expertise. With my evident preference for motivational and collaborative interventions over confrontational ones, the actual role of the therapist as an expert in this area can be lost. There are many times when the clinician's knowledge of both the addictive process and the recovery process are quite useful. At one level, demonstration of understanding the client's experience is an essential component of any clinical intervention. Knowledge of this area is especially relevant, as it does require a certain level of familiarity and comfort in talking the talk. There are a great many specific pieces of information that are important to know to answer relevant fact-based inquiries that a client may have. For example, it is important to be aware of the phenomenon of post–acute withdrawal—this is the period after acute withdrawal, when a client may experience mood swings, irritability, and sleep disturbances, attributed to ongoing dysregulation of the neurotransmitter system (Gorski & Miller, 1986). Even when a client does not directly ask for such information, being familiar with such data will be useful for demonstrating competence and answering legitimate questions.

Ultimately, the balance between expert and collaborative partner is a balancing act, one that is dependent on the dynamics of the client and the clinical acumen of the therapist. There are times when the clinician must maintain a decisive and authoritative stance, and others when reflective listening is what is required. And we may need to solicit advice from the Serenity Prayer, in that we seek "the wisdom to know the difference."

Bill Wilson's Therapeutic Model

Ernest Kurtz (1989) has analyzed Bill Wilson's style of responding to the many letters and inquiries that he received as the founder of AA. He was frequently sought out for his advice on both personal issues and the organization of AA meetings. A conflict within a group about some aspect of protocol might result in a letter to Bill for his opinion. According to Kurtz, Bill's responses generally followed a four-step process:

1. He restated the problem to ensure that he grasped the dilemma. ("So, as I understand it, your situation is . . . ")
2. He compared it to a situation he was already familiar with ("This is like a problem we encountered in a meeting in Akron . . . ") and described that situation in detail.
3. He described how the situation was handled ("What we did was . . . ") and what the outcome was.

4. He solicited the correspondent to let him know how they handled the situation and how it turned out ("Stay in touch and let me know how it worked out").

This strategy, whether consciously thought out or spontaneously developed, provides an excellent model of intervention in substance abuse cases, and may have utility outside this specific clinical area.

Breaking this strategy down, we can note several relevant components. The first step of the process has the advantage of functioning as an empathic reflection and can help the client feel that his concern has been understood. The emotional resonance of such a reflection can be powerful at both cognitive and subcortical levels (Lewis, Amini, & Lannon, 2000). The comparison step serves to normalize the experience of the client, and secondarily can destigmatize the concern. One can use self-disclosure, if comfortable with that, or can compare the situation with composite clinical material, or even with a fictional character.

Although it is a cliché to say so, most alcoholics and addicts tend to be resistant to direct interventions. In the third step, offering a suggestion rather than a directive (however well-intentioned and appropriate) is more likely to solicit the client's active participation in the solution. This was clearly something Bill knew intimately and intuitively.

The fourth step, the solicitation of ongoing feedback, helps to perpetuate the dialogue in therapy. This can refer to both immediate feedback to the suggestions offered or to the ongoing therapeutic relationship.

Personal Recovery in Therapy

Another prevalent cliché in addictions treatment is that only a personally recovering person can offer a therapeutic benefit to an alcoholic or addict. This is widely believed among recovering and nonrecovering staff as well as, all too often, clients themselves.

This belief derives primarily from the experience of persons in AA whose recovery depends on the fellowship of recovering people. It is supported by the poor results obtained from recovering people working with mental health professionals who work from an outmoded personality model of addiction—recall that as recently as *DSM-II* alcoholism was listed among the personality disorders (American Psychiatric Association, 1968).

However, this belief is based on a confusion between the roles of the fellowship and the role of the professional working with patients of any sort, including those addicted to alcohol or drugs. While the role of personal experience in facilitating recovery is central to the 12-step program, it may be less directly relevant in a psychotherapeutic relationship.

Stereotypically, the debate boils down to the addict asking the therapist, "How can you help me if you haven't been where I've been?" The clinician typically replies, "Does the surgeon need to have cancer to be able to operate on it?" or "If you had depression you wouldn't be asking that question." This debate can go in circles indefinitely. The key underlying question ("Can you help me?") is often lost in the confusion, challenge, and defensiveness that encircles this discussion.

The benefits on one side of this argument are apparent. It may very well be that the experience of recovery provides a unique position of empathy from which to address addictive issues. The very presence of a counselor who has recovered from a debilitating addiction is an inspiring example and serves as an irreplaceable role model. A nonrecovering counselor who is ill-informed about this area may very well demonstrate a lack of empathy with the real struggles an addict will go through and may identify less than relevant areas to focus on in treatment.

The liabilities of this position are not articulated as often. There is a type of blind spot that many recovering counselors may demonstrate, in confusing their own experience of recovery with broader principles. Having had a positive experience in working through one's own addiction to a position of recovery may often result in a limited view of the process by which recovery is obtained. "It worked for me" is valuable, but may not be a universally applicable process.

Many recovering people who become counselors also do not have enough understanding of countertransference issues, either as a result of their own experiences or a lack of training. It is not uncommon to encounter such a professional who may be working out a resolution to his or her own issues through working with a client. Surprisingly, this is most often seen in a harsh and punitive attitude toward the client, rather than the empathy that might be expected—it seems to reflect a feeling of "if I can do it, you can do it." This is also sometimes seen in a too-sympathetic approach, in which the counselor sides with the client against members of the family or social circle, who are seen as persecuting the client.

Nonrecovering clinicians may also suffer from a lack of empathy, although the sources of this may be different than for a recovering counselor. Another problem for a nonrecovering counselor can be a lack of familiarity with the material of addiction and recovery (the goal of this book is to offset some of these deficiencies). This can be a fatal flaw in working with this population, with whom it is essential to demonstrate a degree of comfort with this area.

Whether the clinician arrives at this place by personal experience or through study and work experience is less critical than the ability to demonstrate an understanding of the illness, having a road map for recovery, and conveying empathy for the client.

When confronted by a client asking to know your recovery status, it is best (albeit sometimes awkward) to refocus empathically on the presumed underlying question, "Can you help me?" Although a hostile client can easily turn this discussion into an argument aimed at devaluing the therapist's role, it helps to refocus on the relevant question of one's ability to help the client. I am usually comfortable disclosing my own recovering status (I am not a recovering addict) following a brief exploration of the meaning of the client's inquiry. Others may choose a firmer policy of nondisclosure, with a goal of putting this question back on the client. What I have noted, over the years, is that as I demonstrate a greater familiarity with the content and process of addiction, I have been asked this question less frequently.

Chapter 5

Common Treatment Issues

NOW THAT WE HAVE REVIEWED SOME OF the basic concepts and practices in both the TSF and the therapy stance, we will discuss some of the more common issues that may occur in concomitant psychotherapy.

Diagnostic and Triage Considerations

Before even considering your patient's involvement with the TSF, it is prudent to review some important diagnostic considerations. In assessing a patient with a substance abuse problem, it is crucial to be alert to conditions that will require more intensive intervention, such as psychiatric and medical treatment, inpatient treatment, or some combination of these. It is not uncommon to encounter clients who are continuing to abuse substances up to the moment they walk through your door. While our goal is usually to eliminate such substance use (even moderation management programs advocate a period of sobriety prior to attempting controlled drinking) the abrupt termination of some substances can be dangerous and potentially life threatening. Alcohol, barbiturates, and benzodiazepines (e.g., Valium, Xanax) are particularly dangerous, and sudden termination of the use of these can lead to seizures and even death. While heroin and cocaine do not present the same immediate health risks for detoxification, many addicts are unable to tolerate the discomfort of withdrawal and may be unable to successfully abstain without external controls such as inpatient rehab or supportive medications.

On a different note, many addiction problems present initially as psychiatric concerns, particularly depression and suicidal ideation. A thorough assessment may reveal that the depression or suicidal thinking is related to despair about substance use, but this is not always clear, in that the client may underreport usage or omit reference to it altogether. Most clinicians are poorly trained in assessment of substance abuse problems, and even primary care physicians are too often appeased by brief denials of use, without asking even the most basic follow-up questions. In some situations, although it is determined that the primary problem is addiction, a psychiatric intervention or hospitalization may be necessary for the safety and stabilization of the client, prior to any intervention around the substance abuse issues.

I have found that it is usually necessary to ask a series of pointed questions to pin down exactly how much of a substance a client is using, and how often. Daily use is, of course, more problematic, particularly with regard to withdrawal symptoms, but even episodic users (especially of benzodiazepines) may manifest withdrawal symptoms after a few days of abstinence. It is far too easy to accept a patient's offhand remark that his use of a substance is not problematic or "not often," and such assumptions can lead to dangerous mistakes.

> In a recent assessment, a client reported daily alcohol and marijuana use. When I reviewed a list of other substances, he responded that he used cocaine occasionally. I tried to pin him down for specifics. At first he said that he never bought it, but only used if it was available. Two or three questions later, it came out that his roommate was a drug dealer, cocaine was always available, and he was using it virtually daily.

It is beyond the scope of this book to review all the considerations in making such triage assessments. While a complete familiarity with standardized sets of criteria for level of care decisions is ideal (such as the criteria of the American Society of Addiction Medicine, 2001), it is certainly important, at a minimum, to be aware of significant high-risk detoxification situations. It is also important to have referral resources available for such situations, including local detoxification and psychiatric facilities. This is an area of high liability, and some education and awareness is essential for successful practice.

A second assessment consideration concerns the *DSM-IV* diagnostic criteria for substance abuse problems (American Psychiatric Association, 2005). The *DSM* distinguishes between two levels of substance abuse problems: abuse and dependence. Dependence (generally synonymous with addiction) is characterized by three clusters of symptoms: physical dependence, elevated tolerance, and loss of control over use. Abuse refers to a condition in which substance abuse is creating some level of life problems for the client, but physiological signs of dependence, tolerance, and loss of control are absent. Given that a basic assumption of the TSF is that abstinence is required, it is helpful to ensure that the client's clinical picture is consistent with the criteria for dependence, regardless of which substance is being abused. Those meeting the criteria for abuse may also benefit from attendance at a TSF meeting, but they may find it more difficult to "compare in" with the stories being told. Substance abusers may indeed be in an early stage of addiction, but they may also be dealing with difficult life stressors and may require a different sort of intervention. This requires careful assessment, both of the diagnostic criteria and of the surrounding psychosocial situations, to avoid making assumptions that will alienate the client and that may be clinically inappropriate.

A client was referred to treatment by her employer after she arrived at work with alcohol on her breath. She acknowledged increased alcohol intake in the past few months, since the dissolution of her marriage. Assessment revealed that she was indeed drinking heavily, on a near-daily basis, but that her tolerance level had not increased and she did not show symptoms of withdrawal. Her drinking also did not fit the classic picture of loss of control. Her diagnosis was alcohol abuse, not alcohol dependence. In her case, a brief period of supportive counseling and one sample visit to an AA meeting were sufficient to reduce her level of drinking to a more moderate and less problematic level.

The Therapeutic Relationship: Establishing Credibility

Any and all of the recommendations discussed in this chapter, and indeed in this book, presume a decent therapeutic relationship and some knowledge of addiction (the latter of which this book is addressing). Mental health clinicians, regardless of theoretical background, must concern themselves with establishing a sense of safety and security in the therapeutic environment. The quality of the therapeutic relationship is one of the key common variables that affect clinical outcome (Bachelor & Horvath, 1999). It is presumed that readers of this volume are sufficiently experienced at this level of clinical interaction. Demonstrating knowledge of addiction comes with experience that will, hopefully, be aided by this book.

Facilitating Initial Exposure to the Program

How, and even whether, to introduce the client to a TSF will depend on an assessment of the client's stage of readiness for change (Prochaska et al., 1992). Within this Transtheoretical Model, people can be observed to be at different stages of readiness for change; different interventions have been shown to be more useful at each stage. However valid an intervention might be, applying it at the wrong stage will result in a poor outcome. Even the suggestion of AA before the client is ready to hear about it, or before a recognition that addiction is a problem, will most likely be counterproductive. Readers unfamiliar with this model are highly encouraged to consult the work of Prochaska, Norcross, and DiClemente, or even *Changing for Good*, a self-help book they have authored (Prochaska, Norcross, & DiClemente, 1994).

Briefly, the model presumes several levels of readiness:

- Precontemplation (denial or lack of awareness of a problem)
- Contemplation (awareness of a problem without intent to work on it)

- Preparation (intent to make a change, without having taken action yet)
- Action (actively working on the problem)
- Maintenance (relapse prevention)
- Termination (facilitating exit from the stages)

As noted, different intervention strategies have been demonstrated to be more effective at different stages. A recommendation for participation in a TSF will be most effective at the preparation or action stage, when the client is actively seeking direction in how to address the problem he or she has identified and is motivated to work on. In some cases, a referral to AA at the contemplation stage may be useful to help gather and compare information. On the other hand, a suggestion at that stage may be premature and result in a therapeutic backlash. However, a referral at the precontemplation stage is more than likely to be counterproductive; in such situations, the client will usually refuse the recommendation, and the therapist may lose some credibility.

Even without an in-depth knowledge of this system, however, some commonsense rules apply. A discussion about attending a 12-step meeting, even as an experiment, should be based on some level of acknowledgment that there is a problem, and some agreement about the nature of that problem. For example, a heavy drinker may be quite willing to agree that there is a problem, but he may feel that the problem lies with his wife, not with his drinking. In another scenario, a person may agree that her heroin use is problematic, but may think that the real problem lies in an underlying depression and that working on her addiction is merely addressing a superficial symptom. (This is actually a common belief; recall the psychological model described in Chapter 2.) Until there is some consensus between therapist and client, a referral to AA or NA is probably premature. One exception is if the therapist believes that exposure to the TSF might help clients identify with the stories they hear and facilitate acceptance of their condition.

Within the Transtheoretical Model, the goal becomes moving the client from one stage to the next, not necessarily to the goal. In the case of a person in the precontemplative stage, the goal becomes raising awareness of the problem and moving to the contemplative stage. In psychodynamic terms, we are trying to move the problem into an ego-dystonic state. While the temptation is to confront the client with obvious evidence of the negative consequences of his or her behavior (e.g., the recent DUI arrest, the recent near-overdose, the loss of job), it has become increasingly clear that confrontational approaches are not nearly as effective as more subtle motivational methods (Miller & Rollnick, 2002; Miller, Wilbourne, & Hettema, 2003).

What might such a method look like? For example, a client may present with an employer and spouse who have referred him because of concerns about his drinking and marijuana use, but he feels that his use is under control and is not the real problem. In a motivational approach, rather than present the spouse's and employer's evidence, the therapist will ask the client to discuss the complaints that each party is presenting (therefore putting him in the position of making the case) and then asking him to describe his response (increasing the level of discomfort). At any relevant opportunity, the clinician may ask about the connection of these concerns with his actual substance use (e.g., "So, on that day that your boss was angry, had you actually gotten high?" or, better yet, "Your boss must have been really convinced that you were high"—allowing him to validate this if he is ready to do so). Similarly, "That night your wife asked you to leave, how much had you been drinking?" is one way of addressing this, or "Your wife gets so upset when you drink" opens up the discussion as well. These questions or reflective statements are ideally phrased in a nonthreatening, nonjudgmental manner. In my experience, if you phrase the question well (which is more difficult than it sounds), the client will make the connection. When well done, it is not necessary for you to make the connection for them, and, of course, it is better if you do not need to.

A client joined a research project in which she was given either a medication to curb her cravings or a placebo. She was initially asked her goals, one of which was to lose weight for health reasons. After several months in the study she was complaining that she was sure she was in the control group as nothing had happened. In reviewing her Time Line Follow Back (TLFB), a retrospective measure of her drinking in the past few weeks, it was apparent that her drinking had actually reduced by over 50% and she had lost nearly 10 pounds. Even when these two facts were presented to her, she did not see the connection. In this case, the therapist had to state, "Do you think that drinking less may have something to do with your weight loss?" Only after this direct intervention was the client able to recognize that she had actually reduced her drinking and that there was a positive impact on her stated goal.

To complicate matters, there are basic differences between clients who present with substance abuse issues as the chief complaint, and those for whom substance abuse issues emerge from other primary concerns. Although both groups may present some resistance to attending AA, there is a more difficult conceptual challenge with the latter group, who did not seek help for this problem and for whom there are additional obstacles to accepting help for it. They are almost certainly in the precontemplation stage.

If the client is in the contemplation or action stage, he or she may be more receptive to a referral to AA, and you may be surprised that any number of them may have already attended or otherwise had some exposure to the program (e.g., through a friend or relative who has achieved sobriety in AA or NA). Often enough, a simple question will suffice to introduce the topic: "Have you considered going to an AA meeting?" or "Do you know anything about NA?" This is an easy way to begin the discussion. This is far preferable to suggesting or demanding directly that a client should attend. "You really need to go to an AA meeting," or worse, "If you don't attend AA by next week, don't bother coming back" (a sentence a supervisee of mine actually reported using) are not appropriate initial interventions, despite how often these approaches have been used in the past or are still used in some settings. It is helpful to view our role as helping clients to resolve ambivalence about getting help rather than forcing them to get better.

In such cases, depending on your client's level of exposure, you may need to present a brief and concise description of what the program is and what it does. Here is where your own level of familiarity with the program becomes an essential component of your effectiveness in making the suggestion a viable one. Your comfort in making this suggestion is directly related to the client's willingness to accept it.

I have a case that I think of as my most successful case in this vein:

A man sought treatment specifically for his difficulty with alcohol. He did not drink on a daily basis, but whenever he indulged, he found that he could not stop and drank too much. On my initial interview, I told him that he was probably alcoholic and raised the issue of AA. Although he had had no direct exposure to the program, he had certainly heard of it, and was willing to give it a try. I gave him a choice of several meetings in his area and he agreed to attend one during the next week. At our second meeting he reported on his attendance and how positive he felt the experience was—he had been welcomed and was amazed at how much the experiences of some of the others in the room had mirrored his own. However, he had a number of questions that had not been answered—what was a sponsor, what was this "Higher Power" that he kept hearing about? We discussed these issues to some degree and I directed him to return to the meetings, ask questions, and be open-minded. At our third session, he was bright, sober, and more confident. He told me that his approach was successful, that he felt quite comfortable in AA, and that he did not see any need for further therapy. I agreed with him and we parted amicably, with an invitation for him to recontact me if he ever felt the need. Several months later I encountered him and he was still sober and appreciative of our contact.

In "selling" the program, I usually make several key points:

- It is a voluntary fellowship—nobody is going to twist your arm into going, least of all me.
- It is anonymous. You do not have to give your last name or any other identifying information about yourself. You do not even have to admit you have a problem. If anonymity is a more sensi-

tive concern, you can seek out a meeting in another community where you are less likely to be known. Remember that anyone who sees you there is there for the same purpose.

- People are extremely friendly and welcoming. There is no real pressure to speak or participate beyond introducing yourself by first name.
- It beats watching TV. You will hear some interesting stories, at the very least.

When clients agree to try it, I usually make the recommendation that they give it a fair trial, by which I mean that they should agree to attend at least five meetings before making up their mind about it. On any given night a meeting might be bad for a variety of reasons, or may simply be a poor match for a client, so a decision should not be made on the basis of one meeting. I also suggest that they listen carefully for someone who they can relate to speaking in the meeting, and then approach that person afterward and ask for the locations of other meetings they attend.

Almost universally, even when clients return with an unfavorable opinion of the program, they report being made to feel welcome and comfortable by the other members present. Negative reactions to meetings are usually reflective of some internal reservations on the part of the client, not of some actually negative experience in the room.

At other times, clients may be quite hesitant to attend the TSF, for a variety of reasons (which we review below). Recognizing that there are at times somewhat valid reasons for this resistance, it is best to process these reasons with the client. A nonjudgmental, empathic, open-minded approach is the best way to fully explore such issues (Miller & Rollnick, 2002). If a motivational approach is successfully followed, clients will often present the answers to their own reservations.

When a client refuses to attend, I generally do not press the issue. I will solicit other plans from the client and review alternatives. I do, however, feel free to bring up AA or NA as a resource at subsequent sessions. A nonthreatening statement such as, "Have you done any thinking about attending that AA meeting?" can be used to stimulate this discussion.

However, there are times when a direct recommendation to attend a meeting is entirely appropriate. The most common instance of this is when a client has had several failed experiences at establishing sobriety or is isolated. In such a case, I might make a direct suggestion to give the TSF a try. It is often useful to frame such attendance as an experiment, just to see if it can be helpful. Feel free to use any and all of the sales pitches described above. Presenting it as a minimal commitment can also be helpful. Another helpful point to make is "it's only an hour of your time."

As noted above, once clients have agreed to try it, I do attempt to secure an agreement that they will give it a fair trial by attending at least five or six times. This is a good initial contract and allows the clinician a great deal of leverage for maximizing the client's exposure to the program.

One key issue at this juncture is respect for the difficulty and the natural struggle with change of any kind. It is more realistic and useful for us to construe our clients' reaction as ambivalence than as resistance (Miller & Rollnick, 2002). We must make sure to honor the degree to which giving up drug or alcohol use is giving up a familiar and, at some level, gratifying lifestyle. For many of these clients, this lifestyle is the only one they have known for many years, and it is difficult for them to conceive of any type of alternative without using. It is quite easy for us to minimize the degree of this struggle in our natural desire to make this transition smooth for the client. Even as innocent a comment as "you've got nothing to lose" may backfire, if the client has been contemplating the loss of drinking buddies or the prospect of facing fears about social-izing without being high. It is more productive to empathize with clients' ambivalence than it is to try to talk them out of it. "It's not an easy thing to do; I admire your courage in considering it" is better than "You'll see, it will be great." Remember that true courage lies not the absence of fear, but in doing something despite fear.

Abstinence as a Goal: Moderation Management

Some clients are willing to acknowledge that drinking is a problem, and that they need to effect some change, but are not yet willing to accept a goal of total abstinence. Such a goal, of course, is a basic tenet of the 12-step approach, without which there is little point in proceeding. You will frequently hear this expressed in the statement: "I just want to drink like a normal person" or some variant. This is most often accompanied by the introduction of some sort of control strategy (Rogers & McMillin, 1989) to change their use; it could include switching from whiskey to beer or wine, changing the brand they are using, attempts to start use later in the day, buying a smaller quantity, and so on.

A traditional model of dealing with this situation is to attempt to persuade the client that this is not viable, given the diagnosis. Any attempt to resume drinking or using on a moderate level is doomed to failure. In reply, clients will sometimes report that friends or relatives, with as much history of use as themselves, have ended up social drinkers or casual drug users. The traditional reply is, "They won't get away with it for long."

Unfortunately for the hard-core abstinence advocates, there appears to be sufficient evidence that some addicts and alcoholics can indeed return to moderate use, and that in some circumstances, this is a common outcome (Dawson et al., 2005; Rotgers, Kern, & Hoeltzel, 2002). Attempts to persuade a client otherwise are not a profitable or enjoyable enterprise, and are probably not the best way to address this situation.

Interestingly enough, a common solution to this dilemma is found in the Big Book itself (Alcoholics Anonymous, 2001). Although it is often read as an ironic suggestion, there is no doubt that this is a viable strategy:

> We do not like to pronounce any individual as alcoholic, but you can quickly diagnose yourself. Step over to the nearest barroom and try some controlled drinking. Try to drink and stop abruptly. Try it more than once. It will not take long for you to decide, if you are honest about it. It may be worth a bad case of jitters if you get a full knowledge of your condition. (pp. 31–32)

Two immediate objections to this strategy usually arise. The first is an ethical and clinical one: what if the client starts using and never returns? If this is a disease of lost control, how is the client to return to treatment? The second is a liability one: what if the client gets into, for example, a car accident, only to claim that "my therapist told me it was okay to drink"?

The answer to both lies in the therapeutic relationship that must form the context for any of these recommendations. It is important that a recommendation of abstinence be made, even conditionally, to ensure that clients are aware that this is an option and that their choice is paramount. "If you don't drink, you won't have a drinking problem," or "The safest strategy is to cut out drinking altogether" are two simple ways that this stance can be conveyed. If the client chooses to reject these suggestions, this can be acknowledged and documented. Often enough, there is no subtlety about this; clients will frequently directly announce that they have no intention whatsoever of quitting drinking or smoking marijuana. (This is no different than working with a client who may be better off in an inpatient setting but who rejects that option; one documents that refusal, but may continue to work with the client.)

More important, however, is the establishment of a therapeutic relationship within which such experiments can be viewed as part of a process of self-discovery. I would much rather have a client fail at moderation and return to treatment than succeed at sobriety but leave treatment prematurely.

A client presented with a clear-cut loss-of-control drinking pattern— although she could go for weeks without drinking, once she started she was unable to moderate her usage. Although she had prior positive experience in AA, she was ambivalent about abstinence. On naltrexone, however, despite a clinical recommendation for sobriety, she was able to drink moderately for a period. "This is too good to be true—I've never had only one drink in my life," she reported. However, after several weeks, she found that she continued to have heavy drinking episodes that were problematic on several levels. Each week, we processed the experience and she voiced her intent to succeed at moderate drinking. Following a bender after some serious conflict at work, she came to treatment with a new thought. "I guess I can't control it," she concluded. In this case it was far more powerful that this conclusion was her own, not the clinician's. She was then more open to a suggestion that she return to AA for some support for this new decision.

A variant strategy is to suggest that the client attempt a month of abstinence. This can be sold by noting that even moderation management approaches often call for 2 weeks or a month of sobriety to establish a baseline (Miller & Munoz, 2005; Rotgers et al., 2002). This is far safer from a legal and clinical perspective, but may not be accepted by clients. In fact, sometimes a client will fail at this goal but continue to provide rationalizations for the failures; in such a case it makes sense to acknowledge that the goal has shifted from one of abstinence to one of moderation and proceed accordingly. Again, if the moderation goal is not successful, the issue of abstinence can be reintroduced.

In either scenario, the goal is to establish a safe, nonjudgmental environment in which to explore the client's addictive behavior, while building a therapeutic relationship. Only in the context of a supportive relationship can you help the client make changes, even if this may take some time.

There are some situations in which a clinician does not have the luxury to explore such options. When a client presents with clear evidence that drinking or drug use are out of control, such experiments are not indicated and are not to be suggested. Of course, we cannot control the client's behavior outside the consulting room, but in cases where the client continues to drink and drive, have blackouts, engage in high-risk drug behaviors (e.g., sharing needles), go to dangerous corners to cop, and so on, it is imperative to be more clear-cut and directive about the goal of abstinence. As noted earlier, it is best to take a client-centered or motivational approach to helping the client see that abstinence is the healthier and safer route.

For some clients, success at moderation may be quite a relief. It is important to work with them over a period of time, as even a loss-of-control drinker can sometimes maintain moderation for short periods of time. However, there are some for whom moderation becomes the goal. This is quite inconsistent with the 12-step approach, and readers are directed elsewhere if they are interested in pursuing this clinical approach or are interested in this area (Miller & Munoz, 2005; Rotgers et al., 2002).

Ambivalence About the Label Alcoholic or Addict

Some people carry a stereotypical image of an AA meeting in which each person will introduce himself in the same fashion: "I'm Jim, and I'm an alcoholic." For some, considering such an admission is itself a barrier to attending and participating in AA. It is easier to think of oneself as having a drinking problem, being a problem drinker, or having a problem with alcohol than it is to use the word *alcoholic* in describing oneself.

For years I bypassed this issue and told clients that the label did not matter as long as they took appropriate action to better themselves. However, I now believe that within the TSF approach, making such a declaration is a key to acknowledging and accepting one's condition. While a newcomer to the TSF may find it difficult to express his or her condition so simply and directly, eventually this declaration is as fundamental as the First Step and as important (Brown, 1985). (It is relevant to know that newcomers are not pressured into admitting their addictive status, and it is entirely acceptable to say, "I'm just here to listen" or "I'll pass" if asked to speak.)

Theoretically speaking, the rejection of the label alcoholic or addict lies in misunderstanding the meaning of these terms. This is due to the common view of addicts and alcoholics, which derives from the earlier moral and psychological models of this disease (Rogers & McMillin, 1989). Being an alcoholic is a shameful thing if this disorder is due to moral degeneracy or even psychological weak-mindedness. However, if one accepts the disease concept of addiction that is embedded in the TSF, the degree of stigma attached to these labels is likely to dissipate.

A new patient took a seat in the waiting room next to a more experienced client, one who had considerable experience in AA. The man was dressed in his business clothes—a three-piece suit and with a briefcase. The newcomer looked at him nervously and asked, "Are you one of the doctors?" "Nah," came the reply. "I'm a drunk." The newcomer had a look of shock on her face, then broke into relieved laughter. She had never heard anyone use that term as anything but a pejorative.

A chaplain at a local rehab has been known to greet people by extending his arms in an invitation to an embrace, saying, "Hug a drunk!"

One of the most useful comparisons in this area is in viewing addiction as a chronic disease, much like diabetes or hypertension. Both addiction and diabetes are chronic diseases, rooted in physiological conditions and reinforced by psychological, social, and existential factors. The parallels are quite instructive. Neither addiction nor diabetes are caused solely by the client's actions, and both require active monitoring on the part of the client to maintain stability (Milam & Ketcham, 1983; Rogers & McMillin, 1989). Yet a diagnosis of diabetes, however shattering, does not carry the same negative connotation as does a diagnosis of addiction or alcoholism. I believe that this is primarily due to the persistent assumptions that alcoholism and addiction are moral failings of one sort or another, a belief that is slowly eroding in the face of ongoing discoveries about the true nature of these disorders.

This is sometimes a tough stereotype to break. Apart from the social stigma that is clearly evident throughout our society, the degree to which this has been internalized makes it difficult to challenge. Often, as well, the self-disgust with which clients view themselves as "drunken bums" serves as a mask for other forms of self-criticism. Usually, clients have been through all sorts of failed attempts to control or stop their drug or alcohol use. These failures then add to the self-critique they are feeling. It is worth noting that even a clearly physiologically based disease such as tuberculosis was once viewed as a psychological disorder; labeled consumption, it was perceived to reflect an artistic, sensitive temperament.

It can be very helpful to draw a distinction between the inappropriate guilt of having a disease and a rational self-examination of a failure to take personal responsibility for dealing with it.

> A young man with an alcohol problem attended his intensive outpatient program on a Monday, and reported that he had gotten drunk on Saturday night. He had gone to a bar on Friday night to see his friend who was playing in a band. This had been a successful outing, and he had stuck to ginger ale all evening and had a good time. Full of confidence, he returned on Saturday. "I did fine for a while, then I ran into a friend of mine who bought me a beer, and I felt I couldn't refuse. Next thing I knew it was closing time, and I was drunk as a skunk. I should have just stuck to the ginger ale. I'm so stupid." I pointed out that for an alcoholic to drink when in a bar was not stupid, but was what alcoholics do. "Fish swim in water, birds fly in the air, alcoholics drink in bars," I said. "It's not your fault that you have this disease. However, what were you doing in a bar? That was stupid and irresponsible."

This may sound like a fine distinction, but is an important one. It is important to consistently convey that the status of being addicted is just like having any other chronic disease. This is not something one can control, and is not something anyone ever wishes for (certain nihilistic literary types notwithstanding). However, like yin and yang, each diagnosis of a chronic disease comes with an inseparable mandate to take responsibility for its management. I frequently tell the story of a college friend of mine:

> This man suffered from diabetes, but continued to drink, keep odd hours, neglect his diet, and was inconsistent in taking his meds. The first time we came back to the room at night and found him lying on

the floor in a coma, we leaped into action—one person called campus security, another got some juice for him, others got him up and into a chair. We were full of sympathy for him and for his condition. The second time, we were just as helpful, but felt a little less sympathetic. By the fifth or sixth time, we had run out of sympathy: "Why doesn't he just take care of himself?" we would say to each other.

There is also an important distinction to be drawn between honest and sober self-appraisal and negative self-criticism. Learning from one's experience is a positive goal and a basic tool of personal change. "Beating oneself up" is unnecessary and counterproductive. Distinguishing between the two often falls to the clinician treating this person.

The conclusion is that accepting the label alcoholic or addict is not a simple matter and is based to a large degree on the client's understanding and acceptance of the disease concept of addiction. The degree to which the therapist endorses these concepts is critical for facilitating the client's progress toward self-acceptance and recovery.

Powerlessness and Surrender

Along with the concept of the Higher Power, there are no more controversial aspects of the TSF than the concept of powerlessness and the reference to the need for surrender. Our culture propagates the notion that we are self-created people, a nation of do-it-yourselfers (Slater, 1970) and that our ability to persevere and be powerful is the essence of our selfhood. What could be more deflating than to face one's powerlessness in the face of such a critical struggle?

Our society trumpets the message that we can "be all we can be," that we can have it all. For most of us, the struggle to become independent and autonomous has taken up a great deal of our time and energy throughout our adolescence, our young adulthood, and possibly even further. This has become a critical developmental milestone, one that is not compromised readily.

Of course, on one level, the sense of deflation is part of the reason this concept is so important to the process of TS recovery. The founders of AA felt that without a deep sense of deflation, one would not be receptive to adopting the posture of surrender necessary for accepting the Higher Power. This continues to be embedded in much of the TSF.

The Adlerian notion of the inferiority complex comes to mind in this discussion (Adler, 1929; Ansbacher & Ansbacher, 1956). In Adler's theory, all people are faced with a sense of their own limitations and inferiority as a result of the inherent dependence of childhood. As a result, we develop a posture of counterdependence. This veneer becomes a key part of our sense of self, and our sense of potency in the world. Again, accepting our inability to deal with a basic problem such as alcoholism or addiction is totally deflating. This is discussed further in Chapter 7.

A simpler explanation is available, one that may be too safe or soft for some orthodox 12-steppers. In this view, the powerlessness is confined to powerlessness over alcohol or drugs. This is a relatively easier concept to sell and may be sufficient to engage people in the early stages of their involvement in the TSF. At the point a client is considering entering one of the 12-step fellowships, there have probably been some instances in which it was apparent that the drugs were more in control than the person. Of course, this may not be as apparent to the client himself, and this becomes a critical therapeutic task, as discussed above. However, even when clients have difficulty connecting the dots, the evidence is there, waiting for us to help them to see it more clearly. This requires the "simple" admission that the addiction is more powerful than the client.

The deeper implications of powerlessness, however, may not be apparent or even acceptable to a newcomer to the fellowship. In this sense, the guidance of the Higher Power is seen as more influential and powerful than the efforts of the individual client. This is far more overwhelming to clients than simply admitting that alcohol or drugs have defeated them.

Another frightening implication of powerlessness is the dependent and vulnerable position this invokes. Again, like the Adlerian position of inferiority, this admission conjures up a variety of unacceptable feelings of infantile, helpless dependence. For most of us, this is a position we have been struggling to overcome for much of our lives. Furthermore, the experience of addiction is often a solitary one, and trust in others has become a rare commodity.

This plays an even larger role when working with adolescents or young adults. For these individuals the tasks of recovery and the normal developmental milestones are in direct conflict. Normally, the developmental task for young adults is individuation from the family of origin (Haley, 1997). This involves development of one's sense of instrumental potency and autonomy. Imagine the conflict when a 20-year-old, struggling to break away from parents or other family, is faced with the need to accept powerlessness in any part of life.

In this situation, the best strategy is to use the softer approach outlined above, and to defer the deeper acceptance of existential powerlessness. Rarely are young adults ready to directly accept the deeper meaning of this concept. Over time, the more spiritual implications may become more viable.

It is often helpful for the clinician to adopt an educational stance around these issues. Explaining what powerlessness means, in both its superficial and deep meanings, can go a long way toward helping the client accept it. It can be helpful to refer to many of the unrealistic aspirations we have held at various points in our lives. All of us have aspired to some unrealistic goals, whether they involved being president, climbing Mt. Everest, getting a gold medal in the Olympics, or winning the Nobel Prize. Certainly, we do not want to discourage a person's aspirations; however, we must also recognize the opposite side of this equation, that not all of us can be president, climb Mt. Everest, and so on.

The heroic stories of people who defy the odds are inspirational and encourage us to dream about making the impossible into the possible. We thrill to hear about humans walking on the moon or a blind man climbing a mountain. As much as these stories may inspire us to challenge our limitations, it must be recalled that these are the unusual stories, not the typical ones. Holding ourselves up to these standards sets up an unrealistic set of expectations and inevitable disappointment.

Accepting powerlessness requires seeing these daydreams for what they are—daydreams. In some areas (such as controlling the use of drugs or alcohol) it is a doomed effort to challenge the limits.

Yet in the experience of many AAs, the act of accepting powerlessness becomes a liberating experience. In accepting one's limits in this sphere, one gives up having to struggle over and over again to overcome the most difficult tasks imaginable—breaking through real limitations. Accepting these limits becomes a form of relief from this ongoing and repetitive struggle.

This introduces the related concept of surrender, which is a recurring theme in 12-step literature and discussion. In the more limited sense, this refers to giving up the struggle to control one's drinking (Brown, 1985). In this sense, the individual acknowledges that his or her own instincts around drinking and drugging are flawed and dangerous and accepts the need to follow direction (recall one meaning for GOD: "Good Orderly Direction"). This is often referred to as the state of compliance, a stage in the journey toward surrender (Tiebout, 1953), but a potential obstacle.

At the deeper level, surrender refers to giving up one's self-will in deference to the will of the Higher Power. This refers to an act of conversion in one's stance toward the world and is an acceptance of a more humble and more peaceful attitude in general. This implication is explored further in Chapter 6.

In Harry Tiebout's (1949, 1953) work, surrender is the unconscious acceptance of loss of control over one's alcohol use, and an unconscious acceptance of the reality of the world. This contrasts with the more superficial compliance of behavioral change without such internal acceptance. In fact, Tiebout viewed compliance as an obstacle to true surrender, much as an analyst might view defensive compromise structure as an obstacle to access to the deeper repressed material. In this view, superficial compliance acts as a defense against total surrender.

Tiebout also distinguished between surrender and submission. The latter is closer in spirit to the Adlerian sense of inferiority. As such, this can be a major obstacle to recovery for many addicts and alcoholics.

Such submission can breed resentments against the program and against the entire process of recovery.

Shame and Guilt

Feelings of shame and guilt about one's addiction are not only obstacles in treatment; they are often barriers to seeking treatment. Sometimes the primary barrier is shame about having an addiction in the first place, fueled by societal assumptions about the meaning of the terms alcoholic and addict. Most people coming into treatment or into recovery have regrets about things they have done while under the influence.

This is an issue that is best addressed early in the recovery process, as it blocks access to deeper aspects of the program. Negative feelings around being an addict are best validated and then defused by education around the disease concept and the biological nature of the loss-of-control phenomenon (Erickson, 2007). Depending on the degree of self-reproach, this can be a tough sell and is best accomplished incrementally. A typical response is, "But if I'd never had a drink, none of this would have ever happened." I then remind the client that having a drink is a totally normal part of our society, an activity that the vast majority of us can engage in safely and without serious negative consequence. Predicting addiction is a difficult process. For those who then reply, "But I knew that I had a family history of addiction, and that I was at risk," I might reply, "You didn't know for sure, and it's human nature that you had to try." I usually remind people that nobody can predict for certain that they would become addicted, and that nobody would ask for the outcomes that they have experienced. At times, this argument can extend the disease concept of addiction to include the irrational thinking that most addicts display: "Of course you continued to drink despite evidence that it was destructive. That's part of the insanity of the disease."

Generally speaking, this kind of shame dissolves over time and through contact with others in the fellowship. Experiencing the degree of acceptance and humor that so many of the participants in the program display goes a long way toward the kind of self-acceptance that facilitates a remission of this form of self-loathing.

Addressing guilt about specific behavior, is, in many ways, a simpler process. Again, I use the technique of "bookmarking" the issues; acknowledging them and validating them, when appropriate, yet deferring their resolution until later. There is plenty of time for self-examination when the client encounters Steps 4, 5, 8, and 9, and is encouraged to make amends to those harmed by his or her behavior. As noted earlier, Steps 4 and 5 can be done early in recovery, but Steps 8 and 9 usually are deferred until the client's recovery is a bit more stable. Again, more immediately pressing issues may need earlier attention.

Family Dynamics

In addition to the intrapsychic obstacles we have been reviewing, real obstacles often emerge in the interpersonal world of the client. For some, these are primary issues, whereas for others these problems recede into the background in light of the profound insights achieved in the 12-step program.

An initial area of social concern is within the family unit. While this issue can take up an entire volume (and has), a few points are quite relevant for clinicians working with people in recovery, especially in early recovery. Ideally, families are supportive of recovery and are relieved that the nightmare is over. Even with supportive families, however, there is a great deal of variability in their reactions, and some predictable patterns are seen.

Suspicion and Wariness

One pattern is the family's wariness of the client's profession of recovery. Undoubtedly, they have heard this before and have watched their loved one recover and fall, despite all the best intentions. As much as they would like to believe that this time it's different, they typically remain doubtful or wary. In turn, many recovering addicts and alcoholics find this attitude discouraging at best or insulting at worst. In the healthiest of situations, the recovering person can acknowledge the family's doubts and view them as rooted in concern, with at least a kernel of validity. I have found it useful to frame this in the context of the person's last period of sobriety. If a client was clean for 3 months before a relapse, the family can be expected to be concerned for at least that length of time, or perhaps twice as long.

> One alcoholic client of mine noted his wife's tendency to "kiss and sniff" when he came home. As much as this initially irritated him, he had to catch himself, recognize where she was coming from, and accept her fears as somewhat warranted.

Addicts must recognize their own tendency toward impatience and must view this as part of their addictive behaviors.

Conversely, the family should be counseled to have faith in the process and to place the responsibility for the client's recovery on the client, not on themselves. Incessant doubts, nagging about attending meetings, or concerns about who the client is associating with may be reasonable, but take the responsibility off the recovering person and serve to create tension between the family and the client.

Jealousy

In some cases, as relieved as a spouse is to have a clean and sober partner at last, a sense of resentment and jealousy can build up toward the addict's new relationship with the program itself and with new friends made in the fellowship. Evenings spent at the bar or holed up in the basement are now spent at meetings and getting coffee after the meeting. For some family members this represents only a small change—they saw little of their addicted partner during their active addiction anyway.

Others begin to notice the client speaking a new language and spouting new and unfamiliar ideas—what is all this talk about a Higher Power anyway? Who is this sponsor? Suspicion about the client's actual activities (after all, how do we know if she is really going to a meeting?) and about the new relationships formed in the fellowship are quite common and can serve to undermine the client's resolve about sobriety and fully engaging in the program.

The client may react in several ways to this type of feedback from the spouse. A healthy reaction is to accept the spouse's concerns and make an honest effort to balance responsibilities—making some time for family along with the priority of recovery. While this may create pressure to manage increased responsibilities, it provides an opportunity to restore damaged relationships as well as maintain a solid recovery program. Ideally, the family understands the need for the emphasis on program participation and accepts that the recovering person may need to take care of recovery as a major priority toward restoring a healthy family life.

Others, however, may respond in a less mature fashion. The recovering individual may respond with anger and resentment at being doubted and may complain about being placed in an untenable position—encouraged to maintain sobriety while being doubted at every step along the way.

Again, the family is counseled to be aware of the nature of the program and the importance of meeting attendance and sponsorship. Doubts can be validated yet placed in perspective as normal occurrences (for both the client and the family). After all, as clinicians, we may not be privy to an emerging "rehab romance" on the client's part, and it is not our role to defend the client. Our goal should be to allow the recovery process to unfold in as straightforward a manner as possible—there will inevitably be changes in relationships as a result of such a significant change in lifestyle. Our role must be to monitor the process and intervene as indicated to keep the addict on track in recovery, however it plays out.

Old Wounds

Few have gone through a period of addiction without leaving at least some interpersonal wreckage behind. Both client and spouse may be carrying resentments from the period of active addiction. These are lingering wounds which, if not addressed, may fester and emerge as marital conflict later on (if not sooner), typically when a new conflict arises, and they are used as additional ammunition in the conflict.

In these situations, clinicians may find themselves in a double bind. Early in the client's recovery, it is often counterproductive to raise these issues and open up a potentially fractious and disruptive area prior to the client being able to handle it. However, ignoring it is equally destructive, as it invalidates the spouse's quite appropriate anger and concerns, and it becomes the elephant in the room that nobody wants to talk about.

In such a situation, I find it helpful to make a distinction between truly old wounds (events in the past that are no longer active) and issues that are ongoing in the present. The latter usually require some present intervention, preventing them from growing into more serious frictions that will undermine the ongoing process of recovery. For example, an extramarital affair that occurred during the addiction 5 years previously but that was an isolated event is a far different matter than an affair or a pattern of affairs that has continued into the present or recent past. The latter requires immediate intervention, while the former can be deferred to some degree.

I find that an effective way of dealing with the old wounds is to "bookmark" them—acknowledging them, noting the need to work on them, but deferring the discussion to some point in the future when the relationship and the client's sobriety are more stable. As noted earlier, if unacknowledged, the wounds fester, the spouse's concerns remain unacknowledged, and the implicit assumption is that this behavior is not significant. By acknowledging them now, they are validated, and most families are content to let this pass in the present if there is assurance that they will not be ignored.

All these notions around deferring issues find support in the TSF. Recall that the recovering person is encouraged to make amends for damages and hurts caused by his addiction. The 8th and 9th Steps provide a clear process for rectifying old wounds. There is a significant reason why these are placed later in the program. Rectifying old wounds is seen as a task for a person whose sobriety is more secure than someone in the early stages. Reassuring both the family and the client that there is a time and a place for making amends can go a long way toward reassuring all parties that such issues will be addressed, and an attempt to rectify them will be made.

Recall that the 9th Step—making amends whenever appropriate—is a task to benefit the recovering person, and that an appropriate response is not guaranteed. Benefit to the other party is implied but is more of a side effect of this process. The goal of this step is to make the effort, not necessarily to receive forgiveness.

Family Intervention

All of these family issues can be addressed in a conjoint session with the client and relevant family members. Generally, in working with individuals with substance abuse problems, I find it helpful to schedule at least one or two family meetings. Rather than process communication dynamics or old wounds, I find that a psychoeducational stance is best. This is especially helpful if the person has not completed an inpatient rehab, where such educational material is often disseminated.

It is important to distinguish between a session in this context and a true family therapy session. Such a meeting is to be primarily educational in nature—providing the family with information about the nature of addiction and the process of recovery. More immediate interactional issues must be addressed (abuse in the family, extramarital affairs, ridding the house of alcohol or drugs), and older issues can be relegated to a later point. All of the issues delineated above can be openly discussed or predicted, as some of these may not be immediately observed.

Families should also be alerted to common family interaction patterns that threaten the current sobriety of the client, such as enabling and scapegoating. Enabling families have consciously or unconsciously allowed the addiction to flourish. Families have lent money, made excuses, allowed themselves to be lied to, and in many other ways have run interference for the addiction, preventing the addict from experiencing the natural consequences of the behavior.

> A man in his 60s came in for a consultation about his wife, who had a variety of problems, including agoraphobia, obsessive-compulsive disorder, and alcoholism. "She does nothing all day but sit around, complain, and drink," he told me. Eventually, the obvious discrepancy dawned on me: "If she won't leave the house, how does she get access to alcohol?" He replied, partly sheepish, partly defiant, "I get it for her. She'd drive me crazy if I didn't!"

As with abused women who profess love for their abusive spouses, it would seem obvious that such alcoholic or addictive behavior should not be tolerated. Of course, most situations are not that simple. The wife who calls her husband's boss to say he has the flu (when he is actually hung over) can be accused of enabling his disease, but she may also be protecting the family's only source of income and healthcare insurance. The parents who bail their child out of trouble for the umpteenth time usually see themselves as keeping her away from an even worse fate than addiction.

Addicts are also easily scapegoated; when one member of a family has an addiction, it is relatively easy to attribute all problems in a family to this problem. Sometimes, in fact, this may be true. More often, however, an alcoholic family has the usual range of other problems in addition to this one. As in any group structure, it is easy to find a scapegoat, and then other family members can covertly conspire to keep the scapegoat in that role, lest they be the next one chosen. Readers with long memories can recall Eric Berne's (1964) game If It Wasn't for You from *Games People Play*, for a quick synopsis of the dynamics of this pattern.

Enabling and scapegoating families are usually best cautioned to be aware of their own tendencies to engage in such behaviors. It is usually difficult to change these patterns without significant external intervention. Clinical judgment is critical for determining if intervention is warranted sooner rather than later. When such patterns are actively present, it may be necessary to provide some more direct family support, whether that is through yourself or by referral to another clinician to handle the family aspects of the treatment.

Finally, the family should usually be referred for their own support service. This may take the form of referral for supportive family therapy or, preferably, to a 12-step support group such as Al-Anon or Nar-Anon.

Al-Anon and Nar-Anon

Some knowledgeable readers may have noted the absence of reference to Al-Anon or Nar-Anon, a deficiency that is remediated here. Al-Anon is a 12-step organization dedicated to providing support in the form of hope and help for the families and friends of people with addictions, whether they are in recovery or in active addiction. Al-Anon follows a 12-step approach itself and reminds the member that, just as an addict is powerless over the addiction, a family member is similarly powerless over that addiction and over the life of the addict in their midst.

Al-Anon provides a parallel setting for the family member to share the experience, hope, and strength of the more senior members of the fellowship, in learning how to deal with a loved one's addictive behavior. In some cases, this may involve some degree of confrontation or tough love. In other cases, it may involve practicing loving detachment. One of the lessons learned in Al-Anon and Nar-Anon is not to allow the client's addiction to contaminate the rest of the family dynamics.

Al-Anon and Nar-Anon have been caricatured as a group of bitter wives of addicted men sitting around bad-mouthing their spouses. Like any caricature, there is a possible kernel of truth in this picture, as some Al-Anon meetings may yield to such forces. After all, if old issues are put on hold, or if the client is in active addiction, it may be necessary for spouses to find a place to vent their frustrations. However, at their best, Al-Anon and Nar-Anon are powerful groups in their own right and advocate a spiritual awakening in their members, complementary to that promoted in AA and NA. In fact, many people seek out the help of Al-Anon irrespective of their spouse's own recovery status (or nonrecovery status).

Referral to Al-Anon or Nar-Anon encompasses much of the same therapeutic input as does a referral to AA or NA. The therapist must be aware of the dynamics and language of this fellowship and must view this program as supportive of the client's (in this case, a spouse of an alcoholic or addict) welfare and personal growth. In such cases where you may be working with the spouse of an addict but not the addict, the work done in Al-Anon or Nar-Anon can be seen as directly complementary to the work in individual or family therapy. Many of the issues are similar to working with those with dependent personality disorder, although the pathology is often only seen in relation to the spouse and not in general. However, the issues of overdependence, personal control, and power struggles are familiar in this area and the clinician should be prepared to deal with such issues as they emerge.

Family members frequently have a difficult time relinquishing the illusion that they can control or impact their family member's addictive behaviors. There is often a sense that "if he loved me more he'd stop what he's doing." Others have a difficult time biting their tongues when faced with a frustrating situation or with the self-defeating behavior of their partner. This is a difficult lesson for most to learn, and the therapeutic stance in such situations is often one of providing support through this difficulty, while helping the family member set limits with the addicted spouse. Limiting the damage to the rest of the family and setting limits on one's personal victimization are often key steps in having the addict come to terms with the addiction.

A woman whose charming and charismatic husband was alcoholic attempted for years to persuade him that his drinking was affecting their relationship and family life. He provided some acknowledgment, just enough to keep her from drastic measures. She remained unwilling to leave him or make idle threats, feeling committed to him and to their marriage. Eventually she found her way to Al-Anon and made a good connection there. She stopped nagging him, recognizing the futility of this for both of them. When he was available, she was happy to be with him; when he was drunk, she sought social contact elsewhere. She began to live her own life and indulge in her own interests. While not an ideal outcome, she stopped making her life and happiness contingent on him and their relationship, but sought some satisfaction on her own terms.

Difficulties With the Social World

One of the basic precepts found in the TSF is the necessity of avoiding contact with "people, places, and things" (PPT) associated with one's addiction (Alcoholics Anonymous, 1975). This is, of course, usually easier said than done, and in most cases requires some serious manipulation of the social environment. More important, it requires some honest self-appraisal.

The rationale for this admonition is clear but bears some restating. The simplest way is to view such PPT as conditioned stimuli, in the Pavlovian sense, and that exposure to these PPT will trigger cravings and thoughts about using. In this sense, the actual person involved is not culpable—he or she may be supportive of the client's recovery. However, this person's presence can easily cue an urge to drink or get high, which can snowball into a full-blown relapse. Similarly, driving by the bar or house where one used to drink or get high can be a cue to think about using.

When avoiding PPT is not possible (and it often involves some serious therapeutic soul-searching to decide if avoidance is truly impossible or is merely inconvenient), one must learn strategies for dealing with these situations and nip the conditioned response in the bud. The role of Coping Skills Training (Monti, Abrams, Kadden, & Cooney, 1989) can be critical here, in that learning new responses to old situations will often require a structured effort. Cognitive interventions (Beck et al., 1993) are also helpful in allowing the client to examine the cognitions (often of resignation and hopelessness) that facilitate relapses.

For many recovering alcoholics (and for some addicts), alcohol has assumed a place in their sense of personal identity as well as a part of their social world. In such instances, the identity as alcoholic must be challenged and redefined, so that this becomes a positive sense of identity rather than a negative one (Brown, 1985). This also impacts one's participation in the social milieu, especially if drinking has been a key part of that milieu. Alcoholics who avoid drinking situations (e.g., cocktail parties, bars) are also robbed of the association with something that has helped define themselves (e.g., as an adult, as a sophisticate).

> A 27-year-old woman seeking treatment for opiate depend-
> ence balked at the notion of giving up her social drinking. "I
> don't trust people who don't drink," she remarked, sounding
> much like Bette Davis in *All About Eve.*

The actual reconstruction of a social world that does not center on
or feature drinking is often centered on participation in AA or NA and
involves the dimension of social recovery, which is a part of the fellowship. New friends can be met and social relationships can be struck up
that can replace some of the more negative ones contaminated by
involvement with addiction. Sometimes, this can result in a diametri-
cally different view of the social world. A recovering friend wrote me:

> I am often uncomfortable around "earth people," but feel very comfort-
> able around fellow alcoholics. There is a sort of bonding which is almost
> immediate with people who have shared some of the same struggles
> that I have. AA has all but destroyed my ability to make small talk;
> there is an intensity and honesty which I get no where else. I don't get
> this from all individuals necessarily, but from the group. I have been to
> meetings in Boston and Camden, New York where I don't speak indi-
> vidually with anyone and yet come out feeling somehow better—both
> about myself and the world I have to live in.

Sponsorship and Therapy

The relationship between sponsor and therapist can be an awkward one,
particularly if either party is uncomfortable with the work of the other.
They need not be in conflict, however, and if properly coordinated can
be an asset to each other. It is important to distinguish between the
differing roles and goals of each party. The sponsor's goal is simply to
help the client work the steps. While the sponsor-sponsee relationship
can take on additional overtones at times, either consciously or unconsciously, this is the primary focus of this relationship. The sponsor is an
active member of the client's work within the program.

The therapist, by contrast, stands outside the TSF, helping to facilitate engagement in the program by helping the client deal with obstacles to full participation. This may take the form of interpretation of resistance, helping to clarify and resolve ambivalence, clarifying the client's misunderstandings about the program, and offering insights into the meaning of the program in his or her life. The therapist may make suggestions about real-life problems the client may encounter and may also offer some perspective on the client-sponsor relationship if this becomes problematic.

Is it beneficial to make contact with the sponsor? I have rarely had to make actual direct contact with a sponsor to facilitate treatment, except in some cases when a sponsor has referred a sponsee to therapy. In such cases, I have gathered information and gained perspective on the referral issues, and have (with client consent, of course) been able to bounce back some of my concerns. In those rare cases when I have had contact with a client's sponsor, it has been helpful at times to verify the client's claims, such as attendance at meetings, motivation to work the steps, and relations with other members of the fellowship. I have yet to conduct a couples session with a client and sponsor, although theoretically it is entirely possible that such a meeting could be held and could be beneficial.

I do, however, regularly solicit information on the client's relationship with the sponsor. This is important to pinpoint problems in that relationship, whether they involve inflated expectations, suppressed hurt feelings, or feelings that the sponsor may be overstepping his or her bounds. Processing this relationship can be quite helpful in ensuring the client's progress in the fellowship. Monitoring the client's use of the sponsor is also a helpful indirect measure of his or her investment in the program. A client who has not been in touch with the sponsor in several weeks may be slacking off in other recovery areas as well, and this can be an early sign of a relapse process.

Furthermore, the client's reluctance to secure a sponsor in the first place (a not uncommon experience) must be dealt with for its implications of resistance to the program, particularly suggesting a difficulty with surrender or a possible feeling of humiliation about asking for help. In any case, this must be reviewed for the reason behind it and these issues addressed. Sometimes a secondary issue, such as social phobia, may need to be dealt with independently.

The primary difficulty in this triangle usually rests with the therapist's countertransference. We think of ourselves as change agents, and it may be necessary for us to conceptualize our role as coaching a more significant relationship. In helping clients working within the TSF, our role becomes more secondary. This can be difficult for some clinicians, as discussed in Chapter 4.

There are any number of ways in which a newcomer can acquire a sponsor. A person attending an AA meeting can simply raise their hand, introduce themselves and state that they are seeking a sponsor; inevitably, someone (or several people) will approach him after the meeting with a phone number and a discussion. Alternatively, I sometimes encourage a newcomer to scout out a sponsor by listening carefully for someone who has some experience and feels compatible, and approach them directly before or after a meeting. Some meetings keep a list of potential sponsors and their phone numbers, perhaps posted on a bulletin board. A newcomer can pick a number or two off the list and call them to discuss this relationship. I have even heard stories of a new member being approached by an old-timer with a phone number and an invitation to call.

A therapist may be quite useful in the process of acquiring a sponsor. This is often a daunting task for a newcomer, who may be dealing with social anxieties in addition to the difficulties of accepting his addiction. It may be best for the clinician to present herself as a coach, encouraging the client to seek a sponsor, helping him understand his reluctance to make the necessary effort, and helping him process the feelings around creating this new relationship. The clinician must be especially sensitive to the possible implications of the power differential inherent in this relationship, which may activate Oedipal and other related issues for the client. Finally, it is important that the therapist encourage the client to discuss with the potential sponsor any expectations that he may have about this relationship. If a sponsor is more standoffish, it is important to clarify this before the client begins to feel rejected; perhaps it will be better for such a client to get a sponsor who is more apt to reach out.

Conversely, a sponsor who calls the sponsee daily may be perfect for a more reticent person, but may be viewed as intrusive by a more independent person. These experiences and needs are discussed with the therapist to ensure that misunderstandings and crossed expectations do not seriously undermine the sponsorship relationship.

Dealing With Relapse

If dealing with addicted clients on an outpatient basis, sooner or later you will have to deal with a patient who relapses or reverts to some level of substance use. While it is important to give the message that this is not desirable, it must also be seen as part of the ongoing process of recovery. Some distinguish between a slip or a lapse and a relapse, the former being one isolated use of a substance with minimal real consequences, and the latter being a full-blown reversion to a previous level of substance abuse or dependence. Obviously, preventing a slip from developing into a relapse is the role of early intervention in this cycle.

In the case of a full-blown relapse, a brief period of inpatient rehabilitation may be necessary to reestablish stability. All too often a brief lapse or relapse is seen as requiring a return to another 30-day rehabilitation experience. When a removal from the environment may be indicated, I prefer a briefer stabilization period, along with a reassessment of the supports needed for recovery. This is especially true if the client has already demonstrated some ability to establish sobriety in the home environment. Some rehabilitation programs offer distinct treatment tracks for relapsers, addressing unique relapse issues, and this is, of course, preferable to simply repeating a course of primary treatment.

However, a return to inpatient treatment is not always necessary. In the broadest scheme, relapses are best viewed as learning opportunities. Processing with the patient how the lapse happened can be an invaluable lesson in reassessing the risks of the current recovery plan. Developing alternative strategies for such situations as the one that precipitated the relapse can be useful in future planning. It is also usually helpful to consult with a significant other in analyzing the relapse and planning for future sobriety.

Use of Addiction Medications

In recent years, several medications have been developed to assist with the recovery process, in addition to several that have had more long-standing utility in general. These present significant additions to the tools that can be helpful for people in the recovery process. Their use, however, creates controversy within the TSF.

Controversy about the use of methadone in heroin addiction is a good example of some of the issues involved. Methadone effectively relieves the craving for, and withdrawal effects of, opiates and allows the patient to resume a productive life without the constant need to engage in illegal and antisocial activities in order to obtain drugs. Typically, methadone is provided through dedicated clinics that ideally provide ancillary services, including psychotherapy, vocational services, health services, and so on. While the client's addiction is being stabilized on the medication, the client's life is being rehabilitated. Unfortunately, poor funding, politics, and other external concerns have made this idealized picture relatively rare, and methadone maintenance has developed a bad reputation.

In terms of the TSF, is a person on methadone maintenance truly in recovery? While a naive observer may view this person as being engaged in a process of developing stability and coping with addiction, the fact is that he or she is still on a drug that fosters almost as much dependency (some say more) than the heroin or other opiate that it is replacing. From the perspective of a true 12-step proponent, this is not the ideal drug-free state that had been envisioned by Bill W. in developing AA.

This often results in a situation in which persons on methadone have felt unwelcome at NA or AA meetings. They are placed in the awkward position of choosing between full disclosure and honesty or concealing their medical status. Most choose to attend meetings at the methadone clinic itself rather than be placed in this uncomfortable position, yet this limits their access to the power of the fellowship.

Most private practitioners will rarely encounter a client from a methadone clinic, as the clinic tends to provide all services that they need. (I have seen occasional methadone patients when they have felt that the therapy they receive at the clinic is inadequate, or if they are seeking to get off methadone.) Nowadays, we are more likely to work with a patient on one of the new generation of antiaddiction medications, including naltrexone, buprenorphine, or campral, among others still in development.

- Buprenorphine is the next generation of antiopiate medications and promises to replace methadone. Like methadone, it replaces the craving for opiates and eliminates withdrawal symptoms. Unlike methadone, it can be prescribed by doctors (following a brief specialized training) in their own offices, removing all the inconvenience and social problems associated with methadone clinics.
- Naltrexone works for opiates and alcohol. It blocks the opiate receptor sites in the brain and prevents the high that results if a client should use opiates. It may also reduce the high if the patient drinks. It has been shown to reduce the incidence of drinking and minimize the severity of relapses in alcoholics.
- Campral works on a different brain system than naltrexone but offers a similar effect. For those responsive to it, cravings for alcohol are reduced.

For those taking such medications, the conflict with attending a 12-step meeting becomes apparent. For die-hard 12-steppers, the use of such medications is equivalent to the use of drugs that gave doctors a bad rap in the first place (e.g., sedatives and other medications with addictive potential). "A drug is a drug" is a phrase that can be heard at many an AA or NA meeting.

In these cases, clients are encouraged not to openly disclose their use of such medications if they choose to attend a 12-step meeting. Although this blocks their full disclosure in the meeting, it allows them to participate without the potential for a backlash that can be quite destructive, especially in the earlier phases of treatment. Disclosure to one's sponsor, who is hopefully more tolerant of the use of such medications, will help to navigate this area.

It should also be pointed out that, as these medications become more common and their use and pitfalls become more well-known, acceptance of their use is becoming more commonplace. As with the disclosure of drug use in an AA meeting, different meetings have different levels of acceptance of the use of such medications. It is no longer uncommon to hear the sentiment, "Whatever works to help a suffering alcoholic."

Practitioners working with addicts should consider use of these medications. Despite some inflated hype that these meds represent a cure for addiction, they can be quite useful adjuncts for treatment and might be worth considering in any given case. This is a topic left for another forum (Miller & Carroll, 2006; Volpicelli & Szalavitz, 2000; Washton & Zweben, 2006).

Managing Anonymity and Self-disclosure

Many recovering addicts struggle with the issue of how to disclose their recovering status to friends, families, or employers. This is a particularly pressing issue when the client has just disappeared for 30 days to attend an inpatient rehabilitation program.

As noted earlier, the requirement for anonymity has two relevant aspects. One is the grounding in spiritual humility, the need to keep the destructive ego in check. The second is to avoid social stigma. The requirement of anonymity is taken quite seriously in the program. However, the need for anonymity will occasionally come into conflict with the principle of honesty.

In an ideal world, I would advocate a program of total honesty with others. However, I recognize that this may result in difficult consequences, and that sometimes a sin of omission may be warranted. This becomes an individual decision based on the estimate of the importance and degree of the possible consequences. This decision, like so many others in the program, is best reviewed with both the therapist and the sponsor before it is made.

I have often helped clients maintain a tenuous balance between anonymity and self-disclosure by reminding them that this is a program based on honesty, but that Step 9 requires some restraint when disclosure will result in injury to others. This can also be extended to refer to oneself. I have often counseled clients to use discretion in discussing their situation with those who may be in a position to judge them negatively, such as current or prospective employers.

Of course, a significantly greater degree of acceptance of recovery has developed in society at large in recent years. Clients are often surprised to have their "shameful" secret met with warm acceptance. It is often no surprise to the family that the client had a problem, and it is with relief that they greet the client after treatment.

> One client had scrupulously hid the fact of his alcoholism from his landlord, who lived upstairs from him. After engaging in an outpatient program, he was persuaded to attend an AA meeting. To his horror, he recognized his landlord as one of the people greeting him at the meeting. "I didn't expect to run into you here," the client stammered. The landlord replied, "I was wondering when you were going to show up."

> I conducted an outpatient group in which an older man was attending for his drinking problem. I had, after a long period of time, persuaded a younger man, a cocaine addict, to attend the group. When they saw each other, they both showed a shock of recognition. "Hello, Jim," said the older man. "Hi, Coach," replied the younger one.

Dual-Diagnosis Issues

In recent years, the area of addictions treatment has become more complex because of the inclusion of a large number of patients who are considered to be "dual-diagnosis" patients, that is, suffering from an independent psychological disorder in addition to an addiction. This can range from schizophrenic patients who smoke marijuana to mildly depressed patients who abuse prescription medications.

There are a number of controversial issues with this population. One of these lies in the diagnostic area: for example, how is it possible to diagnose a person with a mood disorder in the presence of a chemical dependency? Surely, some degree of sobriety is necessary to get a picture of the person's problems in a baseline condition. History—especially the person's condition prior to the onset of the addiction—can be key in helping diagnose an independent condition. However, this information is frequently unavailable and sometimes irrelevant (for example, if the person's addiction began at an early age). In my experience, it is relatively rare that there is a clear diagnostic picture available from prior to the onset of the addiction problem. A "best guess" is in order, with the important caveat that this guess must be considered to be extremely tentative.

Similarly, psychopathology that was not evident at intake may become more apparent after some period of sobriety. A person whose initial depression appears to be substance-induced may begin to voice more paranoid ideation as he becomes less drug-affected. Someone who is coherent and presentable at intake may become more manic and labile with sobriety. The clinician must be alert and flexible in dealing with such behaviors.

It can be assumed that the client's mental status will be affected by their substance use when they are first seen. In general, mental status improves with sobriety, and this is my general expectation, one that I am quick to share with patients entering treatment. It is reassuring, and usually correct, to predict that the person will feel better within a few weeks.

However, this is not always the case. There are generally two broad sets of reasons for a failure to improve or for a worsening condition. The first is the emergence or persistence of an independent psychopathological condition, which will require its own attention. The second is the realization of the damage caused during the addiction, and the work needed to rectify the situation. The Big Book likens the addiction to a tornado, and the early alcoholic to a man who emerges from his cyclone cellar saying, "Don't see anything the matter here, Ma. Ain't it grand the wind stopped blowing?" (Alcoholics Anonymous, 2001, p. 82). Once he recognizes the damage done, it is not inappropriate to feel some degree of depression. This is an important distinction for the clinician to be attuned to.

A second consideration with this population lies in the question of when to work on abstinence. This may not be an acceptable goal for some patients, especially those with more serious and persistent mental illnesses. Ironically, this group has an additional need for abstinence, since patients are usually on psychotropic medications, and the use of alcohol and other drugs interferes with the efficacy of these medications. It is often easier to engage these people in programs that do not insist on immediate sobriety than to demand an initial commitment to abstinence. Specific protocols for working with the chronically mentally ill are available from a variety of sources (Mueser, Noordsy, Drake & Fox, 2003) as this may be seen as more of a specialty area.

However, many of the same principles outlined in this chapter apply when working with a more high-functioning addicted patient with a diagnosis, for example, of depression or anxiety. For one thing, if they have been on an anti-depressant medication, its effectiveness has been seriously compromised by their substance use. In such a situation it is important to be reassuring that with ongoing abstinence, the medications are more likely to be effective, and the effects of the sobriety itself will likely help relieve some of the depression.

One of the obstacles comes when a patient who is on an appropriate, non-addictive medication attends a 12-step meeting. In an older, more traditional meeting, such a person may encounter resistance to the use of any medications at all. This is partly a throwback to the days in which alcoholics were regularly given sedatives, but then found themselves fighting a second demon. (Dr. Bob himself was dependent on prescription meds in addition to alcohol.) This bias has resulted in some horrific outcomes, as when patients have been discouraged from seeking help for other disorders, or have been convinced to stop taking valuable psychotropic meds. There are stories, possibly apocryphal, of AA members who have committed suicide after being persuaded to stop taking antidepressant meds. I do know of one similar case.

> The father of an addicted adolescent patient reported that he was a recovering alcoholic, with about 7 years of sobriety. This man was also one of the more depressed individuals I've met. He described his early experience in AA, where his ongoing depression was seen as a sign that he "wasn't working the program hard enough"; this compounded his depression with a sense of guilt and self-reproach. He maintained his sobriety while struggling with deep depression. Eventually, he sought psychiatric help. He reported that he was currently stable on several antidepressants, and had been through a course of electroconvulsive therapy (ECT), although some degree of depression persisted and was evident. The true miracle in this case is that he was able to maintain his sobriety in the face of such negative influences.

Fortunately, the use of non-addictive medications has become a more commonplace and more accepted part of the 12-step world in recent years. Increasingly, people have come to understand that the use of such medications is a support for recovery, not a detriment to it. It is critical to distinguish medications with addictive potential from those that do not pose such a risk. It is significant that even many otherwise competent physicians, even psychiatrists, are unaware of the significance of addictive medications in working with recovering individuals. Of course, it is crucial for the patient to actually inform his treating physicians of his addictive status, and to clarify that the doctor is familiar with the complications that this incurs.

All the same, I frequently caution persons first attending AA to avoid mention of psychotropic medications. Over time, as they develop personal contacts in the rooms and begin to get the feel for specific meetings, they may feel freer to disclose their use of these meds, as relevant.

A third consideration is prioritizing the areas to work on when faced with both addictive and psychiatric disorders. In general, the consensus is to work on stabilizing the addiction first, as little psychological gain can occur when an addiction is active. Of course, this is especially true when the person is on a psychotropic medication that is being subverted by their addictive substance, but it is true of the medicine-free client as well.

On some occasions, this must be measured against the presence of a psychiatric disorder that renders effective addictions treatment impossible or extremely difficult. A person in a manic phase of a bipolar disorder who is drinking heavily requires psychiatric stabilization in addition to work on establishing sobriety and working on recovery. In many cases this will require an acute hospitalization, in which both conditions can be addressed. Similarly, a depressed client contemplating suicide may need a more secure and safe environment before he can work on abstinence.

The first time I heard the term "dual-diagnosis" I was the head of an outpatient addiction treatment program. I had a call from a referral source asking if we handled dual-diagnosis patients. My gut level response was, "If they can sit in a chair and participate, we can handle them." I still feel that, with the considerations discussed above, this is a valid perspective. I have seen patients with a wide variety of other psychological ailments sober up, and then be able to deal with their other diagnosis that much more effectively.

Chapter 6
Personal Transformation

First of all, we had to quit playing God. It didn't work.

—Bill Wilson

A client in an outpatient addiction treatment program was seeking help for alcohol and cocaine addiction. He described himself in macho terms—he drove a muscle car, derived satisfaction from his conquests of women, spent a good deal of money on sports betting, and so on. In the course of his work in the program and in AA, he maintained sobriety and began to broaden his worldview. One day he arrived late for group. When he arrived, he was laughing at himself and told the group that he had been detained by a large flock of geese that had been crossing the road in front of his car. He reported that in the past he would have become annoyed at the geese, might have honked his horn repeatedly, perhaps even tried to push his way through them, hoping that they would get out of the way. To his surprise, he did none of those things. He put his car into neutral, watched them pass, and enjoyed the show. "When else would I get a chance to see something like this?" he asked, rhetorically.

Embedded within the 12-step framework are insights that open up the possibility of a larger change in one's view of the world. For those who pursue these insights, the possibility of a more profound personal transformation emerges. For some, this is the true reward of the program, which is often reflected in a member's introduction of himself as a "grateful recovering alcoholic."

This book has already made reference to the distinction between levels of involvement in the TSF; some use the program exclusively to focus on sobriety, while others use it as a means of spiritual development. Some seek primarily social recovery, while others work the steps. While the approach to the program is invariably based on the desire for sobriety, many AAs quickly become aware of the implications of the program, whereas others do not. For those who do recognize this aspect, the 12-step program becomes a means of profound personal transformation.

In the strictest sense, AA sees little distinction between these two levels of participation. The struggle to overcome alcoholism requires significant personal transformation in the process of working the steps. There is no other way for this to happen than admitting personal defeat (Step 1) and accepting help from a Higher Power (Steps 2 and 3). This is the nature of the path of recovery at its root.

However, there has long been an awareness that some distinctions are possible within this path. In 1960, Bill Wilson spoke at a National Catholic Council on Alcoholism convention:

> In this connection, there is an observation to be made about the several motivations we have respecting the practice of AA's Twelve Steps. At first we try the Steps, or at least some of them, because we absolutely must. It is a question of do or die. Then we observe AA principles because we begin to feel they ought to be observed because this is the right thing to do. We may still rebel, but we do try. Then there is a higher plateau which we sometimes touch. In a state of no resistance at all we practice AA's principles because we like to practice them, because we actually want to live by them all.

This distinction is not meant as a pejorative judgment on those who pursue the 12-step program primarily for the ends of sobriety or fellowship. This is, after all, the point of entrance for all members, and the primary purpose of the fellowship altogether, according to the traditions

(Tradition 5: "Each group has but one primary purpose—to carry its message to the alcoholic who is still suffering"). However, the principles of spiritual development underlie the program at all levels, and when articulated and practiced, they form a powerful vehicle for personal growth above and beyond the quest for sobriety.

The distinction between sobriety and recovery, described in Chapter 2, is relevant again here. Sobriety or abstinence, referring to the state of not drinking or not using drugs, is a prerequisite to recovery, which involves self-development, personal growth, and significant changes to self-concept, lifestyle, values, and thinking. It is in the area of recovery, especially in the qualities of humility and honesty that are so central to these changes, that the spiritual and personal transformation dimension becomes a significant factor.

A deeper interpretation of humility can be found embedded in Bill's statement in the Big Book: "First of all, we had to quit playing God" (Alcoholics Anonymous, 2001). This sentence provides a key to our understanding of the larger worldview of the TSF. By giving up our sense of ourselves as all-powerful and all-controlling, we see through the infantile view of our own omnipotence and are forced to accept our finite and limited nature.

This idea appears to be based to a large degree on Bill Wilson's psychological leanings. For him, the infantile nature of the active alcoholic is to be replaced by the spiritual acceptance of the mature recovering individual. There are many examples in the Big Book, the Twelve and Twelve, and *AA Comes of Age* of Bill using language that appears to borrow from Freudian developmental theory.

Several theorists of the TSF have written on this issue. Despite varying perspectives and language, there is a convergence of their views about this deeper meaning. At this point, some of the more relevant ones will be reviewed, with an eye on illuminating this elusive insight.

Ernest Kurtz (1989), the noted historian of AA, wrote eloquently of the philosophical implications and underpinnings of the TSF program, making explicit connections to existential philosophers (Kurtz, 1982). Following the statement about quitting playing God, Kurtz noted that the state of being "not-God" is key to understanding the full depth of the program. In fact, the original title of his seminal history of AA (*AA: The Story*, 1989) was *Not-God*, suggesting the central importance of this concept to his view of AA's intellectual significance. A later book by Kurtz highlights this insight even further: *The Spirituality of Imperfection* (Kurtz & Ketcham, 1992).

For Kurtz, the most fundamental insight of the program is in its rejection of a personal infantile grandiosity in favor of an acceptance of our human "essential limitation" ("essential" in the sense of basic or fundamental). In this view, the limitations of the alcoholic regarding inability to control alcohol use are simply a window onto a more basic sense of limitation, which is inherent in the human condition. For Kurtz, man is his finitude.

Two key implications arise from this observation. The first is that this limitation, in itself, constitutes a form of wholeness—that the alcoholic is complete as he is, defects and all. The acceptance of one's finite nature reaffirms one's humanity. The second and more important implication is that, being finite, we are dependent on each other for mutual support, and this is actually a blessing, not a curse. Not only are we in need of each other, but our very limitation makes us valuable to each other. It is the presence and participation of other alcoholics in the fellowship that creates healing.

An interesting footnote to this discussion is in the development of AA itself. As recounted earlier, AA had its origins in the Oxford Group, which had more grandiose evangelical aspirations. By separating from it, for the single-minded purpose of helping drunks, Bill was affirming the limited nature of his vision of AA. Kurtz quoted Bill: "The Oxford Group wanted to save the world, and I only wanted to save the drunks" (Kurtz, 1982, p. 41).

Kurtz's worldview included numerous paradoxes, in keeping with his existential leanings. He viewed the striving for transcendence in the face of essential limitation as another facet of the human condition, and one that speaks to the desire of the alcoholic quite specifically. The desire for independence coupled with our inherent need for mutuality is another example of the double bind the recovering alcoholic faces.

Similarly, Kurtz discussed the dualistic nature of honesty, a key component of recovery. To be honest, one must be honest with oneself; however, being honest with another helps avoid self-deception, a common pitfall. In the discussion of the 5th Step in the Twelve and Twelve (Alcoholics Anonymous, 1989), discussing one's personal defects with another human being is seen as more important than self-awareness or confession to God. Thus, even in something so basic as self-honesty, we encounter a paradox, one that necessarily involves our interaction with others.

Kurtz, unlike many other writers on the TSF, viewed the activities of the fellowship as a form of therapy. For him, the processes of the program provided a healing experience, despite the absence of professional clinicians. He was also able to pinpoint the source of this healing, in "the shared honesty of mutual vulnerability openly acknowledged" (1982, p. 78). Fellowship and validation are seen as an antidote to the existential terror of the awareness of our ultimate aloneness and finite, limited nature.

Kurtz also bypassed the disease concept of alcoholism in positing the core of the problem not in a disease entity, but in the very nature of the alcoholic. For him, the "alcoholic does not *have* alcoholism—he or she *is* an alcoholic" (1982, p. 39). In this observation, he is reaffirming a structural versus a functional understanding of the problem. Alcoholics do not drink because they have other problems—they drink because they are alcoholics.

Kurtz also saw AA as a significant vehicle for dealing with the shame and self-reproach of the alcoholic. However, he viewed the source of this shame as coming less from external social stigma than from an innate perception of oneself as flawed and deficient. In this view, one source of addictive behaviors is in an effort to conceal the perceived flaw and to avoid self-awareness. It is unclear in Kurtz's telling whether the perceived flaw is in the alcoholism itself, or in a deeper existential sense of failure, of negated possibilities. One is reminded of Alfred Adler's (1929) positing of an inferiority complex as a universal component of personality formation. If so, the shame of the alcoholic may also mask a more enduring underlying factor in human life in general. (Adler's views are discussed further in Chapter 7.)

Gregory Bateson (1972), from the perspective of cybernetics and systems theory, wrote a well-known analysis of the conversion experience involved in AA. Although this essay is quite technical and abstract at times, it contains a few central insights into the qualities of transformation under discussion here.

For Bateson, the fundamental problem of the alcoholic lies in a basic epistemological error; it derives from nothing less than "the strange dualistic epistemology characteristic of Occidental civilization" (1972, p. 321). Bateson saw this error emanating from the reification of the false sense of self conveyed in Western culture. For Bateson, "self" is not a separate governing entity, but rather a single isolated part of a more complex total system, which includes the alcoholic, alcohol, willpower, urges, and so on. By singling out a (false) sense of self from this larger process, the alcoholic is destined to struggle to try to make his "self" control his alcoholism. This sets up the problem of alcoholic pride.

Bateson saw the role of alcoholic pride as an erroneous and inherently self-defeating cycle, and central to this dilemma. This pride exists only in its ability to withstand the temptations of drinking; without this temptation, the struggle ceases to exist and the pride (and the underlying sense of self) ceases to have meaning. This fails to achieve its goal, however, in that once a "victory" is achieved, the battle recedes, the alcoholic relaxes, and the cycle must begin again. The alcoholic loses motivation to control this once he has done so for some period of time—the challenge loses its salience and the alcoholic drinks again to resume the process of struggle. As long as the alcoholic attempts to achieve victory over the addiction, he is validating and encouraging the addiction as strongly as he is affirming his self.

Bill Wilson's stroke of genius, in Bateson's view, occurs in the 1st Step, in which Bill locates alcoholism within the alcoholic's self. Instead of a dualistic struggle of self over alcoholic urge, the two entities are reunited. For Bateson, this is less of an admission of powerlessness than it is the correction of this basic dualistic error. Rather than continuing to assert a self in a cycle of false pride and defeat, the alcoholic can cease the struggle altogether. Rather than positing that the individual has alcoholism, this perspective sees the individual as being an alcoholic. The defect, as it were, is built into the very structure of the self. From this perspective, the correct answer to the question, "Why can't I control my drinking?" is not "Because you have alcoholism," but "Because you are an alcoholic." The parallels to Kurtz's perspective are clear.

This introduces a second key concept in the cybernetic view of alcoholism. Bateson described two basic modes of interaction within the world. Symmetrical relationships are characterized by competition—when one party escalates, the other escalates as well. Complementary relationships are reciprocal—when one escalates, the other recedes, and vice versa. The Cold War between the United States and the Soviet Union is a good example of a symmetrical relationship; dominance-submission or leader-follower are good examples of complementary relationships.

Bateson distinguished between the active alcoholic's symmetrical relationship with alcohol and the complementary relationship of the recovering alcoholic. As he struggles with his self to control alcoholism, he remains in a symmetrical relationship with the addiction. The transition to a more complementary relationship with addiction brings with it a deeper insight: instead of seeing life as a process to be overcome, to struggle with, life becomes a process to embrace and endorse. One comes into a closer and more meaningful relation to life through this perspective. In Bateson's view, this is simply a more correct view of the actual nature of our existence. One is reminded again of the AA aphorism, "Accept life on life's terms."

Here is the key to the personal acceptance and surrender so valued by those in the 12-step program who undergo a spiritual transformation. The process of competitiveness and struggle with life is replaced by a more cooperative and accepting state of mind. This pertains not only to one's relationship with alcohol, but to other relationships as well. The degree of acceptance of one's friends and partners is a significant and often-noted feature of recovering people. This can be seen most readily in the recovering alcoholic's view of active alcoholics, in which a surprising degree of tolerance and understanding can often be observed.

Furthermore, if the self of the addict is merely an interlocking part of a much larger system, a new meaning of "Higher Power" can be seen. In this view, the Higher Power is the totality of the system in which addicts or alcoholics find themselves. It is impossible to fight a Higher Power that includes oneself, and again, it is only by partitioning one's individuality against the world that this is possible even to construe.

This transition also resembles the awakening experienced by students of Zen Buddhism (Ash, 1993). It is presumptuous to assume that participation in a TSF will endow the practitioner with a sort of enlightenment that is otherwise achieved by years of meditation. However, I believe that there is a parallel and somewhat equivalent process at work in this system.

Zen Buddhism, like the 12-step program, places an emphasis on pragmatics rather than intellectualization, in providing a practical program for enlightenment. Zen provides an answer to the struggle of all human beings to overcome the suffering inherent in human life. In the Zen view, much like Bateson's, the fundamental error in approaching life is to be found in the incorrect assumption of a self apart from the world—in other words, in dualistic thinking. Zen provides a method of correcting this misperception in the practice of *zazen*, or meditation, as well as through the rigors of formal Zen training.

The goal of Zen Buddhism is to attain *satori* or enlightenment, a glimpse into his own true nature, the "true substance of our Self-nature" (Kapleau, 1980). In one view, satori is "a turning about of the mind, a psychological experience conferring inner knowledge" that eventually "leads to a transformation of personality and character" (Kapleau, 1980, p. 16). For a Zen practitioner, satori is similar to the spiritual awakening of the recovering addict, whether achieved suddenly or gradually.

There are numerous parallels between the work of recovering individuals and of Zen practitioners. While both have deep spiritual or mystical roots, both are relentlessly pragmatic. Many a 12-step newcomer has been told not to analyze the program but to get involved; Zen meditators are similarly exhorted to let go of their analytic minds in favor of direct experience of reality. Zen Master Yasutani-Roshi (in Kapleau, 1980) is quoted as telling a student, "Why can't you accept things as they are without projecting your own values or judgments onto them?" (p. 123). Zen Master Suzuki Roshi (1988) was fond of reminding his students to always keep a "beginner's mind," that is, avoid intellectualizing or analyzing, and accept one's naive and direct perceptions of reality. This has elsewhere been described as retaining a childlike sense of wonder at the world.

The 12th Step, encouraging AAs to spread the message to still-suffering alcoholics, finds a loose equivalent in the Buddhist ideal of the bodhisattva. The bodhisattva is a person who has achieved Buddhahood (enlightenment), but who delays salvation to help others achieve enlightenment themselves as well. While the 12-step version does not imply a sense of self-sacrifice, the importance of service to others is seen as central to one's own recovery.

Ash (1993), explicitly linking Zen and recovery, pointed to the Buddha's emphasis on his teachings, as opposed to his personal attributes, as a precursor of the Eleventh Tradition, placing principles over personalities. Ash also noted that the 12 steps provide a practical map for recovery, as the Eightfold Path of Buddha prescribes a pathway for spiritual awakening.

The descriptions of the spiritual goal also have striking parallels in both traditions. Bill's emphasis on restoring one's place in the fabric of humanity finds an equivalent in Zen. "Dryness, rigidity and self-centeredness give way to flowing warmth, resiliency, and compassion, while self-indulgence and fear are transmuted into self-mastery and courage" (Kapleau, 1980, p. 16) sounds remarkably familiar to Bill's statement, "Selfishness—self-centeredness! That, we think, is the root of our troubles. Driven by a hundred forms of fear, self-delusion, self seeking and self-pity, we step on the toes of our fellows and they retaliate" (Alcoholics Anonymous, 2001, p. 62).

A Zen practitioner wrote to me regarding the confluence of recovery and Zen: "To me the pertinence of Buddhism here is this: it portrays the perception of the "self"/"ego," as the ultimate addiction . . . we're all perpetual addicts to the delusion of mis-construed selfhood. And the so-called "enlightened" are mostly dry addicts in perpetual recovery" (R. N. Levine, personal communication, 12/20/07.)

In the clinical realm, Harry Tiebout, a psychiatrist colleague of Bill Wilson's, wrote a series of articles in which he portrayed the act of surrender as key in the conversion experience we are discussing here (1949, 1953). For Tiebout, the surrender experienced by the alcoholic is a profound and unconscious recognition of the reality of life, and the surrender of the infantile ego, again, going beyond the simple acknowledgment of loss of control over alcohol.

Tiebout viewed the two key characteristics of the alcoholic that block recovery as defiance and grandiosity. Defiance, akin in some ways to denial, is seen as unique to alcoholics, whereas grandiosity, deriving from "the persisting infantile ego," is more common, and is a feature of all kinds of neurotic personality formation (1949). Both factors serve a defensive function, in that they keep alcoholics safe from the threatening realization that they are engaging in a dangerous, self-destructive behavior.

In characterizing the surrender reaction, Tiebout (1949) distinguished between the act of surrender and the state of surrender. The former is the moment at which the person lets go of defiance and grandiosity, whether in a dramatic or subtle fashion. The latter is a more enduring state of internal peacefulness, although it may take work and nurturance to keep this state alive. Tiebout saw these two elements as being intimately connected—without the act of surrender, a state of surrender is unlikely to develop. However, it is possible for a person to experience an act of surrender without a permanent change in personality leading to the state.

In contrast to the stereotypes around this word, Tiebout saw the surrender reaction as a positive phenomenon, the process by which the defensive forces of defiance and grandiosity become inoperative. (He occasionally used the word *acceptance*, which may be a more palatable alternative for some.) For him, this reaction is one of accepting reality at an unconscious level, and in so doing, the client embraces the true life process. Tiebout saw the act of surrender as "an occasion wherein the individual no longer fights life, but accepts it" (1949, p. 50). The parallels to Bateson's schema is striking.

Furthermore, Tiebout distinguished surrender from submission and compliance. Submission is an analogue of surrender, but the client continues to harbor doubt and resistance; a feeling of humiliation accompanies this phase, and the struggle continues (1940). Similarly, compliance is seen, not as an intermediate state on the way toward surrender, but as a defense against it (1953). In compliance, the client accepts reality at a conscious level, while rejecting it on an unconscious level. In submission, the client pretends to surrender but accepts it at neither a conscious nor unconscious level.

Tiebout (1953) characterized the ego factors involved in surrender as immature and broke them down into three components—omnipotence, poor ability to tolerate frustration, and impatience. These are seen as vestiges of the infantile ego. Therefore, the surrender that Tiebout saw as so central to change, is, in fact, the surrender of the infantile ego itself. A more healthy balance between the ego and the rest of the psyche can then take hold of the personality.

No discussion of personal transformation can be complete without reference to William James's *The Varieties of Religious Experience* (1902/2002). Bill was given this book to read by Dr. Silkworth following his "hot flash" at Towns Hospital. The ideas in the book found their way into the steps and the fellowship because they helped Bill make sense of his mystical experience (which had initially convinced him that he was at last going crazy). James made important observations about transformation and conversion, and about the unification of the divided self.

While not ruling out religious or supernatural explanations, James preferred the explanations offered by natural science. Although he allowed that spiritual conversions could be gradual (the volitional type) or sudden (the self-surrender type), he was clearly more interested in the latter. He viewed the surrender of the personal will as a key element in the sudden conversion experience. Taking a proto-psychoanalytic slant on this phenomenon (the original publication date was 1902), James viewed the conversion experience as the emergence of unconscious material into consciousness.

For James, it was also critical that a period of crisis precede the conversion experience. The deliverance from a "state of sin" appears to be a primary drive for the experience of conversion. The higher motives can emerge when the lower emotional states become exhausted or if the higher state becomes stronger. It is only by replacing a lower state with a higher one that such change can truly become permanent. The experience of such a change, whether accomplished by intellectual means, mystical experience, or affective shifts, is accompanied by a profound sense of relief. This is the relief of an "escape from falsehoods into . . . ways of truth" (James, 1902/2002, p. 206).

James distinguished between personal transformation and conversion by the religious concerns encountered in the latter. However, it is interesting that he cited a case of a man delivered from alcoholism by a nonreligious conversion.

Several of James's ideas can be seen clearly reflected in the TSF. The necessity of hitting bottom as a prerequisite for accepting recovery is presaged in James's work. While Bill saw this as necessary to make the alcoholic hungry for recovery, James did not ascribe a specific function to this earlier state.

The consideration that conversion can be either gradual or sudden is another similarity. Bill noted that the majority of cases were of the gradual type, although his own conversion was more sudden.

James also noted the similarities between the conversion experience and the storms of adolescence, a metaphor that appears to have had an impact on Bill Wilson. Bill's preoccupation with maturity and development may have had its origins in James's volume, as well as in his own personal life experiences.

Finally, James viewed the test of the value of the spiritual life, or a spiritual conversion, as based not on any subjective report of the power or meaning of the experience, but in tangible results. Does the person behave differently after the experience? Are there fruits to be seen? Clearly, this criterion is essential for the role of conversion in the recovery program—the value of the conversion lies in the person's ability to remain sober. In the sense of personal transformation, the other criterion is whether the person manifests qualities of humility and honesty. If these can be seen in his or her behavior, then the person is actively in recovery and can be believed to have gone through a successful transformation. This insight has counterparts in Zen as well.

Freud pointed out that sometimes the best illustration of a psychological point can be found in fiction or in poetry. A good literary example of the kind of transformation described here can be found in Dashiell Hammett's classic mystery novel *The Maltese Falcon*. This book contains a passage which illustrates the changes that are to be found in those who work the program to the fullest.

The protagonist, the detective Sam Spade, begins to tell a story that is apparently unrelated to the main narrative of the novel. He had been sent to search for a missing man, who had disappeared years earlier. He had vanished "like a fist when you open your hand." The man, named Flitcraft, had simply disappeared from a placid, well-organized life, in which there was no evidence of foul play, no signs of any secret life or vices, no indication that he had been planning a getaway. When Spade located him, he was living not far away and had created a similar life for himself: similar job, similar settings, similar wife. He was quite aware of what he had done, but his biggest worry was that he would not be able to make his actions seem reasonable to another.

What had happened? On his way to lunch a beam had fallen from many stories above and hit the sidewalk beside him, grazing his cheek and leaving a small scar. Although scared and shocked, mainly he felt "like somebody had taken the lid off life and let him look at the works."

> What disturbed him was the discovery that in sensibly ordering his affairs he had got out of step, and not in step, with life. He said he knew before he had gone twenty feet from the fallen beam that he would never know peace until he had adjusted himself to this new glimpse of life. . . . Life could be ended for him at random by a falling beam: he would change his life at random by simply going away. (Hammett, 1992, p. 64)

This passage has been widely interpreted to reflect Hammett's belief that life was meaningless. However, it also displays the insights inherent in waking up to a more profound and realistic perspective on life. By accepting the randomness of life and the lack of power we have over it, we are better able to handle its unpredictability and its uncertainty with flexibility and calmness. By accepting uncertainty, we can act with more confidence. This is not merely a matter of resignation to life's cruel nature—it is an active embrace of the way life really is. We are more able to accept life on life's terms.

As the Zen Buddhist proverb has it, what does the woodcutter do after he achieves satori? He chops wood. But the world, and his experience of it, is forever changed.

Chapter 7

12-Step Fellowships and Psychological Theory

A strangely assorted crowd turned up at the early sessions [at the Yale
School for Alcohol Studies] . . . Everybody had his own ax to grind
and his own cast-iron convictions. The drys and wets were hardly on
speaking terms. Every faction wanted us drunks to agree with them.
This was very flattering, but we naturally took the independent course
and agreed with practically nobody!

—Bill W., 1958

EARLIER, I MADE THE ARGUMENT that the mental health practitioner
attempting to understand the 12-step program should seek to appreciate
it on its own terms, not to reduce it to more familiar psychological
constructs. Up to this point, I have kept to this view, and attempted to
provide a picture of the program that is not filtered through any particular psychological lens. However, it would not make sense to ignore
psychological theory entirely, or to not shed light on it from these other
perspectives. Although there may be any number of clinical viewpoints
from which to approach the 12-step program, here I take several specific
psychological theories and use them to illuminate some of the processes
and workings of the AA and NA programs.

Group Dynamics: Irvin Yalom

Although 12-step meetings are structured not at all the way classic
group therapy is, much can be learned about them by analyzing them
from this vantage point. Irving Yalom's (1995) classic text on group
therapy synthesized research findings and clinical observations to
develop a practical approach to the theory and practice of group
therapy. Key to the discussion here is his identification of the therapeutic
factors in group therapy. These factors operate independently and inter-

dependently. Derived from both empirical and clinical sources, Yalom's 11 therapeutic factors in group therapy are:

1. Instillation of hope
2. Universality
3. Imparting information
4. Altruism
5. The corrective recapitulation of the primary family group
6. Development of socializing techniques
7. Imitative behavior
8. Interpersonal learning
9. Group cohesiveness
10. Catharsis
11. Existential factors

Furthermore, Yalom cited two of these factors as being of special importance: interpersonal learning and group cohesiveness. While not all of these factors are equally relevant to understand the functioning of the TSF, each of them can shed light on some aspect of the program.

Instillation of Hope

Yalom considered the instillation of hope to be a central aspect of all forms of therapy. He noted that this is the essential ingredient in forms of faith healing and in the placebo effect (Frank & Frank, 1991). Yalom specifically noted that the presence of recovered alcoholics in the fellowship of AA directly inspires hope in newcomers.

The fellowship directly references the importance of hope in the first sentence of the AA Preamble, read at the beginning of every AA meeting:

Alcoholics Anonymous is a fellowship of men and women who share their experience, strength and hope with each other that they may solve their common problem and help others to recover from alcoholism.

The formula for speakers (to share what it was like, what happened to change that, and what it is like now) also speaks directly to this issue. When patients return from an AA meeting saying that all they heard was war stories, I know that they heard what it was like, but did not pay enough attention to the other two parts of the formula.

The role of hope is discussed more explicitly later, in reviewing the work of Jerome Frank.

Universality

The sense of isolation that plagues most people with mental health disorders is especially difficult for those with chemical dependencies, in that the accepted societal view is that addiction is a failing of personality or of will power. The consequences of internalizing this negative point of view are profound, and the guilt and shame of having this disorder often hobbles any attempt to get help. One of the most common reported consequences of addicts and alcoholics entering treatment is an increased sense of social isolation and a profound sense of shame.

> A middle-class gay male patient was addicted to crack cocaine on a binge basis. Although comfortable with his sexuality, he knew that this could be a difficult point with his boss, who had some vague perception that he suffered from a drinking problem. He also engaged in a variety of unsavory activities, including consorting with street hustlers and petty theft. He was HIV positive, but his sexual activities were minimal—once he and his partner procured cocaine (as he always did), he lost all interest in sex. One day he reported in therapy that he felt relieved that he had disclosed all his problems to his boss. I asked if he had disclosed all his issues—his sexuality? His HIV status? Running with street hustlers? His shoplifting? Yes to all. His cocaine use? "I didn't tell him that! I'm not crazy."

To Yalom, the "disconfirmation of a patient's feelings of uniqueness is a powerful source of relief" (1995, p. 6). In fact, this is often one of the strongest reactions of patients returning from a first 12-step meeting. The feeling that they are not alone in their suffering from this malady is a startling and refreshing perspective, and the fact that many of the members are now sober also increases a sense of hope and optimism.

It has often been remarked that the first word of the 12 steps is *We*, and this is not insignificant. The power of the group is greater than the power of the individual in combating this illness. While there can be a similar relief from learning that one's problems are not unique, as in an individual therapy situation, the power of the group to provide consensual validation is profound.

Yalom also noted that the most common secret disclosed by members of groups he has run is a sense of personal inadequacy. This sense is especially potent for most alcoholics and addicts, who have invariably struggled (on their own) to control their substance abuse and have just as invariably failed. This sense of personal failing (powerlessness) is, in the 12-step program, translated into a source of strength and fellowship.

Imparting Information

While Yalom spoke of groups as imparting information about psychological functioning, one of the specific lessons learned by participants in AA is that their affliction is a disease. The specific nature of this disease may vary according to the understanding of the individual member, but the locus of the dysfunction is consistently placed on the disease pathology itself. Education about other facets of the disease and of its management can be equally important in coming to terms with it, but it all stems from this one basic insight.

> A patient at a rehab center was being seen for an exit interview and was asked what she had learned from her stay. "Once I learned it was a disease, the rest all made sense."

More specific insight about ways of living and managing a recovering lifestyle is often conveyed in meetings and in personal conversations among members. The aphorisms of AA (e.g., "One day at a time," "Meeting makers make it") are also small lessons that are easily remembered, especially by those in early recovery.

In addition to the major volumes published by AA, a small book, *Living Sober* (Alcoholics Anonymous, 1975) is also available; its subtitle, *Some Methods AA Members Have Used for Not Drinking*, conveys its message. This is a semididactic volume with commonsense advice, especially useful for those new to the recovery program. Chapter headings include such suggestions as "Using the 24-hour plan," "Fending off loneliness," and "Remembering your last drunk." This is information of the most practical and valuable variety.

Of course, not all information imparted is readily accepted or incorporated. The difference between comparing-in and comparing-out has already been discussed and is relevant for those in any group setting to recognize. The often-encountered phenomenon of feeling different is not confined to those with narcissistic personality disorder. This is one of the prevalent obstacles to full engagement with the 12-step program.

In the 12-step program, imparting information is not the responsibility of the leader, as it may be in a more traditional group therapy format. Information is typically shared from one member to another member and often takes the form of self-disclosure, not advice or directive.

Altruism

Altruism finds its clearest expression in the 12th step, in which outreach to other suffering alcoholics or addicts is seen as essential to complete one's personal work. Even though some have interpreted this as ultimately selfish in nature (in that one reaches out in order to help oneself), the nature of the help, and the importance of the mission, clearly renders it a form of altruism.

Even the sharing of personal information in a 12-step meeting can be seen as altruistic, in that one is sharing personal experience at least partly in the hope of helping others. The voicing of thanks to a speaker when members comment from the floor emphasizes the role of such sharing in helping others.

Other direct forms of altruism are found in the support offered by one member to another. For some, the essence of the TSF is found in the midnight phone call from one member reaching out to another for help in staying sober; the heart of the matter is the frequency with which members selflessly respond to such calls.

New members in AA may express skepticism that other drunks can help them. While the simplistic answer is that they can be helped by others who are further along the same path, the truer answer is that even newcomers can be helpful to old-timers. The presence of others struggling with the same problem is a relief and is altruistic in itself.

The Corrective Recapitulation of the Primary Family Group

In the TSF, corrective recapitulation is probably one of the least explicitly realized of Yalom's curative factors. There is a great deal of talk in the rooms of the dysfunctional nature of members' childhoods and families of origin. There is considerable theory of addiction as a family disease, although there is little consensus about what that actually means. The absence of clear authority figures also diminishes the role of the 12-step meeting as a corrective emotional family experience.

However, in a more generalized fashion, the fellowship functions as a sort of healthy family that provides a haven for those whose emotional needs go unmet elsewhere. The role of the meeting as a grounding place, to which a member returns to feel closeness and experience an unthreatening, welcoming environment, is often overlooked. The feedback of the group to personal expressions is generally supportive and positive, and it supports ongoing personal growth, as a healthy family should do. For some members, this is the first place in which they have experienced such a warm and accepting welcome, and this provides healing beyond the steps and traditions.

Some treatment centers, especially therapeutic communities, are more explicit about invoking the nature of family dynamics in their structure. In such settings, the sense of loyalty and positive family norms are utilized to promote a specific change in values and character structure.

In one treatment center I visited, the opening greeting by all speakers at the morning community meeting was, "Good morning, family!"

Development of Socializing Techniques and Imitative Behavior

In the TSF, the development of social skills is primarily an indirect phenomenon, often through covert imitation. Social skills are not taught in the fellowship (although they may be taught in treatment centers as part of a coping skills component). However, the role of modeling of healthy social skills is powerful, from the meeting chair to the sharing of other peers. The role of the sponsor in helping an individual member to modify dysfunctional behaviors is also important. A common comment pertaining to this issue, often made to newcomers, is "stick with the winners."

On a different note, the TSF is a springboard for social contacts that are sober and positively oriented. The degree of social contact outside of meetings is one of the significant features of the program, even if it does not figure largely in the literature, steps, or traditions. For many, the program functions as a substitute social system, replacing social contacts in the tavern or on the street corner. The degree of external contact, and the encouragement of such contact, is a clear distinction between the 12-step program and Yalom-style group therapy.

Interpersonal Learning

Interpersonal learning is one of Yalom's two most significant therapeutic factors. It is related to the above two factors, but with an emphasis on the central importance of interpersonal relationships. Yalom stresses the essentially social nature of human existence, and the importance of group therapy in strengthening interpersonal capacities of the group members. He notes that the importance of interpersonal learning is based not only on affective expression but on the development of a "cognitive map" to give that emotional expression meaning. Catharsis without cognition is insufficient for lasting personal change.

The 12-step program approaches this differently. Sharing in a meeting is not a springboard for discussion and analysis, but is left alone. However, the entire worldview of the fellowship serves as a cognitive map, giving context to the content of the sharing. Much of the sharing does indeed take the form of connecting one's personal experience with a component of the program. For example, a man may get up to discuss friction with his employer, which created anger and self-doubt; however, he is likely to connect this to the Serenity Prayer and invoke the need to accept things he cannot change. The precepts of the program are there, almost floating in the air, and do not generally require explicit elucidation.

However, the conscious exploration of interpersonal dynamics is not the central focus of the fellowship or of any one meeting. Interpersonal advice, when offered, is usually in the form of a parallel self-disclosure, intended to teach by example or by comparison. (Such offerings can just as easily be how not to act in a situation, by revealing a personal failure; e.g., a participant can state, "I tried what you're attempting and it didn't work for me.") Rarely is direct advice or interpersonal feedback offered, at least not in the context of a meeting.

Interpersonal learning does occur in the TSF, but it appears to be based less on recapitulation of personal behaviors in the group and insight about those behaviors, as in the Yalom model, than on modeling and observation. The process of socialization appears to be a more meaningful determinant of change. The role of the sponsor cannot be overstated in this regard. While the choice of a sponsor has been little studied, it is most likely that the newcomer chooses a sponsor who embodies some aspect of his or her idealized self. This is an entirely different process than that espoused by Yalom.

However, in a broader sense, the role of interpersonal learning remains important to both endeavors. As Yalom notes, there is no "demonstrated relationship between the acquisition of genetic [e.g., deep] insight and the persistence of change" (1995, p. 46). Personal change requires an interpersonal component, regardless of the method by which this change occurs.

Group Cohesiveness

The second of Yalom's two most significant therapeutic factors is group cohesiveness. Cohesiveness, defined as the force by which members feel a part of, and attracted to, the group, is seen as therapeutic in its own right, as well as a precondition of change for the other factors. Therefore it is one of the most essential components of successful group therapy.

However, the nature of AA makes this a quite different task than in a regularly meeting interactional therapy group. For one thing, the membership at two consecutive AA meetings is not likely to be identical—people come and go with more frequency than in a stable therapy group. The sense of cohesiveness must be with the entire organization of AA, and with the rooms, rather than with a specific set of people. In some cases an allegiance with a home group or a clubhouse will serve as the point of identification, despite the transitional membership.

A second difference is the transitional nature of leadership within AA. Any given meeting will have a chairperson, but this chair rotates (often on a quarterly basis) and the leader's function is more limited than in a therapy group. The leader is also chosen from among the membership of the meeting; a leader on Tuesday may be in the audience on Wednesday, and may not be the leader at all a few months later. Leaders are trusted servants, not authority figures. The issues of transference and similar attitudes toward leadership are therefore more diffused and vague.

For Yalom, cohesiveness has two functions. For one thing, the degree of cohesiveness in the group provides a sense of safety for the expression of affective issues, and the preconditions for other therapeutic work. For another, "the sheer experience of being an accepted, valued member of a group" (Yalom, 1995, p. 70) may in itself have a healing function.

Twelve-step programs provide a setting for either form of cohesiveness. The closeness experienced in the rooms provides a ready setting for the sharing of deeply held personal experiences. For some, just being in a room of people sharing the same affliction is a healing experience.

The degree of cohesiveness in a 12-step meeting is clearly due, in large measure, to the shared common experience of alcoholism or addiction. Whereas much of Yalom's work presumes that the task of the therapist is to develop such a cohesive experience, the conditions of membership in a TSF accept such cohesion as a near given. Furthermore, the ongoing nature of the majority of 12-step meetings ensures that a sense of connectedness exists in any given meeting from day to day, or week to week. Usually, a newcomer joins an established meeting that already has its own norms, traditions, and cohesiveness.

Catharsis

Yalom views catharsis as a necessary, but not sufficient, factor of change in group therapy. As indicated above, catharsis must be coupled with some form of cognitive learning to be meaningful in making therapeutic gains. One role of catharsis is in promoting group cohesion—the expression of affect, whether positive or negative, results in greater affiliative bonds among members, if properly worked through.

Catharsis is not seen as a major part of the AA program. However, much of people's personal sharing may include affective displays and may be considered cathartic. This may facilitate members' closeness to the group and may enhance their sense of belonging; others may also respond to such input with caring and connection.

Existential Factors

Existential factors—the recognition that life is not fair, accepting personal responsibilities, the inevitability of some degree of pain—were relatively highly ranked by patients in research cited by Yalom. In particular, he noted that an item, "taking ultimate responsibility for the way I live my life," was ranked highly by many patients. Yalom pointed to an inherent paradox in the existential view of life and of treatment: although group therapy aims at helping improve interpersonal relationships, there is an ultimate limit to the degree of intimacy that can be obtained, either in therapy or in life itself.

The 12-step *weltenschauung* addresses these concerns in a spiritual manner. While seeing the essential incompleteness and imperfection of each of us as individuals, it also recognizes the need for each of us to attempt to secure an interpersonal connection. The dialectical nature of this, and the recognition of human dependency needs, is a profound awareness, one that is difficult to sustain. It has elements of empowerment as well as terror. However, this insight is key to the deeper meaning of the 12-step ideology (Kurtz, 1982). Thus, existential concerns undergird the TSF, even if they are not immediate and conscious concerns of individual members.

The essence of this existential perspective may be summed up in one of my favorite 12-step aphorisms—"Accept life on life's terms." The newcomer to AA often struggles with the task of accepting powerlessness and surrendering egotism. This perspective allows him or her to relinquish an egocentric perspective in favor of a more complementary one (Bateson, 1972).

To sum up, many of the factors that have been found by Yalom to be therapeutic in group therapy are also active in the TSF. Their form of these factors may be different, and they may differ in importance, which is only logical, given the differing formats and goals (self-exploration of psychological functioning vs. sobriety). Future research into the TSF may be helpful in articulating the relative importance of each of these factors, and this may, in turn, assist treatment professionals in designing more effective interventions.

Hope and Meaning: Jerome Frank

Jerome Frank originally published *Persuasion and Healing* in 1961, and the expanded third edition, coauthored with his daughter Julia Frank, was published in 1991. This book is widely seen as a landmark study of the art and science of psychotherapy, and an attempt to derive the common roots of a variety of schools of therapy and behavior change. Their observations about the process of such change, including direct reference to AA itself (pp. 249–252) help illuminate the processes of change found in the fellowship.

For Frank and Frank (1991), a primary role of psychotherapy is to provide hope to combat a sense of demoralization. One of the keys to this is to provide a modification to the patient's "assumptive world," in order to change a negative experience into a more favorable one.

To accomplish this, Frank and Frank (1991) identified four components of successful psychotherapy, as follows.

A Relationship

The first essential element of psychotherapy is "an emotionally charged, confiding relationship with a helping person (often with the participation of a group)" (Frank & Frank, 1991, p. 40). The existence of a healing relationship underscores the interpersonal nature of psychopathology and the need for relatedness in restoring functioning. This is explicitly referenced in Bill's writing that the goal of AA is to restore the alcoholic's sense of belonging to the family of man, from a position of self-centeredness, of "self-will run riot" (Alcoholics Anonymous, 2001, p. 62). In the case of the TSF, this relationship is diffused among the membership, although the relationship with one's sponsor may be especially salient for the member. Frank and Frank, understanding the human capacity for symbolization, allowed for the possibility that the relationship need not be with an individual, nor must the individual be constantly present. Their reference to the popularity of self-help books as an example obviously brings up the image of the Big Book in AA or NA.

In the actual practice, the experience of most AA members is one of warm acceptance, and of the approval, even necessity, of personal confiding (sharing) for the process to work. This is the centerpiece of 12-step practice. Individual relationships can be formed, but the primary relationship, as Yalom would concur, is with the group, or with the institution of AA itself.

A Healing Setting

The Franks point to the tradition of healing being conducted in a special setting, both to enhance the prestige of the therapist (and the patient's expectation of help) and to convey a sense of safety. While a church basement may not pass for a Park Avenue psychiatrist's office, there is a similarity in function. The affectionate reference to "the rooms" of the TSF conveys the consistency and reliability of what is to be found within the fellowship, whether in a basement or a penthouse.

An Explanatory Myth

The second component of psychotherapy is "a rationale, conceptual scheme, or myth that provides a plausible explanation for the patient's symptoms and prescribes a ritual or procedure for resolving them" (Frank & Frank, 1991, p. 42). This component speaks directly to the patient's need to make meaning of his situation. According to the Franks, Freud referred to the psychoanalytic worldview as "our mythology." Explanatory myths are invariably culture bound, which enhances their plausibility.

From this perspective, the veracity of the disease concept is of secondary importance. What matters is that the 12-step member believes the explanatory rationale and that it is plausible. In this regard, the 12-step worldview is quite comprehensive in scope. While somewhat vague in elucidating the origins of the disorder, it relegates this concern to secondary status and focuses on a procedure for dealing with the problem in the here and now.

As noted earlier, the Big Book comes closest to providing an explanation of the origins of the disorder in "The Doctor's Opinion," a chapter originally in the book itself, but now found in the preface. (Some have argued that because it is moved, fewer people actually read it.) This chapter, drawing on the work of Dr. Silkworth, describes alcoholism as an allergy combined with a compulsion and suggests that these are constitutionally inherited traits. While not measuring up to more scientific explanations of the disease, this explanation provides a simple, easily understood description of the origins of the problem. Whether this is true scientifically (e.g., Erickson, 2007) or is purely metaphorical, this explanation can still be heard discussed in the rooms of AA and NA.

A Ritual

The third element of successful psychotherapy is "a ritual or procedure that requires the active participation of both patient and therapist and that is believed by both to be the means of restoring the patient's health" (Frank & Frank, 1991, p. 43). Here, the role of the 12 steps themselves becomes immediately apparent. There are few therapeutic rituals that are as clear and explicit as these. The participant's faith in the healing power of the steps is reinforced by the regular testimony of speakers at meetings sharing the "experience, hope, and strength" of their own stories. The oft-quoted passage in the Big Book, "rarely have we seen a person fail who has thoroughly followed our path," (p. 58) directly invokes the importance of the member's belief in this process.

The Franks also point out that a ritual also allows a face-saving way for the patient to make changes that may otherwise have been difficult to make on a social level. This consideration allows for the client who is motivated to change but lacks a means of doing so.

> I recall a client who was successful in quitting her cocaine use, and thanked the program staff for informing her that it was bad for her, as if this was not common knowledge.

Although apparently taking a psychological understanding of alcoholism (p. 13), the Franks spoke positively of AA under the rubric of "directive psychotherapies." They noted that although positing a disease entity underlying alcoholism, the cure provided by A. A. is to assume responsibility for one's recovery and to apply moral remedies (such as making amends). They also noted that the First Step in AA (accepting powerlessness over alcohol) paradoxically may increase a sense of self-efficacy—by acknowledging their own role in contributing to the problem, members open the possibility that they may be able to be active in overcoming it.

The Franks' emphasis on ascribing meaning to the symptoms and to the cure also invokes the contribution of Viktor Frankl (1946/1984), whose system of psychotherapy rests completely on his belief that mental health depends on having a sense of meaning in one's life. His observations as a prisoner in the Nazi death camps led him to recognize that those who survived were not necessarily the most physically fit, but those whose belief systems provided a meaningful rationale for survival. For example, one man was persuaded to go on, having faced the deaths of his entire family, in order to bear witness to his experiences, and to seek to prevent a second Holocaust.

The role of AA in helping patients make sense of their experience cannot be overstated. Invariably, patients suffering from addiction blame themselves for their suffering, and it is easy to understand this attribution, given that the problem appears to be self-created by the ingestion of alcohol or drugs. The notion that they are largely blameless for the creation of their loss of control (although entirely responsible for its resolution) is an exhilarating relief for those who come to accept it.

Inferiority and Social Interest: Alfred Adler

It is interesting that Bill Wilson made a connection with Carl Jung over the issue of spiritual conversion, but made no reference to the work of Jung's former colleague, Alfred Adler (1929; Ansbacher & Ansbacher, 1956). In retrospect, Adler's work was remarkably syntonic with that of Wilson, as there are some striking similarities in their views of human nature and of the cure for psychological illness.

For Adler, the fundamental drive of man is for superiority, and dominance over others. This results from a perception of inferiority, based on childhood dependence. This drive for superiority (often termed "masculine protest" by Adler) is a direct contradiction to the more healthy social interest that comes naturally. This drive is fundamentally antisocial—it pits the individual against society. The drive for superiority is also quite difficult to circumvent, as any attempts to point it out to the patient are perceived as threats to his sense of superiority and reminders of his earlier helpless condition.

This situation essentially recapitulates the situation of many an addicted individual (in addition to any general personality formation). The perception of defect or inferiority is triggered by the inability of the addict to control substance use, despite many efforts to do so. This results in the posture of defiance and grandiosity (think of "masculine protest"), which has been described elsewhere (Tiebout, 1949).

For Adler, the solution to this situation was the restoration of the person's connection with the social fabric, a return to interpersonal functioning. "To cure a neurosis and a psychosis it is necessary to change completely the whole up-bringing of the patient and turn him definitely and unconditionally back upon human society" (Adler, 1929, p. 24). Compare this to the AA approach of taking inventory, making amends, and affiliating with other recovering alcoholics: The AA member "puts down the bottle and learns to replace 'booze' with people and meetings" (Spiegel & Fewell, 2004, p. 126). In Adler's terms, social interest is the antidote to masculine protest.

The method of Adler's individual psychology differs markedly from that pursued in the 12-step program. Adler, for example, did not pursue the spiritual dimension in the same way that Bill Wilson and Carl Jung did. However, the goals of both appear quite similar, in reconnecting individuals with the social group from which they have become estranged by virtue of their disease, and in reducing the individual's degree of egocentricity.

Attachment and Transitional Objects: D. W. Winnicott

The function of AA in serving as a transitional object has been discussed by Spiegel and Fewell (2004). Drawing on the object relations work of Winnicott and the attachment theory of Bowlby, they propose that much of the value of a 12-step meeting derives from its role in helping the client bridge the gap between the drinking world and the sober one. Seen this way, engagement with the 12-step program is a developmental process, in which the program gradually becomes internalized, much the way a child internalizes images of a secure mother to allow more autonomous functioning.

Winnicott and Bowlby stress the infant's need to internalize the soothing of the mother, to be able to learn self-soothing, which will allow for more independent functioning. To some degree this function is facilitated by transitional objects, items that come to symbolically replace the mother and permit the infant to feel secure even in the absence of the actual nurturing parent figure.

In this view, the desperation with which newcomers initially approach the TSF is a form of regression and allows access to more primitive ego states. This approximates a more authentic experience of self, requiring soothing and stabilization. The program thereby serves as a form of transitional object, allowing the client to experience the safety and security of the meetings and internalize this particular way of being, much as the infant internalizes the reassuring mother. To Spiegel and Fewell, the early feelings of relief upon encountering and entering the fellowship (the oft-mentioned "pink cloud" of the newcomer) revive primitive feelings of bonding and connection. The common practice of 90/90 (i.e., attending 90 meetings in 90 days) ensures a consistent proximity to the program and facilitates this sense of bonding. Many newcomers, indeed, make a practice of hanging out at clubhouses, attending multiple meetings in a day, and generally allowing themselves to experience a dependent regressive state vis-à-vis the program.

The use of the program as a transitional object replaces the use of drugs for much of the same effect of security and self-soothing, but allows for a higher degree of functioning and autonomy. Whereas the drug can provide a reliable form of gratification, the program itself is also available on a constant basis via the use of "telephone therapy" (Alcoholics Anonymous, 1975) or frequent meeting attendance. Ultimately, the goal is for the AA member to internalize the presence of the program, along with its values and norms, and reattain autonomous functioning, while still utilizing the program for ongoing support and dependent regression. The use of the steps is seen by Spiegel and Fewell as providing guidelines for further individuation, with the program and the meetings functioning as a secure base from which to explore, much as a small child returns to the parent for reassurance after forays into the independent world.

A Developmental Model of Recovery: Stephanie Brown

Spiegel and Fewell's (2004) observations find support in the work of

Stephanie Brown (1985), who made an empirical study of the process of recovery in AA and also took a developmental approach. Brown concurred that the member must relinquish an attachment to alcohol, but that it can be replaced by an attachment to the program of recovery. She also noted an internalization of the attitudes and beliefs of the 12-step program.

Brown, however, focused on both the cognitive and affective shifts AA members go through in the process of recovery. She identified three components of change: the alcohol axis, environmental interactions, and the interpretation of self and others. She also identified four phases of change: drinking, transition, early recovery, and ongoing recovery. The relative importance of each of the axes varies according to the phase of change, which in turn affects the focus of psychotherapy at that point.

The alcohol axis represents the person's preoccupation with alcohol and the form that this preoccupation takes. During the drinking phase, the person struggles with attempts to control drinking, with an underlying belief that this is a problem subject to personal willpower. With the experience of hitting bottom, during the transition phase, the alcoholic comes to accept that the fundamental problem is the inability to control the drinking. While the emphasis on alcohol, and the identification as an alcoholic, must remain in the client's focus for recovery to progress, the nature of that identification changes, from one of a drinking alcoholic to that of a recovering alcoholic, and its centrality fades as other concerns emerge with sobriety.

Environmental interactions broaden as the focus on alcohol changes and diminishes. Consistent with the view of Spiegel and Fewell (2004), AA members use the fellowship as a base of safety from which they can explore new interactions in the world, yet return to the program to review them and compare notes. In the early phases, the need for support from other recovering AAs is paramount. However, Brown pointed out that members may affiliate with the program, yet can regulate their own level of intimacy and dependency on the fellowship. As members maintain sobriety and progress in their recovery, they recognize the importance of the interdependent nature of the fellowship and expand this awareness to the external environment as well. The nature of this dependency also shifts, from a more passive dependence to a more mature mutual sense of interdependence.

The process of exploring environmental interactions also applies to clients working through personal problems that had been masked or neglected during the course of their active addiction. Clients are more able to approach these issues from the perspectives of the program and utilize tools that were initially applied to their sobriety. These may include the capacity to let go of things they can not control or the ability to solicit help from others to resolve problems.

Interpretation of self and others expands as sobriety progresses. The reevaluation of one's personal relationships is an inevitable step in the process of recovery. Some relationships in the active drinking stage are reassessed as having little meaning or value; one often hears about old friends now being viewed as associates or drinking buddies rather than friends. This may also pertain to more intimate relationships.

> One client in rehabilitation expressed fear about returning home to her husband. She had been drinking and abusing prescription medications for the entire duration of their marriage, even though it had not escalated out of control until the last few years. She expressed the concern, "I've never known him sober, and he's never known me sober."

The reassessment of self goes beyond the transition from drinking to recovering alcoholic. Most people in active recovery describe significant changes in their views of themselves, of their values, and of the nature of their interpersonal relationships.

Brown's schema provides a useful guide for therapists working with alcoholics or other addicts. In the early phases, the focus must be on attaining sobriety and on conveying the importance of accepting the loss of control that is one of the defining characteristics of addiction. As the client moves through the process, the therapist must not allow the client to lose sight of his or her addictive status, but must broaden the focus to review ongoing interactions with others, reevaluations of self, and negotiating the world from a more sober and more egalitarian perspective.

One important implication of Brown's work is that the process of recovery is a distinct and unique process, and is not simply the mirror image of the decline that the addict experiences as active addiction progresses. This runs counter to some of the more simplistic and static notions of earlier theorists. Furthermore, Brown's schema allows for a wide variety of individual progression through the phases of recovery, with regression and relapse possible as variations within an overall progressive movement.

Chapter 8

Challenges in Research on the 12-Step Fellowship

History has shown that, whatever their several merits, neither preaching nor moralizing nor other efforts at reform have ever made much impression on alcoholics as a whole. But factual education about the malady has in the last few years shown great promise.

—Bill Wilson, 1958

IT HAS BEEN WIDELY ACCEPTED BY MANY observers that AA does not support research and that there has been little actual research into the 12-step fellowships (e.g., Fingarette, 1988). In fact, it appears that there has been a great deal of research into AA, although much of it (particular the older studies) has been of poor methodological quality (Emrick, Tonigan, Montgomery, & Little, 1993; McCrady, Horvath, & Delaney, 2003; Miller & McCrady, 1993). More recently, AA research has increased and has become more sophisticated. The number of publications on this topic in the 8 years between 1993 and 2001 ($n = 118$) is nearly as great as the total between 1940 and 1992 ($n = 125$) (Owen, et al., 2003). While AA does not, in fact, frown upon research efforts, there are a number of reasons why it is difficult to engage in rigorous methodological studies of such a fellowship.

Bill W. himself commented on this issue. As quoted in Miller and McCrady (1993), Bill issued a "Memo on Participation of A.A. Members in Research and Other Non-A.A. Surveys." In this memo, he welcomed "any new light that can be thrown on the alcoholic's mysterious and baffling malady" (p. 9) and generally encouraged the participation of AA members in such efforts, with several important reservations. First, he suggested that researchers become "thoroughly familiar with the Fellowship" and demonstrate respect for the traditions of the program (e.g., Nowinski, 1993). He also suggested that both researchers and AA members engage in open communication about the research, and cautioned that researchers might not receive the same level of cooperation from an organization as decentralized as AA, and that decisions about participation are always made at the local level. Finally, Bill stated firmly that research must not interfere with the primary purpose and goals of the program, namely, to help alcoholics attain and maintain sobriety—any research that obstructs this cannot be tolerated.

Bill wrote elsewhere on this topic (a 1958 essay in the AA magazine *The Grapevine* has been reprinted as a pamphlet, "Let's Be Friendly With Our Friends," Bill W., 1958), encouraging support and cooperation with others who are pursuing alternative approaches to dealing with the alcohol problem. "We don't care too much whether new and valuable knowledge issues from a test tube, a psychiatrist's couch, or revealing social studies . . . we regard all who labor in the total field of alcoholism as our companions on a march from darkness into light" (p. 2). Bill's own extended personal research into other approaches to recovery is well documented (Cheever, 2004) and reflects his ongoing search for solutions to the problem.

Bill's concerns were appropriate and formed the basis of much of the standard critique of research into the TSF, but there are other methodological issues that were not within his domain. As he noted, the lack of a central organizing structure makes data gathering difficult; it is not possible to secure data from one central source. This renders archival studies impossible, as no central membership records are kept. Just as significant, it makes it difficult to make any general inferences about AA from a study of one local area. Regional differences in practice, policy, and tradition make any broader generalizations about research findings quite tenuous at best. How does one generalize about an organization that gives such wide latitude to each local group to establish its own rules and practices?

A fundamental weakness in any study of AA will be the inherent difficulty of establishing a double-blind condition and a random assignment to "treatment" condition. AA functions as a program of attraction;

part of its power depends on the member making a choice to attend, rather than being coerced to attend. In fact, the few studies of random assignment have generally been conducted with mandated clients, and they appear to demonstrate that this condition results in negative outcome (McCrady et al., 2003). Given this fact, any study that assigns clients to a 12-step condition places a basic obstacle on the interpretation of the results; they are at least one step removed from the natural conditions in which AA exists. Correlational studies, which form the bulk of 12-step research, yield interesting findings, which are less persuasive in terms of determining causality. Yalisove (2004) considers an ethical constriction as well—it would be unethical to prohibit clients in the control group from attending AA should they wish to do so.

Conversely, another implication of this fact is that it will invariably be difficult or impossible to distinguish the effects of the fellowship from the inherent motivation of the members who have chosen to affiliate themselves with it; any naturalistic study must deal with this critical confounding variable. As several researchers have pointed out (e.g., Vaillant, 1995), AA attendance itself may simply be a correlate of highly motivated individuals.

Generalizations about AA have been made from studies of treatment programs employing 12-step principles. Nowinski and colleagues (Nowinski & Baker, 1992; Nowinski, Baker, & Carroll, 1992) developed a structured program called Twelve-step facilitation, which provides a manualized program for researchers on 12-step programs. The program facilitation works to enhance the client's awareness of his or her addiction as a disease and to encourage attendance and participation in AA. It provides introductions to AA practices and traditions in a semididactic format. However, like other research on treatment, it is not AA itself, and as such is only an indirect measure of the impact of AA on sobriety (Yalisove, 2004). Similarly, the outcomes of treatment programs (outpatient or residential) based on AA cannot be said to reflect the utility of AA itself, in that the degree of compliance with the recommended attendance at meetings can be highly variable (Tonigan, Toscova, & Miller, 1996). In any such study, the relationship between participation in 12-step facilitation and actual involvement in a 12-step program must be assessed as part of the measurement of treatment utility, if the impact of AA itself is the primary variable examined (McCrady et al., 2003).

Researchers also face the problem of translating the ideas of the TSF into operational constructs that are then testable (Nowinski, 1993). While some studies measure duration of AA attendance or number of meetings attended, there is also a need to assess the degree of involvement in the TSF (see Tonigan, Connors, & Miller, 1996, on the Alcoholics Anonymous Involvement Scale and the Recovery Interview of Morgenstern, Labouvie, McCrady, Kahler, & Frey, 1997, for examples). Such constructs as spiritual awakening, commitments, sponsorship, and step work are loosely defined in the first place and translate poorly into operational terms. "God *as we understand him*" is a difficult place to begin a rigorous empirical study.

While not problematic for some researchers, the goals of treatment can present an obstacle for interpretation. If abstinence is considered the only valid goal, then substantial reduction in drinking accompanied by significant improvements in life functioning may be considered treatment failures, if the client continues to drink episodically or at a moderate level (Yalisove, 2004). Several alternative measures have been utilized in studies (e.g., number of abstinent days, days till onset of relapse, number of heavy drinking days) to tease out some of the subtle distinctions of alcoholic drinking. However, in the world of AA research, abstinence remains the gold standard goal of treatment.

However, the major obstacle to research into the utility of TSFs is in the minds of researchers themselves. Researchers are an empirical bunch and are generally skeptical of the more faith-based tenets of the 12-step program (Vaillant, 1995). Furthermore, there is an understandable tendency to examine the psychological intervention as the primary independent variable, with the role of AA seen as an adjunct to the treatment intervention. In other words, studies frequently ask, "Does AA add any value to a treatment intervention?" In many ways, this is the opposite of the stance that is really needed to determine the value of a 12-step program—the more relevant question is whether formal treatment adds much value to the impact of the 12-step program itself. Only recently have researchers begun to realign their work and see AA as an entity worthy of study in its own right.

Dropouts from studies, a problem in all clinical research, are a special issue in research on AA (Tonigan, Bogenschutz, & Miller, 2006), as it can prove difficult to track members of an anonymous organization. The dropout rate from AA is fairly high, and, as discussed in Chapter 9, it is difficult to make assumptions about the success or failure of such noncompleters.

Emrick et al. (1993), in a meta-analysis, described problems in the research on AA to that point. The pool of subjects in the 107 studies reviewed comprised a relatively homogenous group, largely male, with a mean age of 42. The generalizability of this group to the whole of AA is uncertain. Generally, the sample descriptions are poor and the diagnostic criteria used are vague, making comparisons between studies quite difficult. More studies were obtained from inpatient than outpatient sources; while making the researcher's job more manageable, it does not allow for the study of AA in its more natural setting. This bias is especially significant in view of the finding (Tonigan, Toscova, et al., 1996) that outpatient samples yielded more significant relationships between AA attendance and outcome than inpatient samples. Emrick also noted that a significant problem in most studies is the lack of random assignment to treatment groups; as noted earlier, this is an inherent limitation in this area.

Tonigan, Toscova, and Miller (1996) presented another meta-analysis that moderates some of Emrick's findings. Again, they reminded us that the bulk of the research in this area has been on treatment utilizing AA concepts (e.g., such as Nowinski's 12-step Facilitation), not on the fellowship itself. As noted above, they observed stronger relationships between AA participation and positive drinking outcomes in outpatient samples than in inpatient samples. They provided no explanation for this finding. However, R. Moos (personal communication, 6/7/08) notes that the social network benefits of AA are more relevant in community settings.

Although Emrick et al., (1993) do not touch on this issue (McCrady et al., 2003, mention it in passing), almost all of the research into self-help groups has been on AA. Even less is known about NA, Overeaters Anonymous, and other groups based on the 12-step model or on alternative models. For the time being, we too will focus on AA and make cautious extrapolations to other TSFs.

Reviewing the Research

The following selective research review is not intended as a full scholarly review of the literature and is probably a biased one at that. In keeping with the title of this book, it is intended to help clinicians understand the dynamics of the fellowship and assess indications for referral or nonreferral to such programs. The following questions are addressed as most relevant for the practicing clinician:

- Does AA attendance enhance drinking outcomes?
- Who is more likely to attend and benefit from AA?
- Does AA attendance enhance secondary outcomes?
- How much AA is enough?
- What are the curative components of AA?

Does AA Attendance Enhance Drinking Outcomes?

Bill Wilson reported on his own informal outcome study in the foreword to the second edition of *Alcoholics Anonymous* in 1955:

> Of alcoholics who came to AA and really tried, 50% got sober at once and remained that way: 25% sobered up after some relapses, and among the remainder, those who stayed on with AA showed improvement. Other thousands came to a few AA meetings and at first decided they didn't want the program. But great numbers of these—about two out of three—began to return as time passed.

Bill's report is more quaint than statistically sophisticated.

Critics of AA can refer to the well-known major review by Miller et al., (2003). The authors reviewed 381 studies on alcoholism treatment that met their criteria and gave each one a methodological quality score (MQS) reflecting the quality of the study and an outcome logic score (OLS; from +2 for positive effects observed to –2 for no evidence of benefit). The product of the MQS and the OLS was computed for each study and the scores from each study within a given modality were totaled, yielding a cumulative evidence score (CES) for that modality. The CES therefore provides a summary score of the evidence for each modality's beneficial effect. It then allows a rank ordering of all treatment modalities included in the review.

In this review, AA ranks 38th in the list (just behind 12-step facilitation), with a negative CES score, hardly an impressive outcome. However, there are several problems with this assessment, noted by the authors themselves. First, as noted above, the methodological quality of much of the work on AA to that point was admittedly quite poor, affecting the overall MQS ratings of the studies (the MQS for the AA studies is among the lowest in the review). Second, the CES score clearly favors a larger number of studies—the highest ranking modality, brief interventions, included 34 studies, whereas the AA rankings were based on 7 studies.

However, it must be noted that the CES for the AA studies was a negative number, indicating a lack of positive results for the studies included. This largely reflects the fact that several of the studies included used clients who were mandated to treatment, for example by courts or employers, hardly an unbiased sample. The authors concluded that, on the basis of this review, the efficacy of AA remains largely untested. Heather (2007) made the point that these data, rather than reflecting the negative efficacy of AA, "should be interpreted as providing no support for *compulsory* attendance at AA" (p. 255, emphasis in original).

Within the limits of correlational research, the answer to the question of AA's overall efficacy appears to be a qualified positive one. Generally, those who attend AA are more likely to maintain abstinence than those who do not. McCrady and colleagues reported that "one of the most consistent and robust findings is that there is a positive correlation between AA attendance and drinking outcomes," whether studying a clinical or nonclinical population (2003, p. 182). Again, whether the sobriety is due to attending AA or whether both behaviors are the result of some other variable (e.g., high motivation) is impossible to determine from these data.

For example, Hoffman and Miller (1992), reviewing inpatients and outpatients in their CATOR database, found that clients attending AA were significantly more likely to be abstinent than those who did not at a 2 year follow-up point. Attendance at professional aftercare treatment increased this likelihood in an additive fashion: 90% of those who attended both weekly AA and aftercare for a full year were abstinent. In an earlier study, Hoffman, Harrison, and Belille (1983) noted a much higher abstinence rate (73%) among AA attendees than among nonattendees (33%). Again, the motivation factor cannot be ruled out.

Data demonstrating the value of AA was found by Ouimette, Moos, and Finney (1998). Studying clients for the first year after formal treatment, they found that participation in both aftercare and AA yielded the most favorable outcomes. In this study, patients were categorized into one of four aftercare groups: no aftercare, outpatient only, 12-step participation only, or outpatient and 12-step participation). Patients who attended only 12-step groups had better outcomes than those who participated only in outpatient treatment. The results for abstinence were powerful. Of those in the combined outpatient–12-step, 63% were abstinent, compared with 49% in the 12-step only group, 29% in the outpatient group, and 24% in the no-aftercare group. Interestingly, level of motivation was associated with choice of activity (with aftercare and AA involvement associated with higher levels of motivation) but was not directly associated with outcome, suggesting that AA attendance provided some benefit independent of motivation. The presence of an Axis I disorder did not impact these findings related to substance abuse outcomes. Both the number of meetings attended and the degree of involvement in the TS program (e.g, working the steps, reading literature) were associated with both abstinence and remission, as well as several secondary variables.

In a 16-year follow-up of earlier data (Moos & Moos, 2004), Moos and Moos (2006) were able to provide a rare view of the long-term impact of AA attendance on drinking outcome. They found that both treatment and AA involvement were predictive of better outcome 16 years later. However, after the initial treatment episode, continued participation in AA was associated with better outcome at 16 years, whereas this was not true of further treatment. One of the implications of this study was that treatment was beneficial by fostering participation in the 12-step program. The authors stated, "Some of the contribution of treatment reflected participation in AA, whereas the contribution of AA was essentially independent of the contribution of treatment" (p. 745).

McKay, Alterman, McLellan, and Snider (1994) examined the degree of 12-step involvement on drug and alcohol use at 4 and 7 months posttreatment in a day hospital treatment program. They found a positive relationship between 12-step involvement and outcome even when pretreatment substance use and treatment completion were controlled for. This again suggests that the 12-step involvement itself was relevant to outcome, independent of the level of motivation of the client.

Fiorentine (1999) studied a sample of outpatients and distinguished those with any 12-step attendance as well as those with at least weekly attendance. He found lower rates of both drug and alcohol use among those attending any 12-step programs in a 2-year follow-up (drug use: 27% vs. 44%; alcohol: 32% vs. 61%). Attending a 12-step meeting weekly, or more frequently, was also associated with even lower rates of drug and alcohol use: (drug use: 22% vs. 44%; alcohol use: 24% vs. 60%).

Studies of 12-step-oriented treatment programs themselves provide an indirect analogue of the efficacy of the 12-step program, although they remain one step removed from measuring actual attendance or involvement. Ouimette, Finney, and Moos (1997), studying a Veterans Administration population, compared 12-step treatment with cognitive-behavioral treatment, a relatively well-studied modality. Although they did not utilize a random assignment protocol, they did include follow-up at 1 year postdischarge. They found that although all three groups (12-step, cognitive-behavioral, and mixed) showed improvement on several outcome variables, only the 12-step group demonstrated significant improvement in abstinence (reflecting again the relevance of the outcome measures used). Interestingly, they found no differences for subgroups of patients who had been mandated to treatment or who had comorbid psychiatric diagnoses.

Project MATCH, a large multisite study attempting to assess the merits of patient-treatment matching, also provided some data on the relative efficacy of 12-step treatment (Project MATCH Research Group, 1997, 1998). Project MATCH compared three treatment modalities: 12-step facilitation (TSF), cognitive-behavioral treatment (CBT), and motivational enhancement treatment (MET). The study was based on five outpatient and five aftercare sites, with a total of 1,726 subjects. Subjects were randomly assigned to one of the three treatment groups. Treatment in the TSF and CBT groups consisted of weekly sessions over the 12 weeks of treatment, while MET patients had four sessions, consistent with the philosophy of MET (Miller & Rollnick, 2002). Although the study benefited from random assignment, it did not include a no-treatment control group. Outcome measures included percentage of days abstinent (PDA) and drinks per drinking day (DDD), as well as abstinence. Treatment in Project MATCH was delivered individually, although those in the TSF condition were, of course, encouraged to attend AA meetings.

The results of Project MATCH demonstrated no significant differences in PDA and DDD between the three treatment groups. However, in the outpatient sample, TSF patients had the highest rate of abstinence (24%, vs. 15% for CBT and 14% for MET). In the 3-year follow-up (Project MATCH Research Group, 1998), drinking patterns were assessed for the 3 months prior to the 3-year interview. TSF patients again demonstrated the highest rate of abstinence (36%, vs. 24% for CBT clients and 27% for MET clients). Among the few predicted patient-treatment matches that were confirmed, patients with low psychiatric severity (a significant confounding variable) did better in TSF treatment than in CBT.

Another significant finding emerged from the 3-year follow-up data (Owen et al., 2003). It was discovered that a substantial portion of the

MET and CBT patients had voted with their feet (p. 526) by attending AA and becoming involved with some aspect of the program. In fact, 45% of the MET subjects and 39% of the CBT subjects reported at the 3-year follow-up that they had attended some AA meetings.

In a study of the role of behavioral couples therapy (BCT; Owen et al., 2003), three treatment conditions (BCT alone, BCT and AA, BCT and relapse prevention) were found to have no differences in percentage of days abstinent at an 18-month follow-up point. However, the number of AA meetings attended correlated positively with percentage of days abstinent; this correlation was greater in the group including AA than in the other two groups.

It may be observed that most of these studies assess AA participation following formal treatment. Some research has addressed the role of AA both with and without formal treatment. Timko, Moos, Finney, and Lesar (2000) used a naturalistic design to study the relative contributions of treatment and AA attendance. Although either form of formal intervention was better than no treatment at 8-year follow-up, it was noted that the AA-only group had better outcomes at the 1- and 3-year points than the formally treated group or the combined AA/treatment group. One possible interpretation is that the treatment-based groups continued to demonstrate improvement in subsequent years—in a sense, they caught up with the gains achieved by the AA-only group. It was also noted that participation in either AA or formal treatment during the first year was associated with better drinking outcomes at the 8-year follow-up.

The issue of motivation was examined by McKellar, Stewart, and Humphreys (2003) using structural equation modeling or path analysis. Although employing a naturalistic design, the relationships between hypothesized variables can be examined for causal inference. Following patients for 2 years, the researchers found that AA affiliation (attendance and involvement in 12-step activities) predicted better clinical outcome, and not vice versa (suggesting that the positive outcome was not strictly due to dropout of less successful members). Level of motivation did not appear to be a factor in the positive outcomes, nor did psychopathology.

It must be noted that not all of the research on AA is positive. In his earlier review, Emrick (1987) noted that 36% of the studies reviewed found no significant relationship between AA attendance and outcome, and that 10% reported a negative relationship.

Who Is More Likely to Attend and Benefit From AA?

One of the more consistent findings from the meta-analysis of Emrick et al. (1993) was the observation that the more severe the drinking, the more likely someone is to make use of AA (e.g., McLatchie & Lomp, 1988). This is true whether one measures the actual amount of drinking, the concern about drinking, the experience of loss of control, or anxiety or compulsiveness about drinking. A secondary finding is that those who engage in AA are more likely to seek help in general and have external supports available. Holding religious or spiritual beliefs was another variable associated with AA participation. Again, it is noted that these are correlational findings and cannot be considered causal. Emrick et al. (1993) also noted that most of these correlations are modest at best. Morgenstern et al. (1997) observed that the client's perception of consequences, rather than actual drinking behavior, affected the decision to affiliate with AA.

This finding is consistent with the traditional observation that to join AA one must hit bottom first. Those with less severe alcohol problems may find other paths to recovery—they may simply quit on their own or may moderate their consumption, but they generally do not feel the need to seek help from AA. In this light, AA is seen as a last-ditch effort, an interpretation that Bill W. and Dr. Bob would probably find satisfying.

Vaillant (1995), reviewing longitudinal data in his Boston-based sample, noted that the most significant factor predicting positive engagement with AA was Irish ancestry. He posited that the social aspect of AA may have influenced this outcome. However, he also noted that the Irish population in his study appeared to have more severe drinking problems, an observation consistent with that of Emrick et al. (1993).

Observations from the Project MATCH research, as cited above, are relevant: those patients with low psychiatric severity did better in TSF than in CBT. Similarly, those with a high level of anger did better in

MET than in TSF or CBT. Those with a social network that was supportive of drinking did better in TSF, possibly due to the great deal of emphasis in the 12-step program on connection with others and on interpersonal service.

Does AA Attendance Enhance Secondary Outcomes?

Moos and Moos (2004) evaluated drinking outcomes and possible mediating variables at 1-year and 8-year posttreatment intervals, in a study looking at the duration and frequency of AA attendance in the first year of sobriety. They found differential effects for the duration of a person's involvement versus his frequency of attendance on secondary functioning. At the 8-year follow-up point, increased duration of involvement in AA predicted better self-efficacy and social functioning, whereas increased frequency of attending meetings affected improved social functioning. They found evidence that continued attendance at AA after the first year also improved clients' level of social functioning, if they attended at least four meetings a week.

Moos and Moos (2006), in a 16-year follow-up of earlier data (2004) found that those who attended AA for 27 weeks or more in the first 3 years were not only more likely to be abstinent than those who had not attended, or who had attended for less than 27 weeks, but they also rated higher in self-efficacy and social functioning. They did not measure the degree of personal involvement in AA, which might have yielded even more significant findings.

Ouimette and colleagues (1998) measured amount of AA attendance and degree of involvement in the program (such behaviors as reading 12-step literature, contact with sponsor). Both variables were negatively correlated with level of depression—that is, the more one attended the program and the more one was actively working the program, the less depressed one was likely to be. Interestingly, involvement with the program (but not the number of meetings attended) correlated with employment status and with support from partners or spouses.

Montgomery, Miller, and Tonigan (1995) found an increase in a sense of meaning in life associated with an increased level of involvement in 12-step related activities, not necessarily in number of meetings attended.

The area of studying personality changes that co-occur with TS participation is one that is ripe for future researchers.

How Much AA Is Enough?

A question that patients often ask (not always out loud) is, "How often should I attend?" Although there is a tradition of initiating AA participation with a 90/90 (attending 90 meetings in 90 days), there has been no direct empirical study of this practice. However, a few studies have addressed this concern in a more general way.

In a study mentioned above, Moos and Moos (2004) examined duration of participation and frequency of attendance at AA in the first year of recovery, reviewing outcome at the end of the year and at an 8-year follow-up. Their data suggest that two meetings a week appears to be a cutoff point for frequency of attendance; less than this level of participation was equivalent to no participation. However, abstinence rates at the 8-year point were affected by the frequency of AA attendance in the first year. No AA participation in the first year resulted in a 35% abstinence rate, 2–4 meetings per week in a 57% abstinence rate, and more than 4 per week resulted in a 73% abstinence rate.

Interestingly, they observed that those who did not immediately become involved in AA after initial referral but waited a year to begin participation derived less benefit from it. They suggested that these people were displaying a greater level of resistance, and their participation was more erratic—for example, they attended at times of crisis but then stopped going.

However, in reviewing their overall data, Moos and Moos (2004) concluded that the duration of involvement in AA was more important than the frequency of such attendance. The longer a subject remained involved in AA, the better the outcome was likely to be. They suggested that the tradition of 90/90 is less important than ongoing consistent participation over time.

Morgenstern et al. (1997), evaluating subjects at 1 month and 6 months, also noted that increased involvement (as measured by several indices of participation) in AA was correlated with decreased use.

However, they did not specify an amount of participation that would be beneficial.

Hoffmann, Harrison, and Belille (1983) assessed the frequency of AA attendance and outcome at 6 months posttreatment. They found that weekly attendance resulted in a 73% abstinence rate at 6 months, whereas abstinence for those attending "several times a month" was 69%, "once a month" was 45%, and "not at all" was 33%. They noted that the statistical break occurs between the "several times a month" group and the "once a month" group, although even the irregular attendees had a higher rate of sobriety than those who did not attend at all. They also pointed out that most participants either attended weekly (21%) or not at all (33%), suggesting an either/or approach to the 12-step program. They did not measure the degree of involvement in the program.

McLatchie and Lomp (1988) took the interesting approach of categorizing their subjects as successes or failures; successes included abstinent patients as well as those drinking in a nonproblematic manner. They found that both nonattendance and regular attendance at AA were predictive of a successful outcome. However, irregular or inconsistent attendance was predictive of a poor prognosis for recovery. They suggested that this group had a "misaffiliation" with the fellowship, and that those who affiliated with AA on a more regular basis were those who had hit bottom and made a more complete identification with the program. The success of the nonattenders remains unexplained. The observation that some people may attend AA only in moments of crisis is consistent with that of Moos and Moos (2004).

Montgomery and colleagues (1995) concluded from their data that the number of meetings attended was not associated with drinking outcome. However, the degree of involvement in 12-step-related activities was positively associated with successful outcome, even when the degree of AA attendance was controlled for. They suggested that future research make sure to assess the degree to which the client is working the program in addition to attending meetings. Their results also shed some light on the negative results obtained in samples of patients who are mandated to attend meetings but who may not become invested in the process.

What Are the Therapeutic Components of AA?

Morgenstern et al. (1997) identified two competing theories about the mechanism of benefit in the TSF. The first theory holds that the 12-step program works by inducing certain specific changes in the member. Specifically, the program works by facilitating a conversion or spiritual experience, also called the surrender phenomenon. The second theory holds that AA works by mobilizing other common self-change mechanisms (Hubble et al., 1999). In this study, Morgenstern and colleagues identified hypothesized mediating variables, which are common to a variety of change processes. These include commitment to abstinence, awareness of the costs of the addictive behavior, and self-efficacy. Their research provides support for the common factors model rather than the specific factor theory. However, there is potential circular reasoning here, in that they reported that awareness of costs and commitment to abstinence at intake are themselves predictive of AA affiliation. It may be that AA works by keeping such initial motivation active. The authors noted that these two factors did not change over the course of treatment, implying that this represents a lack of movement. However, it could also be argued that participation in AA served to maintain these variables at a salient level, or they otherwise might have dissipated.

Tonigan (in Owen et al., 2003) expanded on this line of inquiry. His results suggest that the relationship between AA attendance and drinking outcome is mediated by a sense of self-efficacy fostered by participation in the program. In this view, AA increases the patient's self-confidence that he or she can avoid taking the first drink. In contrast, although AA attendance predicted the degree of spiritual awakening, changes in spiritual awakening itself did not relate to drinking outcome.

Connors, Tonigan, and Miller (2001) utilized Project MATCH data to examine the relationship between initial drinking severity, AA attendance, and outcome. They found that more serious drinking problems at intake predicted greater involvement in AA in the first 6 months posttreatment. Participation in AA then predicted subsequent abstinence. The impact of AA on abstinence was partially mediated by an increased sense of self-efficacy.

Litt, Kadden, Kabela-Cormier, and Petry (2007) attempted to increase network support for abstinence as a means of promoting improvement in drinking behaviors. They utilized an intervention based on the TSF manual developed for Project MATCH, with less emphasis on the spiritual dimensions. They noted that the changes in social networks observed in their sample occurred not by eliminating drinking contacts but by adding sober contacts. The role of AA in this outcome appears to have been critical. They found that AA involvement was a major factor in the change in patient social networks as well as a significant direct contributor to the drinking outcomes. Both AA attendance and AA involvement were significantly correlated with a variety of positive outcome measures at 9- and 15-month follow-up; these variables were the strongest predictors of drinking outcomes. That clients in the Network Support intervention group participated more in AA than those in the control conditions suggests that patients can be induced to participate and benefit from AA.

Similarly, Kaskutas and Humphreys (Owen et al., 2003) reported that those with greater involvement in AA had better outcomes, but that these results were mediated by enhancing changes in the patient's social network. They also concluded that even when the patient had support from others in the social environment, the kind of support offered by AA members appeared to differ and to be significant in facilitating recovery. Similarly, Bond, Kaskutas, and Weisner (2003) found evidence that an increase in social supports from AA sources was particularly helpful in facilitating abstinence at 1 and 3 years follow-up. AA involvement in the year prior to contact was a significant predictor of abstinence.

Owen and Slaymaker (Owen et al., 2003) utilized a path model to explore the possibility that AA influences abstinence via the mediating variable of lifestyle changes. Their data supported the hypothesis that AA affected drinking outcome by the mediating variable of working lifestyle changes. However, they also found a direct relationship between AA participation and abstinence, which was not mediated by any known variable.

William Miller, one of the leading researchers on alcoholism, provided a summing up of current AA research at a presentation of the

Research Society on Alcoholism in 2001 (Owen et al., 2003). He made seven points (p. 531). These points, with my own commentary, follow:

1. AA cannot be ignored in understanding treatment outcomes. The finding that subjects in all three arms of the Project MATCH study attended AA underscores this conclusion. Chapter 1 of this volume documents the value of studying AA in general.
2. It is possible to facilitate AA attendance. The degree to which TSF enhances AA participation is an illustration of this finding.
3. Treatment is the time to promote AA attendance. This is supported by the findings of Moos and Moos (2004) that early intervention seems to be most facilitative.
4. Attendance is not involvement. Although these two are modestly correlated, each appears to have a different impact on outcome. Differential results have been observed (e.g., Ouimette et al., 1998). There appears to be a difference between clients who only attend meetings and those who actively work the program.
5. AA participation predicts better outcomes. This is a common although not universal finding, with involvement often accounting for more of the variance than simply measuring attendance.
6. Abstinence is the outcome most likely to be affected by AA. Measures of drinking moderation appear to be less affected than measures of abstinence in AA research.
7. The abstinence message of AA does not seem to be deleterious. Miller concludes that the "abstinence violation effect" (the sense of guilt and failure experienced after an initial slip) (Miller & Gordon, 1985) is not always relevant, especially in the context of AA-based treatment.

To sum up, the research appears to demonstrate that AA provides real benefit to clients, especially those pursuing the goal of abstinence, rather than moderation or reduction. The generalizability of these findings beyond the male, middle-aged population currently served by the program remains uncertain.

Future research must utilize some of the insights of the prior research (e.g, measuring involvement as well as attendance, utilizing better and more reliable outcome measures, studying AA in nonclinical settings). Given that there is some demonstrated benefit, an appropriate direction for future research will be to assess who is more likely to benefit from the program and how to best facilitate that level of engagement. Maximizing the client's sense of self-efficacy, both within and outside of AA, appears to be a promising direction for treatment professionals, one that could utilize the insights of cognitive-behavioral therapy (Beck et al., 1993).

Chapter 9

Critiques and Controversies

For myself, I have come to set a high value on the people who have criticized me, whether they have seemed reasonable critics or unreasonable ones. Both have often restrained me from doing much worse than I actually have done. The unreasonable ones have taught me, I hope, a little patience. But the reasonable ones have always done a great job for all of AA—and have taught me many a valuable lesson.

—Bill Wilson, Letter, 1955

CRITICISM OF AA IS ALMOST AS OLD AS the fellowship itself. The primary initial response to the publication of *Alcoholics Anonymous* in 1939 was indifference and skepticism. The *Journal of Nervous and Mental Disease* reviewed the book and pronounced it as having "no scientific merit or interest" (White, 1998). This was the general popular consensus until the publication of a laudatory article in 1941 in the *Saturday Evening Post*. Scholarly critiques of AA have been published regularly since the early 1960s (Bufe, 1998). In 1963, Arthur Cain published an article critical of AA for evolving into a religious cult, and a second one was published a year later in the *Saturday Evening Post* (Cain, 1964). Some of Cain's critiques have contemporary relevance to the evolution of the TSF, which are reviewed in Chapter 10.

Prominent contemporary critics of the TSF include Stanton Peele, Charles Bufe, and Herbert Fingarette. Although there is a great deal of overlap in their critiques, each is considered separately.

Stanton Peele: Diseasing America

The most important critic of the TSF and the disease concept is Stanton Peele, a social/clinical psychologist who has written extensively on this topic. Over the years, Peele has published a number of books critical of the disease concept of addiction and of AA, and has been an outspoken critic of the treatment establishment. While he makes some valid points, his argument is frequently overwrought; his arguments are often muddled and are based on misrepresentations or misunderstandings of the program and the tenets of the disease model. However, given the incisiveness of some of his points and his general influence, it would be foolish to ignore his position. Note that his seminal book, *The Diseasing of America*, was published in 1989, prior to much of the current research on brain functioning that has supported the disease model. However, a brief perusal of his Web site (http://www.peele.net/) suggests that his views are largely unchanged since the writing of that volume.

Peele's argument against the TSF and the disease model can be broken down into the following points (Peele, personal communication, 2008).

1. The use of the concept of disease to describe addiction and other behavioral problems is a way for addicts to avoid responsibility for their actions. The portrayal of problems as diseases in general creates a passive victim stance.
2. Addiction is more of a psychosocial problem than a biological one, arising from a failure to develop meaningful life activities and values. Addiction is more prominent in lower class settings, where options for personal development are limited. There is little evidence for a biological inheritance of alcoholism.
3. AA proponents maintain that AA is the only effective treatment for alcoholism, whereas the evidence for AA's effectiveness is weak or nonexistent.
4. The concept of alcoholism as a disease serves to create a negative self-fulfilling prophecy for addicts, condemning them to a life of unnecessary struggle.
5. The ubiquitous goal of abstinence is unrealistic and unnecessary for the majority of those with alcohol problems. A more appropriate approach is to understand that substance use and abuse are normal and that we should be striving for harm reduction rather than abstinence.

6. The progressive nature of addiction portrayed by disease concept adherents is a fiction, and, in fact, the majority of those with substance abuse problems will mature out of these problems.
7. The dominance of the 12-step approach in the treatment settings does a disservice to clients by limiting their choices about recovery.

Each of these points is considered below.

Disease as an Evasion of Responsibility

While some may use their disability status as an excuse for antisocial behaviors, within the TSF it explicitly does not work that way. The acceptance of one's disease carries with it an implicit responsibility to care for it. Like other chronic diseases, the mandate for stability rests with the patient, not the doctor.

Many of the critiques of the disease concept fail to distinguish between chronic and acute disease states (Rogers & McMillin, 1989). In an acute medical illness, the doctor does take an active role in treatment—prescribing medications to fight pneumonia, for example, or putting a cast on a broken limb. In chronic illness, the clinician diagnoses the disease and describes a plan for stability and remission, but the responsibility for compliance with the treatment plan lies with the patient. Consider again the example of diabetes; the doctor can prescribe medication and a diet, but the responsibility for managing the disease is up to the patient. Here there is no question of the physical and medical nature of the disorder—however, the resolution requires the active involvement of the patient.

The parallels with addictive disease are clear. For 12-step adherents, there is little debate about the reality of the disease. The responsibility for managing it, as well as for taking responsibility for one's own life, are part of the evolving maturity of the recovering person.

A patient in an outpatient group reported a story he had heard in an AA meeting, and which may be apocryphal. An AA member was late for a meeting and was stopped by a policeman for speeding.

Thinking he might be able to talk his way out of the ticket, the driver told the policeman that he was a recovering alcoholic, that he was late for his AA meeting, and that his sobriety depended on attendance at the meetings. The policeman listened attentively as he continued writing the ticket. He handed it to the driver and said, "Why don't you reread Chapter 5 in the Big Book?" The officer, obviously an AA member himself, smiled and walked off. The driver repeated this story in the meeting with a hearty laugh.

True or not, this story accurately depicts the attitude of AA members about the responsibility of living life on life's terms. It is entirely consistent with Bill's insistence on the developing maturity of the recovering individual. Using AA, or one's disease status, as an evasion of responsibility is usually symptomatic of a poor level of involvement in the program.

Addiction as a Problem of Values Rather Than Biology

This is hardly the appropriate setting for reviewing the literature on the biological or genetic components of addiction, and the reader is directed to other sources to learn more about this area (e.g., Erickson, 2007; Goodwin, 1994). By a conservative estimate, there is abundant evidence that for a substantial proportion of the addicted population (if not a majority), dysfunctional brain chemistry or other biological mechanisms play a significant role in the etiology and maintenance of chemical dependency. Peele's contention that there is little evidence of a biological component is undermined by much recent research and is simply incorrect.

Peele is correct, however, in challenging the simplistic notion that addiction is nothing more than a biological abnormality. Such unidimensional approaches (White, 1998) as that offered by James Milam (Milam & Ketcham, 1983) tend to be overly reductionistic and miss important psychosocial determinants of addiction. Similarly, the publicity campaign of NIDA a few years ago ("Addiction Is Brain Disease") misses the more commonly regarded biopsychosocial conception of addiction, however imprecise that definition may be.

However, Peele's substitution of what is essentially a moral model of addiction is regressive and unidimensional in the other direction, and appears to be based on stereotypes about junkies and drunks. It does not take much direct experience with addiction to find many people whose lives would be productive and fulfilling if not for the destructive impact of their loss of control over alcohol or drug use. George Vaillant (1995), reviewing longitudinal data on male alcoholics over a 40-year period, concluded that the disorder and unmanageability of the lives of many of his subjects were caused by their alcohol addiction, not vice versa.

Interestingly, the conception of addiction shared by many 12-step members would probably fall closer to Peele's view than to the biological. Many members of the fellowship locate the source of the addiction in their character, not their biology (e.g., Kurtz, 1982). The importance of values in recovery cannot be ignored, and the change in values manifested by recovering people is clearly and often noted.

Social class is certainly a variable in addiction, but the rate of alcoholism in the general population is a far more complex phenomenon than the simplistic race and class generalities that Peele portrays. It may be that social class is more relevant in mitigating the damage of addiction and altering the course of the disease (by presenting more opportunities for treatment and recovery) than it is relevant in determining the base-rate prevalence of alcoholism in the first place. Certainly the ubiquity of upper-class AA meetings and celebrity rehabs argues against a simplistic notion of addiction as a disease of the lower classes.

AA as the Only Cure for Alcoholism

In this assertion, Peele is simply wrong and may be choosing the statements of some overzealous 12-step adherents over anything to be found in the writings of the founders or anywhere in the literature of the fellowship. Bill's purpose in writing the original version of *Alcoholics Anonymous* was to share a method that had worked for himself and 100 others. Although there are passages within the Big Book that imply absolutes, these must be understood within the context of the fellowship and program. In any number of places, the book refers to the limits of knowledge of the program as it stands. Bill Wilson famously stated,

"AA has no monopoly on recovery" and he was well known for continuing to explore alternative approaches to recovery. Later in his life, he explored vitamin therapy and LSD in a search for other ways to help more suffering alcoholics recover. He would quite likely approve of the current search for medications to alleviate cravings and mitigate relapse (Volpicelli & Szalovitz, 2000).

As reported in Chapter 8, evidence for the efficacy of the TSF is primarily hampered by methodological issues. While some critics portray AA as a secret society, resistant to exploration by outsiders, the workings of the program are actually transparent—open meetings can be attended by anyone, and insider's views have been widely published (e.g., Robertson, 1988). AA publishes a triennial membership survey (Alcoholics Anonymous, 2004). As noted earlier, the primary purpose of the fellowship is the recovery of its members; beyond this, local meetings and individual members are free to decide whether or not to participate in any research study.

The principal confounding variable for researchers is the nature of the program as one of attraction rather than promotion, as stated in Tradition 11. Assigning or mandating a client to AA automatically violates this premise and is likely to promote poor outcome. (As a colleague said of court-mandated clients, "If he knew, Bill would be turning over in his grave.") Therefore there is an inherent selection bias in who attends AA and who benefits. It is not apparent that any double-blind study can overcome this obstacle. However, this is a problem for researchers, not for AA itself.

A related issue is the relationship between treatment and recovery. Peele appears to confound these two very distinct realms in his analysis. He portrays a recovery establishment that believes that treatment is the only way for addicts to get sober, and implies that this is driven primarily by a profit motive. Treatment is seen as a necessary precursor to engaging in the TSF, and the two are seen as one monolithic structure. There may be some truth in his assertions that treatment programs and the AA-based establishment have an undue level of influence on policy-makers and legislators.

However, Bill Wilson, principally in the Twelve and Twelve, made a clear effort to distinguish AA from professional agencies and personnel employing the program. What goes on in a rehab center is not AA or any other TSF, however much the treatment regimen may draw on 12-step insights. While AA or NA meetings are often offered as a part of the treatment protocol, these are a distinct and separate activity. This remains a point of confusion for some people and is an ongoing concern for recovering people working in the field, but the guidelines are fairly clear for anyone who reads Twelve and Twelve or who thinks it through carefully.

Disease as Self-Fulfilling Prophecy

Peele resists the idea that alcoholics suffer from a chronic disease that condemns them to a life of ongoing wariness and monitoring of their proximity to alcohol. In fact, he maintains that the very belief in this concept will create a full-blown relapse when even a small lapse has occurred. This has been called the abstinence violation effect (Marlatt & Gordon, 1985). In this view, once an alcoholic has a drink or a sip of liquor, any resulting relapse is due to belief in the inevitability of the relapse, not to a physiological reaction to the alcohol. Fingarette (1988) reviewed some of the same evidence that Peele presents, including a frequently-cited study by Marlatt, Demming, and Reid (1973) in which alcoholics responded more to their belief that a drink contained alcohol than to the actual presence of alcohol in the drink.

Part of the problem with this approach derives from the creation of a caricature of the disease concept, in which even a sip of alcohol will inevitably produce a relapse. It is probably far more realistic to assume that alcoholism occurs on a continuum, like other disorders. Some pneumonias are mild, walking pneumonias that produce a relatively small impairment in functioning; others are fatal. Some diabetics can be managed with diet, while others require medication. Similarly, some cases of addiction are so severe that even a small taste of alcohol, even a hint in food, can produce a tragic relapse. Others may be quite resistant to small lapses and can tolerate a periodic slip, while still being vulnerable to alcohol in general.

Abstinence as the Only Valid Goal

According to Peele, a majority of young people with alcohol problems resolve these naturally, in the course of growing up and maturing. The outcome for the majority of these people is moderation of their alcohol use, not abstinence. He also reports that the majority of recoveries in other countries involve attaining moderation goals, not abstinence goals. Peele, in general, subscribes to the goal of harm reduction, that is, diminishing the impact of addiction, not eliminating it. A classic example of the harm reduction philosophy in action is the creation of needle exchange programs for intravenous drug users to reduce the spread of HIV due to sharing needles. This strategy accepts that some people will not stop their drug use, but we can intervene to minimize its personal and social impact. In this view, reducing the number of drinks a person has is a more realistic goal than total abstinence.

Although Peele barely references this in his written work, he has communicated that he believes that "especially for longer-term, severe alcoholics, abstinence may be the most viable alternative," although not all may be able to achieve that goal (Peele, personal communication). In acknowledging this possibility, the discussion may have shifted from one of disagreement to one of where to draw the line between those who can moderate and those who must abstain if they are to function fully. Perhaps the difference between Peele and disease proponents is mainly one of degree.

One basic problem in Peele's work, specifically on this point, is his lack of diagnostic specificity. His definition of alcoholism and, in fact, addiction in general is quite vague and makes no reference to *DSM* criteria, which should form a general consensus in the field. In short, Peele does not clearly distinguish between those with alcohol abuse and those with alcohol dependence. It is only the latter, whose problems are marked by the physiological symptoms of dependence, tolerance, and loss of control who can appropriately be called alcoholic. It is to this population that the rules about alcoholism apply, and to whom the TSF is primarily relevant. It is no contradiction to the disease concept to observe that those with alcohol abuse can learn to moderate their

drinking, mature out of this stage, respond directly to external consequences, and so on.

In this context, I recall a conference about a decade ago at which
both George Vaillant and Linda Sobell were presenting. Vaillant is the
author of *The Natural History of Alcoholism* and an advocate of the
disease concept, while Sobell, along with her husband Mark, is a pioneer
in studying controlled drinking outcomes. The two spoke together on a
panel, and rather than sparks flying, they found central points of agreement. The basic consensus was that the more severe the degree of alcoholism in a given individual, the more likely it was that he would be
unable to learn moderation and would have to work on abstinence as a
goal.

Alcoholism as a Progressive Illness

Peele specifically challenges this point, noting that many young people
with addictive symptomatology are able to reverse this course as a result
of developing more meaningful life pursuits. Progression of the disease
is a major article of faith to those in the TSF. While not found as clearly
in the Big Book as it is in Jellinek's *Disease Concept of Alcoholism* (1960),
it is strongly implied. Generations of patients in rehabs have encountered the J Chart or the Jellinek Chart documenting the progression of
the illness and of possible recovery in an inverted bell curve.

In fact, more recently this concept has come under criticism, as the
course of alcoholism and addiction has come to be seen as more varied
than this relatively simplistic idea (Dawson et al., 2005) The idea that
unaddressed addiction will inevitably result in jail, institutionalization,
or insanity may be more myth than reality. In this context it is important to remember that much of Jellinek's work was based on surveying
the membership of AA, so a limit to the generalizability of his findings
is certainly appropriate, if not always understood.

Here, too, the notion that there is a continuum of severity of the
disease may help reconcile two diverging points of view. For some
people the progression of the disease is quite apparent and is spontaneously noted. For others, the capacity to arrest the potential progres-

sion of the disease may be more robust, and early symptoms of addiction may not lead to further damage.

The Dominance of the TSF in the Treatment Field

Peele is accurate in portraying the TSF as the dominant ideology in the treatment field, if not in academic or other areas. By some estimates (Bufe, 1998; Rotgers et al., 2002) over 90% of the treatment programs in the United States are oriented toward an abstinence-based 12-step model. While other models of the disorder and of treatment are utilized in other parts of the world, most programs here endorse AA exclusively.

Peele notes, correctly, that other methods have empirical support that the TSF lacks (Miller et al., 2003). However, it has to be noted that most of these alternate models have had limited trials in the real world. A few rehab centers offer alternative programs, including aversion therapy (the Shick-Shadel Institute), but in general, these research-based alternatives have not seen widespread development outside of the laboratory. Their broader utility is largely untested.

In many quarters, members of the TSF have been skeptical about alternative procedures. The resistance of some AA members to the use of medications to curb cravings (e.g., naltrexone, campral) has been noted, and use of other psychotropic medications to treat ancillary conditions (such as antidepressants) has sometimes been discouraged, despite the lack of addiction potential in most of these drugs.

This was not the attitude of Wilson, Smith, or any of the original members of AA, who were desperate to discover any ways to help others. Bill's early writing on the subject was quite clear—let doctors address medical conditions. In the early days, however, inappropriate use of some medications (especially benzodiazepines) led many AA members to a great deal of suspicion of the medical profession. However, this attitude has been lightening up in recent years, and there has been an increasing level of acceptance of some medications, if not of alternative methods in general.

Upon reflection, it is not hard to understand the loyal commitment of many AAs to the program that they credit for saving their lives. Most have tried other methods for gaining sobriety, including psychotherapy, willpower, and moral reframing, prior to coming to accept and benefit from the 12-step program. As with many organized social movements, the followers are usually more rigid than the developers, and the original creative spark can be lost on subsequent generations. Hence, I have certainly heard AA or NA members tell me that the only route to recovery possible was through their program, and that those seeking alternatives were in denial; this is not a thought that would have occurred to Bill Wilson or Bob Smith.

In sum, Peele clearly has an axe to grind, and creates some caricatures of the 12-step program which he then attacks quite broadly and energetically. In some areas his critiques of the program and the treatment establishment miss the mark. However, he has raised some cogent points that even the most fervent admirers of the TSF must come to deal with. Peele's emphasis on the development of alternatives to the AA program, his raising awareness of the processes of natural recovery, and his recognition of the psychosocial components (in contrast to the purely biological thrust of much of today's research) deserve serious consideration by all who work in the field. Ironically, it is obvious to me that Bill and Dr. Bob would support these efforts.

Bufe: Cult or Cure?

It would be hard to recognize the Twelve-Step Fellowship portrayed in these pages from reading Bufe's *Alcoholics Anonymous: Cult or Cure?* (1998). Despite Bufe's stated intention to "produce a more balanced, more realistic public view" of AA (p. 7), he introduces his readers to "a typical AA meeting" in this fashion: "You walk through the front door of the AA hall, a large, dingy room reeking of stale tobacco smoke. You walk across the grimy linoleum floor to the coffee urn, pour yourself a cup of what appears to be used motor oil (rumor has it that the stuff will dissolve pencils)." He goes on to describe the speaker as "slurping coffee" and speaking of "his more lurid drinking episodes." A speaker from the floor is described as "incoherent" and a quarter of the participants are "looking pained or disgusted" (pp. 11–12). Bufe makes repeated reference to "coffee-slurping, cigarette-smoking ex-drunks" (e.g., pp. 12, 105,

123). This is hardly the balanced perspective promised in the introduction and undermines some more reasonable points that Bufe has to make.

Bufe makes a great deal of the connections between AA and its predecessor, the Oxford Group. In his view, there is a guilt by association in this connection, and he spends a great deal of time portraying the Oxford Group's evolution from an evangelical Christian fellowship into a conservative political organization (Moral Rearmament). Bufe is also critical of Oxford Group founder Frank Buchman's predilection for attracting the rich and famous to his organization, his flirtation with Nazism, and his hypocritical stances. Furthermore, he charges AA with deception in hiding its connection with the Oxford Group. Although the Oxford Group is not mentioned by name in *Alcoholics Anonymous*, the debt owed by AA to the Oxford Group is quite explicitly depicted in the Twelve and Twelve, published in 1953, and placed in its historical context in *AA Comes of Age* in 1957 (Alcoholics Anonymous, 1990). Bufe never explicates the significance, if any, of this omission in the earlier book, which, of course was concerned principally with describing the nature of the program, not with its origins. Interestingly, Bufe makes little mention of (and attaches no significance to) the break between the two groups, which was perhaps motivated more than a little by the very tendencies in the Oxford Group that he himself dislikes so much.

Bufe is at his worst in his smug dismissal of the spiritual dimension of the 12-step program. He labels the program as religious rather than spiritual and is contemptuous of the program's use of, and belief in, a Higher Power—"This poses obvious problems for those who believe that the existence of God is no more likely than the existence of Mother Goose." While this may be his personal belief, it hardly constitutes a reasonable critique of the 12-step program.

In noting the prominent "coercion" of alcoholics into AA, Bufe stretches the meaning of the word. While it is clear that some are coerced into attending 12-step meetings by probation officers and other legally mandated parties, much of the coercion that Bufe speaks of is more accurately described as the natural consequences of alcoholism. Is it coercion if a wife yells at a husband about his drinking? If an employer threatens an employee to get help or face losing her job? There is a vast difference between situations like these and the threat of going to jail if a parolee refuses to attend AA. Bufe ignores the high number of AA members who are self-referred (30%) or referred by another AA member (31%; Alcoholics Anonymous, 2004). Only 12% report being referred by a court order or a correctional facility. (Bufe apparently does not realize that this practice is controversial within AA, as many members feel it violates the 11th Tradition, attraction rather than promotion).

Bufe makes selective use of the literature on the effectiveness of the 12-step program. He discusses two studies that demonstrate negative outcomes of AA, while only briefly noting the significant confounding variable that the subjects of these studies were court-ordered individuals. He makes no reference to the fact that the outcome variable in one of these (rearrests, not alcohol consumption) is inappropriate to the topic at hand. On the other hand, he makes a brief, and inadequate, dismissal of Project MATCH, and relegates another positive outcome study to a footnote (pp. 93, 103).

Furthermore, Bufe plays fast and loose with the numbers presented. It is telling that, at one point, he concludes that AA is ineffective, because it only helps about 2.6% to 3.5% of all the alcoholics in the United States. This is hardly a useful or relevant comparison.

Bufe is correct, however, in attributing political power to those who espouse the 12-step philosophy, including the many programs that provide treatment along 12-step lines. Funding for research has often been affected by political pressure from advocacy groups and political organizations who are wedded to the 12-step model. However, the more recent trend of funding studies dealing with pharmacological agents would tend to undermine this argument.

Bufe's view of the tradition of anonymity verges on the paranoid. Rather than viewing anonymity as a tool for personal development, Bufe sees it as a mechanism by which AA proponents can advocate for AA without divulging their membership status, therefore making it appear as if their feedback is neutral and unbiased. This reaches an absurd point when Bufe cites a negative review of his work in a journal written by "an addictions 'professional' who was almost certainly an AA member, but who did not disclose her membership in the review" (p. 63).

Interestingly, despite the relatively sensational title of his book (*Alcoholics Anonymous: Cult or Cure?*), Bufe concludes that AA is probably not a cult (it should be obvious that he does not view it as a cure, either). Using criteria that he developed (he provides no reliability or validity data to support these criteria), he compares AA to cults such as the Church of Scientology and the People's Temple. Borrowing a term from Stanton Peele, he dubs AA "Cult Lite," noting that, although AA's characteristics are less dangerous than other cults, its widespread influence renders it perhaps more dangerous in the long run.

Bufe praises the anarchic organization of the 12-step program, appreciating the casual nature of the proceedings and the lack of a hierarchy. He draws appropriate attention to the implication that, in locating the source of the disease within the person, AA tends to ignore the social and cultural factors which perpetuate it, and which may have causative elements as well.

Overall, Bufe tends to rely too much on personal impressions and pejorative insinuations, and rehashes material that Peele has covered perhaps more thoroughly. He strikes new ground in his research on the origins of the TSF in the Oxford Group, but this is largely meaningless or insignificant. He raises questions about Bill's fiscal management of the funds involved in publishing *Alcoholics Anonymous*, but arrives at no clear conclusion about it.

Other Critiques

A more reasonable critique comes from Herbert Fingarette, a philosopher and consultant to the World Health Organization on alcoholism. Fingarette (1988) addresses the TSF peripherally, as his primary target is the disease concept itself. Fingarette reviews much research on the loss of control phenomenon, demonstrating that the concept of loss of control is more malleable than diehard advocates of the disease concept might maintain. Interestingly, he notes in passing that more recently scientists such as George Vaillant and Mark Keller have adopted a more nuanced modification of the disease concept; however, he quickly dismisses that and goes back to critique the classic model.

Reviewing some of the same data discussed by Bufe and Peele, Fingarette's primary critique of the TSF is that it remains underresearched and its effectiveness unproven. He notes, appropriately, that some of the improvements in 12-step attendees may be due to the self-selection bias of its members and their elevated social class status. He also reports, significantly, that people who attend and who benefit from AA may be a specific subset of the overall population of alcoholics, therefore rendering some of our generalizations about the disease less universally applicable than has been assumed. This is especially relevant to the work of Jellinek (1960).

Fingarette, Peele, and Bufe, among other critics, have some valid critiques of the 12-step program and the disease concept, but suffer from several forms of myopia. They paint the TSF and the disease concept in quite one-dimensional and stereotypical terms. A consistent theme of the critics is the failure of the disease concept to fulfill a caricature—that even a taste of liquor will induce a full-blown drinking frenzy in an alcoholic. While this may be one interpretation of the disease concept, it hardly does justice to the more subtle variations that exist in this disease as well as any other form of disease.

Another common critique is that the treatment offered for what is purportedly a medical disease is hardly medical at all, largely consisting of education, support, and, in the case of the TSF, spiritual direction. Fingarette (1988) even states that "people who are seriously allergic to some food need only to be informed of what triggers the allergic reaction in order to be motivated to avoid eating that food" (p. 74). This would come as a surprise to those working with diabetics or hypertensives, for whom compliance with a treatment regimen is a central concern. Fingarette and his colleagues overestimate the amount of medicine that is involved in much medical treatment, and severely underestimate the role that nonspecific factors play in recovery from all sorts of diseases. The relevance of psychotherapy to this discussion is hardly mentioned, despite its demonstrated utility with other medically grounded illnesses such as depression, schizophrenia, or bipolar disorder.

In this context, it is relevant to remind readers (and hopefully the critics) of the distinction between acute medical conditions and chronic illnesses, including alcoholism and addiction. In an acute illness, the doctor takes an active and instrumental role in working the cure— prescribing medicine, splinting a broken bone, applying active treatments. In a chronic disorder, the patient must take the active role in recovery. This distinction appears to be lost on the critics. The lack of a "medical" treatment for a "medical" illness is hardly unique to the addiction field.

In fact, when compared to other chronic diseases, treatment for addiction and alcoholism fares relatively well (McLellan, Lewis, O'Brien, & Kleber, 2000). Relapse rates for insulin-dependent diabetes, hypertension, and asthma are all roughly equivalent to the relapse rates for addiction (including alcoholism). And as has been noted by many recovering addicts, we do not consider a relapse of asthma or hypertension to be a treatment failure the way many do with relapses to active addiction, a vestige of the old moral model of addiction.

Another common critique of the 12-step program is the notion that, in promoting attendance and participation at meetings, the addict is substituting one dependency for another. This criticism is also voiced by spouses of recovering addicts, who, having lost their spouse to bars and the streets, now may find them lost to the rooms of AA or NA. While there may be an element of truth to this charge, it may be a necessary condition for recovery. As with other habits, the substitution of a less destructive habit may be useful to smoothly transition away from the problem. And attending AA is clearly less destructive than a night of drinking or drug use.

Each of the critics has noted that there is a substantial dropout rate from AA. Their general assumption is that these represent treatment failures, and that the majority of the dropouts have likely resumed drinking and drugging. Although I am unaware of any studies of this phenomenon, it is also possible (and anecdotal evidence supports this interpretation) that some portion of this group are doing well—that a small dose of AA was enough to send them on a more productive path. Given the robust phenomenon of spontaneous recovery or maturing out from addiction, there is plenty of reason to suspect that many of these people are recovering from their addiction, whether they are abstinent or moderating.

Another caricature of the 12-step program painted by the critics is that of a self-fulfilling prophecy in AA, abetted by significant peer pressure. In this view, a participant who does not conform to the norms of the program will be browbeaten and pressured to conform—a person whose experience does not match the J Chart will be charged with denial and pressured to recall the ways in which his or her experience matched the prototype. Similarly, those who relapse will be ostracized and made to feel guilty, and will not return to the program.

There may be some truth to the notion that there is peer pressure, both overt and subtle, in the rooms of AA. Charges of denial may meet newcomers who are uncertain about their alcoholic status. On the other hand, it is also common that such a person may be told something like, "I thought so, too. Keep coming back," and encouraged to verbalize doubts to get support and feedback. While it is true that some who relapse will avoid returning to the program out of guilt, the near-universal response that greets relapsed members is warm and welcoming. It is impossible to rule out the self-fulfilling prophecy hypothesis, but if so, it is of the most benign sort imaginable (Vaillant, 1995).

A client of mine, a man in his early 20s with a significant addiction history, took to the 12-step program like a drowning man grabs a life preserver. Although he dutifully followed the program precepts and the advice of his sponsor, it was not always easy for him to give up many of the alluring pleasures of his former life. One day, feeling especially frustrated, he got up to speak in a meeting and spouted off. "I hate recovery! I hate AA! I hate this lifestyle! I hate everybody in this room!" As he reported it to me, he was met with a brief silence, then a chorus of "Thanks for sharing," "Keep coming back," "It works if you work it." "I never expected that kind of response," he told me. "I couldn't help but crack up. Where else could I curse out a room full of people and have them be supportive of me?"

Other forms of self-criticism of AA for its demographic limitations are reviewed in Chapter 10.

Chapter 10

The Evolution of the Fellowship

In the years ahead, AA will, of course, make mistakes. Experience has taught us that we need have no fear of doing this, providing that we always remain willing to admit our faults and to correct them promptly. Our growth as individuals has depended upon this healthy process of trial and error. So will our growth as a fellowship.

Let us always remember that any society of men and women that cannot freely correct its own faults must surely fall into decay if not into collapse. Such is the universal penalty for the failure to go on growing. Just as each AA must continue to take his moral inventory and act upon it, so must our whole Society if we are to survive and if we are to serve usefully and well.

—Bill Wilson

What happened to the 600,000 who approached AA and left?

—Bill W.

READERS MAY HAVE NOTICED THAT MUCH OF the preceding material has been based on Alcoholics Anonymous, far more than on any of the other TSFs. One reason is that AA has been the prototype for all TSFs. As the first group of its kind, it has set the standard by which other groups have formed and evolved. Many of the principles that have been articulated are equally valid for other TSFs, but found their earliest and clearest explanation in AA.

A second reason is simply that much more has been written about AA than all of the other TSFs combined. A recent Psych Lit search yielded 1,544 results for the term "Alcoholics Anonymous," while searches for Narcotics Anonymous, Gamblers Anonymous, and Overeaters Anonymous yielded 116, 108, and 138 results, respectively (a combined total of 362, or 23% of the results for AA). With due respect to our friends in Gamblers Anonymous, the deck is stacked in favor of literature on AA.

However, it should be apparent now that, given the flexible nature of the fellowship, the program was bound to evolve, and the program may be seen as being in tension between the forces of conservation of the original message and mission, and the forces for expansion and extension. Not only has the AA program evolved over the years, but it has served as the springboard for other similar programs. Moreover, the general philosophy and worldview of the TSF has been extended to other areas; some of these are logical extensions, while others are more tenuous. This chapter reviews some of the evolving practices and implication of the 12-step program.

Other 12-Step Programs

The most obvious example of the influence of AA has been in the formation of other fellowships explicitly patterned on the 12-step model. Early in the development of the program, the role of AA in handling other addictions was discussed and debated. Some felt that the process of these addictions was so similar to alcoholism that the inclusion of pill and morphine addicts was only logical. The prevailing opinion, however, promulgated by Bill W., was that the AA fellowship should be reserved for alcoholics exclusively, and that other addicts were welcome to form their own organizations for recovery.

This decision has not been without controversy. Bill wrote a column for the AA *Grapevine* in 1958 (reprinted as a pamphlet, "Problems Other Than Alcohol") in which he reviewed the issues surrounding this question. He recognized that alcoholics and drug addicts were "first cousins of a sort," but insisted that AA should be restricted to those who have alcohol problems. This would not exclude an individual who had alcoholism as well as a drug problem, but would not include someone with purely drug problems. Bill suggested that some AAs could join with addicts to form a special group to work on the drug problem, but that such a group should not call itself AA. Bill's concern (following the 5th and 10th Traditions) was that inclusion of addicts would dilute the message and appeal of AA, just as dabbling in political areas had diluted the message of earlier recovery programs such as the Washingtonians. "Our first duty, as a society, is to insure our own survival" he wrote, and while limiting AA's focus to alcoholism, he also encouraged others to form similar groups using the 12-step principles he had outlined.

The origins of Narcotics Anonymous (NA) are a bit murky, as it seems that there were several independent attempts, in different parts of the country, to adapt the steps and traditions of AA to the problem of drug addiction. The first reference to a 12-step-oriented program for drug-addicted individuals appears to have been a suggestion for a "Hopheads Corner" at the Lexington Federal Narcotics Center in 1944 (White, 1998). In 1947 an Addicts Anonymous meeting was formed at Lexington, ultimately changing its name to Narcotics Anonymous to avoid confusion with "the other AA." Similar groups were begun in Texas and Virginia in the same time period.

The origins of NA as we now know it appear to lie in a group formed in California in 1953. The group's progress was quite erratic until the 1960s, when the first true NA literature appeared, and the founders learned to adhere more closely to the traditions first developed in the AA fellowship. In certain areas, notably New York, the development of the NA fellowship was hampered by laws forbidding the gathering of drug addicted individuals; NA meetings were, in effect, illegal. The value of the fellowship was enhanced by the publication of an article about it in the *Saturday Evening Post* (which had also published the famous Jack Alexander article praising the AA fellowship) in 1954 (Ellison, 1954). It was not until 1972, with the development of a World Services Office, that true stability was achieved in the NA fellowship.

NA bases its program on three "disturbing realizations":

1. We are powerless over addiction and our lives are unmanageable.
2. Although we are not responsible for our disease, we are responsible for our recovery.

3. We can no longer blame people, places and things for our addiction. We must face our problems and our feelings. (Narcotics Anonymous World Services, 1988, p. 15)

Narcotics Anonymous explicitly references its debt to AA on the first page of the introduction of its basic text (Narcotics Anonymous World Services, 1988). NA describes addiction as "an incurable disease of body, mind, and spirit." Like AA, little effort is expended on discussing the etiology of the disease; the focus is on helping the addict to recover, not on discussing the disease. A similar emphasis is placed on the importance of desperation in bringing the addict to NA. The fellowship welcomes alcohol addicts as well, making reference to alcohol as another drug.

The basic text of *Narcotics Anonymous* (1988) combines aspects of the Big Book and the Twelve and Twelve. It includes an explanation of the program, a discussion of the steps and traditions, and personal stories of its members. The steps and traditions are adapted almost verbatim from those of AA. However, one change in phrasing in the 1st Step proved to have significance beyond the NA and AA fellowships. Rather than using the AA phrase, "We admitted that we were powerless over alcohol . . . ," the NA 1st Step states, "We admitted that we were powerless over *our addiction* . . . " (emphasis added). While it has been often noted that the only reference to substances in AA occurs in this step, NA omits reference to substances altogether, and more explicitly locates the problem within the individual. This has implications for the formation of other fellowships for other types of addictions.

NA remains the second largest such 12-step group, after AA. According to their Web site, the program grew from less than 200 groups in 3 countries in 1978 to over 25,000 groups holding nearly 44,000 weekly meetings in 127 countries (http://www.na.org/basic.htm). Based on a survey of about half of the 13,000 attendees at the 2003 NA World Convention, approximately 55% were male, 70% were Caucasian, and average length of recovery was 7.4 years. Further, 72% were employed full time, and about 71% were between 31 and 50 years old.

Other 12-step groups have emerged to deal with specific substance abuse problems. Cocaine Anonymous was founded in 1982 in Los Angeles and claimed 30,000 members in 2,000 groups by 1996. Its basic text (generally seen as the mark of maturity of a 12-step fellowship) appeared in 1994. Unlike AA, however, Cocaine Anonymous does not restrict its membership to any one drug. Its 1st Step reads: "We admitted we were powerless over *cocaine and all other mind-altering substances—* that our lives had become unmanageable" (emphasis added). In this way it is more similar to NA in its stance of openness to substance addictions in general.

Similarly, there are fellowships for other substance abusers, including Crystal Meth Anonymous, Heroin Anonymous, Pill Addicts Anonymous, Methadone Anonymous, and Marijuana Anonymous. The struggle in this growth is for some balance between the comfort and familiarity for abusers of a specific drug of abuse versus the desire for more unity in a more inclusive fellowship (such as NA). The greater growth of NA than any of the individual fellowships may reflect the value of the inclusive fellowship as well as the greater numbers available with such a framework. A problem associated with this is the dilution of strength in one fellowship when others emerge. Members of these younger fellowships may drift into AA over time, as some members feel that there is a greater "quality of sobriety" in the older, more established fellowship (White, 1998). This may place a limit on the development of these newer fellowships as more seasoned members mature out and enter AA.

The reframing of the problem as addiction rather than alcohol has opened the way for a slew of other 12-step programs to deal with problems that are not based on any substance at all. These are often referred to as process addictions and, in this view, share more similarities with other addictions than with the equivalent mental health diagnosis. The inclusion of such behavior as compulsive gambling and compulsive sexual patterns in an addictions framework represents a shift in worldview for mental health practitioners, which may be as significant in its implications as the shift to a trauma-based worldview that has occurred for other disorders. To treat compulsive gambling as an addiction, rather than as an impulse control disorder (American Psychiatric Association,

2005) requires a rethinking of the entire view of this pathology, in what has been termed a shift from a disease model to a recovery model.

Gamblers Anonymous (GA), one of the first of such fellowships, was founded in 1957, and now numbers about 1,000 groups nationwide. The GA fellowship utilizes the 12 steps adapted from AA, but also has some of its own procedures, such as pressure groups, a form of confrontational engagement with a member. GA members will also help sponsees negotiate with creditors and will assist with budgeting.

GA explicitly disavows a need to understand the reasons for the "illness called compulsive gambling," but does identify the personality characteristics they feel underlie the problem. These include an inability to accept reality, emotional insecurity, immaturity, and a "a strong inner urge to be a 'big shot'" (www.gamblersanonymous,org). These are all consistent with Bill's conception of the characteristics of alcoholics. (The reasons why one develops, for example, alcoholism rather than compulsive gambling are rarely addressed in these fellowships.)

There are several fellowships for those suffering from compulsive sexual behavior, including Sex Addicts Anonymous (SAA) and Sex and Love Addicts Anonymous (SLAA), both founded separately around 1977. Because of the possibility of exploitation by outsiders, these groups do not make meeting lists public and will screen potential members before disclosing the sites of meetings. SAA clearly acknowledges their debt to AA and the use of the 12 steps on their Web site, and SLAA was founded by an AA member who continued to struggle with his compulsive sexual behavior.

Given the role of sexuality in human life, defining sobriety can be a tricky matter. Both groups ask each member to define a set of personal behaviors that constitute abstinence. SAA posits three circles of behaviors, with the outer circle representing acceptable behaviors, the middle circle representing potentially dangerous behaviors, and the inner-circle representing unacceptable behaviors. "Sexual sobriety" consists of refraining from engaging in any of the inner circle behaviors. For example, soliciting sex from a prostitute may be an unacceptable behavior, whereas renting a pornographic video or flirting at work may be seen as dangerous behaviors that may potentially lead to a relapse. Sex in a committed relationship may be one of the behaviors seen as acceptable in this scenario. Similarly, SLAA asks each member to define bottom-line unacceptable behaviors, which are the targets for abstinence, defining sobriety.

Similarly, Overeaters Anonymous (OA; not to be confused with Food Addicts Anonymous) defines sobriety as "the action of refraining from compulsive eating." Their view of this disease assumes that compulsive eating is a maladaptive response to stress. In addition to the steps and traditions adapted from AA, OA utilizes eight tools of recovery. These consist of an eating plan (no one diet or eating plan is endorsed), sponsorship, meetings, telephone support, writing (journaling is encouraged), literature, anonymity, and service. A key phrase in OA is "I put my hand in yours, and together we can do what we could never do alone."

Views on this use of the 12-step program for a wide variety of problems other than drugs or alcohol can be highly variable. The more nonspecific the problem (e.g., Emotions Anonymous is much less specific than AA) the more difficult it becomes to define terms and the less comfortable some clinicians become with this mode of working with these problems. There are two defining criteria that could serve to establish these as more legitimate modes. The first is simple efficacy—do they work? Empirical study is as difficult to conduct in these groups as it is in AA, and relatively little work has been done in this area. The second criterion is to determine if these disorders (or which of them) have characteristics similar to drug and alcohol addictions—do patients exhibit similar patterns of dependence, tolerance, and loss of control? For example, there is evidence that naltrexone, a medication that is effective in controlling relapse to alcohol and opiate use by blocking endogenous opiate receptors in the brain (Volpicelli, Alterman, Hayashida, & O'Brien, 1992) is also effective in reducing compulsive gambling (Grant & Kim, 2002). These are tantalizing findings, and further research may help us define which syndromes may be more appropriately classified as addictions and which may not be. However, these two arguments may not be related. It may be that people will respond to 12-step-oriented interventions even with disorders that do not appear to be addictions in any sense of the word.

12-Step Programs Related to AA

In the early days of AA, when the membership was almost exclusively male, concern was expressed for the impact of alcoholism and recovery on the wives and families of members. The chapter "To Wives" in the Big Book was written by Lois Wilson as a way of engaging the wives of alcoholic men. It contains her advice to these women. Some of the advice appears dated and sexist—treat him with love, as you would any other ill person, avoid resentments and anger, do not nag. However, the strategy advocated in this chapter is really about the wife's own spiritual development. Wilson notes that these long-suffering wives are "like everybody else, afflicted with pride, self-pity, vanity and all the things which go to make up the self-centered person; and we were not above selfishness or dishonesty" (Alcoholics Anonymous, 2001, p. 116). Lois advocates the wife seeking her own spiritual program (as well as encouraging her husband to read the Big Book).

This sentiment led to the formation of Al-Anon. In the early days, wives often attended meetings along with their husbands (White, 1998), but eventually they began meeting separately. Similar to the synchronous emergence of several NA groups, wives of AA members began to meet together in various areas, using such names as AA Auxiliary and the Non-AA Group. Eventually, in 1948, these groups adapted the 12 steps to their own purposes and formulated a 1st Step acknowledging their own powerlessness: "We admitted we were powerless to help the alcoholic." In 1951, Lois began to organize some of these efforts, leading in 1954 to their incorporation as the Al-Anon Family Group. This group also began to produce its own literature and was helped by sympathetic portrayals in the media.

The basic message of Al-Anon is that members must recognize that their spouse (men are included in Al-Anon, although they remain in the minority) suffers from a disease neither party can control, and that they should practice a form of loving detachment, recognizing that the alcoholic's behavior is not a sign of lack of caring, but is due to an entirely independent disorder. The achievement of this capacity for serenity in the midst of chaos and despair is the program of Al-Anon.

A significant misconception about Al-Anon is that this is a program to help the alcoholic get sober. Rather, this is a program intended to help the spouse to achieve peace, "to learn a better way of life, to find happiness whether the alcoholic is still drinking or not." This is often difficult for newcomers or outsiders to grasp, given the sense of crisis with which many come to Al-Anon.

Another serious misconception about Al-Anon is that the program consists of a bunch of unhappy women complaining about their husbands and urging newcomers to leave their spouses. While this may occur at times, a good Al-Anon meeting aims at helping the member reach a point of clarity and serenity in his or her own life.

The 12 steps of Alcoholics Anonymous, verbatim, serve as the steps for Al-Anon as well. This emphasizes the importance of spiritual development for both partners. People generally come to Al-Anon in one of two ways—they come after the spouse has achieved sobriety to help cope with the changes in their lives, or they come while the alcoholic is continuing to drink. In the latter case, it is especially important to remember the purpose of the fellowship is detachment from alcoholism, and personal development, not learning strategies to induce the partner's sobriety.

Perhaps surprisingly, there seems to be as much resistance in referring patients to Al-Anon as there can be to referring alcoholics to AA. Most people believe the problem belongs to the alcoholic, not to them. To some, the themes of Al-Anon may seem like blaming the victim; having lived with an active alcoholic, many resist looking at their own personal issues. It is not uncommon to hear someone say, "If my spouse gets sober, I'll be fine. I don't need any other help."

It is critical, in making a referral to Al-Anon, to be quite clear that this is for the benefit of the person being referred, not as an adjunct to the other's treatment. I often simply state that Al-Anon is a support group for those living with an alcoholic or addict, without reference to the spiritual or developmental aspects of the program. As with any other TSF you make referrals to, it is helpful to have some personal knowledge of the local groups. I had a woman I worked with, who made excellent use of Al-Anon in the course of her husband's attempts at recovery, make a list of meetings she had attended that were better and did not lean toward the complaining mode. This list has been very useful to me in working with the families of patients referred for addictions.

A 2006 membership survey revealed that there were nearly 15,000 Al-Anon groups in the United States. The vast majority of the members were Caucasian and over 50 years old; 85% of the membership was female. Most reported tremendous benefit from attending, but it must be remembered that this was not a random sample, and that the sample size (645) reflects a tiny proportion of the total membership.

Interestingly for clinicians, the members reported that nearly 60% were also engaged in psychotherapy, and that therapists were among the most common referents to this program. Between 76% and 80% of those also in treatment referred to their psychotherapy as important or very important to their recovery. Clearly, there is a tremendous potential for collaboration between therapists and 12-step programs in this area.

Similar to Al-Anon, Alateen serves as a support group for the children, ages 12–20, of alcoholics, and espouses a similar philosophy. Meetings are usually facilitated by an Al-Anon member and are generally timed to coincide with Al-Anon meetings. Although there are fewer of these groups than AA or Al-Anon groups, there were an estimated 3,300 Alateen groups in the United States by the late 1990s.

There are also equivalent support groups for friends and relatives of members of other 12-step fellowships. These include Nar-Anon (NA), COSA (Sex Addicts Anonymous), and Co-Anon (Cocaine Anonymous).

Codependents Anonymous presents a special case, as it does not have a counterpart in any type of addiction. Recognizing that the personality characteristics of the spouses and children of alcoholics and addicts may exist in relationships independently of addictions, Codependents Anonymous was founded in the mid-1980s. In this fellowship, members deal with their own futile efforts to control the behavior of others, and their neglect of their own welfare. For this fellowship, the 1st Step reads,

"We admit that we were powerless over others—that our lives had become unmanageable." Part of the preamble reads, "The only requirement for membership is a desire for healthy and loving relationships." This is an addiction in one of its purest forms. The rise of codependency as a disorder has been lumped in with other movements of the same era (Peele, 1989), such as the Adult Children of Alcoholics program and the Inner Child movement. However, the codependency movement appears to have a resiliency of its own, and meetings and literature continue to thrive (Beattie, 1990) with over 1,000 groups in the United States. Apparently, this concept has resonated with a fair number of people who would not otherwise be associated with addictive diseases.

Non-12-Step Groups

Although the focus of this book is on the 12-step approach to recovery, it is necessary to make reference to a range of other, non-12-step-oriented programs. Most of these would not exist without AA or NA as a catalyst, and some were explicitly organized as a reaction to the precepts put forth in AA. They are often cited in surveys of recovery methods and can be useful to a clinician who encounters someone who appears to be more suited for their approach than for a traditional 12-step program.

Secular Organization for Sobriety (also known as Save Our Selves or SOS), was begun in California in 1985 by James Christopher. SOS is a hybrid of 12-step and non-12-step views, without the emphasis on spiritual growth. Similar to AA, SOS believes that abstinence is the only solution to alcoholism. SOS positions itself as a friendly alternative to AA and offers itself to those for whom the references to God and Higher Power are unacceptable. Rather than believing that addicts are powerless over their addiction, SOS offers a program of empowerment. SOS stresses individual responsibility for recovery, with the support of other SOS members and attendance at SOS meetings as an adjunct.

SOS arose out of the secular humanist movement. Christopher had initially sought sobriety through AA, but found that his "fearful and guilty" alcoholism was converted to a fearful and guilty sobriety in the

12-step program. He posited that recourse to a Higher Power was obsolete, given the increasing evidence that alcoholism was a physiological disease. Some of the influence of AA can be felt in SOS, for example in their statement that "All those who sincerely seek sobriety are welcome." There are currently SOS meetings in every state.

Rational Recovery (RR) was founded by Jack Trimpey, a social worker who overcame his own drinking problem on his own initiative, by "stubbornly refusing to drink" (Trimpey, 1996, p. 1). RR presents a program quite distinct from both AA and SOS, a program more consistent with cognitive therapy approaches. Trimpey posits an "addictive voice" inside people encouraging them to drink; recovery depends on awareness and resistance to this inner voice via AVRT—addictive voice recognition technique. RR no longer conducts meetings, providing its program via books and the Internet. RR eschews the belief that addiction is a disease, viewing it as a maladaptive voluntary response to stressors, and will view veterans of the program as cured, not recovering.

Perhaps the most significant difference between AA and RR is that RR is not a self-help group of any kind—it is a for-profit corporation. A Crash Course on AVRT is offered online, and suggests that you may be able to terminate your addiction merely by reading the introduction to it.

As opposed to SOS, which positions itself as a friendly alternative to AA, RR is actively opposed to AA, citing its theological underpinnings as destructive to individual responsibility. RR has gone so far as to challenge court-mandated referrals to AA as being unconstitutional on the grounds that it violates the separation between church and state. In RR's view, AA is a religious organization, to which the state should not be referring individuals. Despite objections by AA that it is a spiritual group, not a religious one, there have been a series of court reviews supporting the RR position. Ironically, I suspect that Bill and Dr. Bob would agree that coercing anyone into AA would be counterproductive.

Trimpey made more waves by announcing that, as of December 31, 1998, all recovery groups (including AA, NA, SOS) were cancelled, and declaring that the "recovery group movement is over." While perhaps a bit facetious and deliberately provocative, this message was aimed at all those RR sees as having sacrificed their own independence for reliance on any recovery group. The only exceptions were for groups "supervised by Rational Recovery"; all others were "counterproductive, pose numerous personal risks, and unnecessary" (www.rational.org). The reaction to this message ranged from amusement to outrage, but the actual impact on the recovery movement appears to have been negligible.

SMART Recovery (Self-Management and Recovery Training) was founded in 1992 and appears to have been a spinoff from Rational Recovery, as that program veered into polemics and extremism. It is a nonprofit organization and offers about 300 meetings per week, in several countries, but primarily in the United States. SMART Recovery shares some theoretical assumptions with RR, but takes a much more centrist approach. SMART utilizes motivational and cognitive approaches to managing recovery and encourages abstinence, self-reliance and, assistance to others in relinquishing dependence on support groups. SMART consists of four points:

1. Enhancing and maintaining motivation to abstain
2. Coping with urges
3. Problem solving (thoughts, feelings, and behaviors)
4. Lifestyle balance

Membership in SMART is short-lived, as the individual learns the principles of self-management and life skills necessary for sobriety. SMART has achieved more legitimate recognition than RR, but its influence is still quite limited.

Women for Sobriety (WFS), founded by Jean Kirkpatrick, is a nonprofit corporation, based in Quakertown, Pennsylvania. Dr. Kirkpatrick founded WFS on the observation that female alcoholics had different needs and a different process of recovery than male alcoholics. Dr. Kirkpatrick was particularly put off by the emphasis on powerlessness and surrender in the TSF, and felt that this was particularly troublesome for women in recovery, who typically felt demeaned in their addictions in the first place.

Instead of the 12 steps of the AA model, Kirkpatrick developed a set of 13 principles forming the core of her New Life program:

1. I have a life-threatening problem that once had me.
2. Negative thoughts destroy only myself.
3. Happiness is a habit I will develop.
4. Problems bother me only to the degree I permit them to.
5. I am what I think.
6. Life can be ordinary or it can be great.
7. Love can change the course of my world.
8. The fundamental object of life is emotional and growth.
9. The past is gone forever.
10. All love given returns.
11. Enthusiasm is my daily exercise.
12. I am a competent woman and have much to give life.
13. I am responsible for myself and for my actions.

Clearly, WFS shares some theoretical precepts with RR and SMART Recovery in positing a cognitive-behavioral approach to recovery. It also shares some elements of the TS program in its emphasis on emotional and spiritual growth as a core underpinning of recovery.

The growth of WFS has been surprisingly slow. Meetings can be hard to come by (even in my area, which is quite near Quakertown). Many women attending AA favor women-only meetings, which may contain much more of an empowerment message than is evident in a literal reading of the 12 steps, so an audience for WFS may not be as large as presumed. However, given the critiques of AA as a male-dominated program (discussed below), it is difficult to understand why this program has not become more widespread.

Moderation Management (MM) is different than the other programs described in that it does not posit abstinence as the only resolution for alcohol problems. Its history is entwined with the tragic biography of its founder, Audrey Kishline; I will describe the two separately.

Kishline (1994) founded MM as a nonprofit organization in the early 1990s, targeting problem drinkers who do not meet criteria for alcoholism. She is explicit in stating that moderation is not for those "chronic drinkers who are dependent on alcohol." However, she notes that there were no programs for those whose drinking is problematic, but who do not meet the more severe criteria; these drinkers have been estimated to outnumber alcoholics four to one (Kishline, 1994).

The MM approach uses a nine-step program for learning to monitor cues for excessive drinking and replace them with alternative behaviors. A key element in the MM program is doing "a 30," that is, 30 days of abstinence to begin the program. This serves a twofold purpose. It screens out those whose drinking is so severe that this period of abstinence is not viable. It also establishes a baseline for the subsequent experimentation in moderation. For those who may have difficulty in doing this right away, Kishline suggests working up to it, with an increasing number of abstinent days each week.

Eventually, Kishline reviewed her own difficulties adhering to this program and made a decision to go to AA, WFS, and SMART Recovery. She sent out a message to MM in January 2000, stating that, although she still supported the goals of MM for those with less severe drinking problems, she recognized that she was unable to maintain these goals herself. Several months later, while driving during an alcohol-induced blackout, Kishline was in an accident, killing two people. She pleaded guilty to two counts of vehicular homicide and was sentenced to jail time. A media uproar ensued, with finger-pointing and blame on both sides of the controversy. Some cited this event as evidence that moderation does not work for alcoholics; others blamed AA for failing to "cure" her. A letter, signed by several prominent members of the moderation movement and 12-step proponents, advocated that both approaches were needed.

MM is a useful tool for clinicians working with this population. For one thing, some early stage problem drinkers may be able to secure a stable moderate outcome, and it is dangerous for us to automatically assume that anyone who arrives in our offices is an alcoholic. A careful diagnostic interview can help distinguish between an alcohol abuser and one who is alcohol dependent (this is reviewed in Chapter 5). More important from a motivational standpoint is that some clients, regardless of the severity of their alcoholism, may not be ready to accept a goal of abstinence. In such cases, moderation may be a useful interim goal and may lead to a decision to pursue abstinence, of the client's own accord. Readers are directed elsewhere for literature on this topic (Kishline, 1994; Miller & Munoz, 2005; Rotgers et al., 2002).

Controversies Within the Fellowship

What issues are currently facing those within the TSF? Is it going stronger than ever, with ever-increasing membership and growing influence? Is there a sense of stagnation within the program?

There is, of course, evidence that both of these opinions have validity. AA continues to grow, and new 12-step-oriented groups are being formed regularly (I recently became aware of Neurotics Anonymous). New members continue to discover old truths, and AA continues to extend its hand to diverse members of the population at large. However, there are some concerns, often expressed in whispers, that something of the old spirit is often missing, that the program has become reified and lost some of its original intent.

A particular concern has been the relevance of AA and NA to the lives of women and minorities. As has been pointed out, the membership of the fellowships has remained heavily oriented toward middle-class or working-class Caucasian males. While women and minorities have increased their levels of participation overall, the numbers still reflect a preponderance of male Caucasian members.

One of the stumbling blocks remains the concept of powerlessness so central to the 1st Step and to the fellowship in general. This has been a difficult notion to convey successfully to those who have already felt disenfranchised in society in general. For many, the explanation of this as a spiritual phenomenon is sufficient to bypass resistance. For others, it remains a stumbling block and has clearly led to the creation of such organizations as Women for Sobriety.

Women made the first to attempt to enter what had primarily been an all-white-male domain. The first edition of *Alcoholics Anonymous* contains only one story by a female alcoholic, and one by a wife of an alcoholic. Many early women members were viewed with great suspicion by the male members, and were seen as a threat by the wives of these members. A variety of restrictions were imposed—they were barred from certain meetings; they were asked to leave before the discussion ensued; and they were asked to sit separately. Then, as today, there was also a tendency for women entering the program to be seduced by men taking advantage of their vulnerability—this has been termed the 13th Step and is frowned upon, but remains all too common.

A major breakthrough for women in the fellowship came when Marty Mann, the first woman to achieve lasting sobriety in AA (White, 1998), began speaking extensively on her experiences. In addition to founding the National Council on Alcoholism, she published a book on alcoholism (Mann, 1958) and encouraged other women to acknowledge their problems and seek help. Although her decision to abandon the tradition of anonymity was controversial within the fellowship, her actions brought many women into the program.

One of the ways in which the program has adapted to meet the needs of women is the regular establishment of women-only meetings. Some women attend these meetings exclusively, feeling a sense of safety that they do not experience in mixed-gender meetings. (Men-only meetings also are common and many men avail themselves of these as well.) Sponsorship is almost always conducted with a member of the same sex, to avoid distracting and potentially destructive entanglements.

The experience of racial minorities, especially African Americans, in AA has also been marked by the kinds of prejudices prevalent in American society in general. According to White (1998), both Bill and Dr. Bob were open to engaging black alcoholics in AA, but there was little progress on this front until the mid-1940s. Bill himself brought two African American alcoholics to a meeting in New York in 1940, and was subject to criticism by the other members. In the earlier days, Bill suggested that this was an issue best left for each individual AA group to decide for itself, recognizing the wide variance in local customs and cultures. In addition to his respect for the integrity of the local group, he was concerned about involving AA in a controversial area that could undermine its early unsteady status.

A story related by White (1998) is quite revealing in portraying Bill's attitude toward integration within the fellowship:

> Jimmy F. told a particularly poignant story. When he met Bill Wilson at a Founders' meeting in Akron, Bill asked him what group he was affiliated with. Jimmy responded that he was a member of the "Interracial Group" in Ann Arbor. Bill wanted to know why it was called an interracial group, since the whole fellowship was interracial. Jimmy and his fellow local members were so struck by Bill's question that they subsequently changed the name of the group to the Ann Arbor Community Center Group. (p. 160)

Both women and members of a wide variety of minority groups have achieved sobriety through the fellowships, but there remains a notable gap in reaching these populations. White (1998) noted that there is a tendency for many African Americans to seek sobriety within institutions that are more familiar within that culture, such as the church. This has given rise to an increase in faith-based forms of recovery, which may actually embody much of the original spirit of the early AA.

Some have expressed concern at a variety of threats to the integrity and future of the fellowship, from both internal and external sources (Delbanco & Delbanco, 1995). The number of people referred to AA by courts or probation officers (despite the legal precedents) remains high, and threatens a program based on attraction, not promotion.

More sinister may be the internal stagnation that can set in after the initial heady rush of success and expansion wears off. Now that the first generation of founders has passed on, the original sense of spirituality and discovery may have become diluted in the current generation. A rigid codification of the program may have replaced Bill's willingness to experiment for solutions to the problem, and to challenge himself and his fellowship on an ongoing basis.

The Evolution of the Fellowship

Recovery and 12-step programs have received a great deal of media attention in recent years, with celebrities seeking asylum in rehab centers and proclaiming their own sobriety. Nowadays, many attend AA for its social aspects as much as for the spiritual and developmental growth originally promised (and required). An article in the *Philadelphia Inquirer* titled "Dangerous LiAAisons" (Kolson, 1990) pointed out that as recovery was becoming chic, many people with minimal claims to addiction were seeking out AA or NA as a means to feel cool, and as a way of finding a romantic partner. The thrill of a sexual encounter can be extraordinarily tempting to a newly recovering person, whose primary source of pleasure has just become off-limits and who is experiencing a profound sense of loss; the rooms are full of people in just such a state, and the 13th Step beckons.

The prevailing victim mentality decried by Peele (1989) remains a threat. This can be seen as the inadvertent byproduct of the 12-step ideology, one that is antithetical to a seasoned AA member. However, many people have adopted this view of their problems. Delbanco and Delbanco (1995) report that some old-time members have taken to calling out, "Shut up and don't drink" when a member is perceived as whining.

I have heard stories from recovering friends about meetings that are "off the books," that occur in people's living rooms, as much in an attempt to recreate the original spirit of the fellowship as to avoid the posers encountered in an open meeting. This in itself poses a problem for the fellowship, by robbing it of more experienced members.

How AA and the other 12-step programs will deal with these threats remains to be seen. It may be that the essence of AA remains to be rediscovered periodically (White, 1998) and it may take different forms than what we now know (e.g., in the faith-based programs mentioned earlier). What is most likely is that it will continue to grow and evolve, and perhaps may take a trip underground.

References

Adler, A. (1929). *The practice and theory of individual psychology.* London: Routledge & Kegan Paul.

Alcoholics Anonymous. (1958). *Problems other than alcohol.* New York: AA World Services.

Alcoholics Anonymous. (1967). *As Bill sees it: The AA way of life.* New York: AA World Services.

Alcoholics Anonymous. (1975). *Living sober: Some methods AA members have used for not drinking.* New York: AA World Services.

Alcoholics Anonymous. (1980). *Dr. Bob and the good oldtimers.* New York: AA World Services.

Alcoholics Anonymous. (1984). *Pass it on: The story of Bill Wilson and how the AA message reached the world.* New York: AA World Services.

Alcoholics Anonymous. (1989). *Twelve steps and twelve traditions.* New York: AA World Services.

Alcoholics Anonymous. (1990). *AA comes of age.* New York: AA World Services.

Alcoholics Anonymous. (2001). *Alcoholics Anonymous* (4th ed.). New York: AA World Services.

Alcoholics Anonymous. (2004). Membership survey [pamphlet]. Available at: http://www.aa.org/en_pdfs/p-48_04survey.pdf.

American Psychiatric Association. (1968). *Diagnostic and statistical manual of mental disorders* (2nd ed.). Washington, DC: Author.

American Psychiatric Association. (2005). *Diagnostic and statistical manual of mental disorders* (4th ed., text rev.). Washington, DC: Author.

American Society of Addiction Medicine. (2001). *ASAM patient placement criteria for the treatment of substance-related disorders* (2nd ed.). Washington, DC: Author.

Annavi, M., Taube, D., Ja, D., & Duran, E. (1999). The status of psychologists' training about and treatment of substance-abusing clients. *Journal of Psychoactive Drugs, 3,* 441–444.

Ansbacher, H., & Ansbacher, R. (1956). *The individual psychology of Alfred Adler*. New York: Basic Books.

Ash, M. (1993). *The zen of recovery*. New York: Jeremy P. Tarcher.

Bachelor, A., & Horvath, A. (1999). The therapeutic relationship. In M. Hubble, B. Duncan, & S. Miller (Eds.), *The heart and soul of change* (pp. 133–178). Washington, DC: American Psychological Association.

Bateson, G. (1972). The cybernetics of "self": A theory of alcoholism. In G. Bateson (Ed.), *Steps to an ecology of mind* (pp. 309–337). New York: Ballantine Books.

Beattie, M. (1990). *Codependents' guide to the twelve steps*. New York: Prentice Hall.

Beck, A. T., Wright, F. D., Newman, C. F., & Liese, B. S. (1993). *Cognitive therapy of substance abuse*. New York: Guilford.

Berne, E. (1964). *Games People Play*. New York: Grove.

Bond, J., Kaskutas, L. A., & Weisner, C. (2003). The persistent influence of social networks and Alcoholics Anonymous on abstinence. *Journal of Studies on Alcohol, 64*, 579–588.

Brown, S. (1985). *Treating the alcoholic: A developmental model of recovery*. New York: Wiley.

Bufe, C. (1998). *Alcoholics Anonymous: Cult or cure?* Tucson, AZ: See Sharp Press.

Cain, A. H. (1963, February). Alcoholics Anonymous: Cult or cure? *Harpers*, pp. 48–52.

Cain, A. H. (1964, September 19). Alcoholics can be cured—despite AA. *Saturday Evening Post*.

Cheever, S. (2004). *My name is Bill*. New York: Washington Square Press.

Chiert, T., Gold, S., & Taylor, J. (1994). Substance abuse training in APA-accredited doctoral programs in clinical psychology. *Professional Psychology: Research and Practice, 25*, 80–84.

Connors, G. J., Tonigan, J. S., & Miller, W. R. (2001). A longitudinal model of intake symptomatology, AA participation and outcome: Retrospective study of the Project MATCH outpatient and aftercare samples. *Journal of Studies on Alcohol, 62*, 817–825.

Dawson, D. A., Grant, B. F., Stinson, F. S., Chou, P. S., Huang, B., & Ruan, W. J. (2005). Recovery from DSM-IV alcohol dependence: United States, 2001–2002. *Addiction, 100,* 281–292.

Delbanco, A. & Delbanco, T. (1995, March 20). A.A. at the crossroads. *New Yorker,* p. 50.

Ellison, J. (1954, August 7). These drug addicts cure one another. *Saturday Evening Post.*

Emrick, C. D. (1987). Alcoholics Anonymous: Affiliation processes and effectiveness as treatment. *Alcoholism: Clinical and Experimental Research,* 11, 416–423.

Emrick, C. D., Tonigan, J. S., Montgomery, H., & Little, L. (1993). Alcoholics Anonymous: What is currently known? In B. S. McCrady & W. R. Miller (Eds.), *Research on Alcoholics Anonymous: Opportunities and alternatives* (pp. 41–76). New Brunswick, NJ: Rutgers Center of Alcohol Studies.

Erickson, C. (2007). *The science of addiction.* New York: Norton.

Fingarette, H. (1988). *Heavy drinking: The myth of alcoholism as a disease.* Berkeley: University of California Press.

Fiorentine, R. (1999). After drug treatment: Are 12-step programs effective in maintaining abstinence. *American Journal of Drug and Alcohol Abuse, 25*(1) 93–116.

Frank, J. D., & Frank, J. B. (1991). *Persuasion and healing: A comparative study of psychotherapy.* Baltimore: Johns Hopkins University Press.

Frankl, V. (1984). *Man's search for meaning.* New York: Pocket Books. (Original work published 1946)

Goodwin, D. W. (1994). *Alcoholism: The facts.* Oxford, U.K.: Oxford University Press.

Gorski, T. T. (1989). *Understanding the twelve steps.* New York: Fireside.

Gorski, T. T., & Miller, M. (1986). *Staying sober: A guide for relapse prevention.* Independence, MO: Herald House, Independence Press.

Grant, J. E., & Kim, S. W. (2002). Effectiveness of pharmacotherapy for compulsive gambling: A chart review. *Annals of Clinical Psychiatry, 14,* 155–161.

Gregson, D., & Efran, J. S. (2002). *The tao of sobriety*. New York: St. Martin's Press.

Haley, J. (1997). *Leaving home: The therapy of disturbed young people* (2nd ed.). New York: Routledge.

Hammett, D. (1992). *The Maltese falcon*. New York: Vintage. (Originally published 1930)

Harwood, H. J., Kowalski, J., & Ameen, A. (2004). The need for substance abuse training among mental health professionals. *Administration and Policy in Mental Health, 32*(2), 189–205.

Hazelden Foundation. (1987). *The twelve steps of Alcoholics Anonymous interpreted by the Hazelden Foundation*. San Francisco: Harper/Hazelden.

Heather, N. (2007). Alcohol problems. In C. Freeman & M. Power (Eds.), *Handbook of evidence-based psychotherapies* (pp. 251–268). Hoboken, NJ: Wiley.

Hoffman, N. G., Harrison, P. A., & Belille, C. A. (1983). Alcoholics Anonymous after treatment: Attendance and abstinence. *International Journal of the Addictions 18*(3), 311–318.

Hoffman, N. G. and Miller, N. S. (1992). Treatment outcomes for abstinance-based programs. *Psychiatric Annals, 22*, 402–408.

Hubble, M. A., Duncan, B. L., & Miller, S. D. (1999). *The heart and soul of change: What works in therapy*. Washington, DC: American Psychological Association.

James, W. (2002). *The varieties of religious experience*. New York: Modern Library. (Original work published in 1902)

Jellinek, E. M. (1960). *The disease concept of alcoholism*. New Haven, CT: College and University Press.

Kapleau, P. (1980). *The three pillars of zen*. Garden City, NY: Anchor/Doubleday.

Ketcham, K., & Mueller, L. A. (1983). *Eating right to live sober*. New York: New American Library.

Khantzian, E. J., Halliday, K. S., & McAuliffe, W. E. (1990). *Addiction and the vulnerable self: Modified dynamic group therapy for substance abusers*. New York: Guilford.

Kishline, A. (1994). *Moderate drinking: The moderation management guide*. New York: Crown Trade.

Kolson, A. (1990, August 23). Dangerous liAAisons. *Philadelphia Inquirer*.

Kurtz, E. (1982). Why AA works: The intellectual significance of Alcoholics Anonymous. *Journal of Studies on Alcohol, 43*, 38–80.

Kurtz, E. (1989). *AA: The story (previously published as not-God)*. San Francisco: Harper/Hazelden.

Kurtz, E., & Ketcham, K. (1992). *The spirituality of imperfection: Storytelling and the journey to wholeness*. New York: Bantam Books.

Leupnitz, D. (1988). *The family interpreted*. New York: Basic Books.

Lewis, T., Amini, F., & Lannon, R. (2000). *A general theory of love*. New York: Random House.

Litt, M. D., Kadden, R. M., Kabela-Cormier, E., & Petry, N. (2007). Changing network support for drinking: Initial findings from the Network Support Project. *Journal of Consulting and Clinical Psychology, 75*, 542–555.

Mann, M. (1958). *Marty Mann's new primer on alcoholism*. New York: Holt, Rinehart and Winston.

Marlatt, G. A., Demming, B., & Reid, J. B. (1973). Loss of control drinking in alcoholics: An experimental analogue. *Journal of Abnormal Psychology, 81*(3), 233–241.

Marlatt, G. A., & Gordon, J. R. (1985). *Relapse prevention*. New York: Guilford.

McCrady, B. S. (1994). Alcoholics Anonymous and behavior therapy: Can habits be treated as diseases? Can diseases be treated as habits? *Journal of Consulting and Clinical Psychology, 62*, 1159–1166.

McCrady, B. S. Horvath, A. T., & Delaney, S. I. (2003). Self-help groups, in Hester, R. K., & Miller, W. R., *Handbook of Alcoholism treatment approaches*, (pp. 165–187). Boston: Allyn & Bacon.

McKay, J. R., Alterman, A. I., McLellan, A. T., & Snider, E. C. (1992). Treatment goals, continuity of care, and outcome in a day hospital substance abuse rehabilitation program. *American Journal of Psychiatry, 151*(2) 254–259.

McKellar, J., Stewart, E., & Humphreys, K. (2003). Alcoholics Anonymous involvement and positive alcohol-related outcomes: Cause, consequence, or just a correlate? A prospective 2-year study of 2,319 alcohol-dependent men. *Journal of Consulting and Clinical Psychology, 71*, 302–308.

McLatchie, B. H., & Lomp, K. G. E. (1988). Alcoholics Anonymous affiliation and treatment outcome among a clinical sample of problem drinkers. *American Journal of Drug and Alcohol Abuse, 14*, 309–324.

McLellan, A. T., Lewis, D. C., O'Brien, C. P., & Kleber, H. D. (2000). Drug dependence, a chronic medical illness: Implications for treatment, insurance, and outcomes evaluation. *Journal of the American Medical Association, 284*, 1689–1695.

Milam, J. R., & Ketcham, K. (1983). *Under the influence*. New York: Bantam.

Miller, W. R., & Brown, S. A. (1997). Why psychologists should treat alcohol and drug problems. *American Psychologist, 52*, 1269–1279.

Miller, W. R., & Carroll, K. M. (Eds.) (2006). *Rethinking substance abuse*. New York: Guilford.

Miller, W. R., & McCrady, B. S. (1993). The importance of research on Alcoholics Anonymous. In B. S. McCrady & W. R. Miller (Eds.), *Research on Alcoholics Anonymous: Opportunities and alternatives* (pp. 3–11). New Brunswick, NJ: Rutgers Center of Alcohol Studies.

Miller, W. R., & Munoz, R. F. (2005). *Controlling your drinking*. New York: Guilford.

Miller, W. R., & Rollnick, S. (2002). *Motivational interviewing* (2nd ed.). New York: Guilford.

Miller, W. R., Wilbourne, P. L., & Hettema, J. E. (2003). What works? A summary of alcohol treatment outcome research. In R. K. Hester & W. R. Miller (Eds.), *Handbook of alcoholism treatment approaches* (3rd ed.) (pp. 13–63). Boston: Allyn and Bacon.

Minkoff, K. (1989). An integrated treatment model for dual diagnosis of psychosis and addiction. *Hospital and Community Psychiatry, 40*, 1031–1036.

Minkoff, K. (2001). Developing standards of care for induviduals with co-occurring psychiatric and substance abuse disorders. *Psychiatric Services, 52*, 597–599.

Montgomery, H. A., Miller, W. R, & Tonigan, J. S. (1995). Does Alcoholics Anonymous involvement predict treatment outcome? *Journal of Substance Abuse Treatment, 12*, 241–246.

Monti, P. M., Abrams, D. B., Kadden, R. M., & Cooney, N. L. (1989). *Treating alcohol dependence*. New York: Guilford.

Moos, R. H., & Moos, B. S. (2004). Long-term influence of duration and frequency of participation in Alcoholics Anonymous on individuals with alcohol use disorders. *Journal of Consulting and Clinical Psychology, 72*, 81–90.

Moos, R. H., & Moos, B. S. (2006). Participation in treatment and Alcoholics Anonymous: A 16-year follow-up of initially untreated individuals. *Journal of Clinical Psychology, 62*, 735–750.

Morgenstern, J., Labouvie, E., McCrady, B. S., Kahler, C. W., & Frey, R. M. (1997). Affiliation with Alcoholics Anonymous after treatment: A study of its therapeutic effects and mechanisms of action. *Journal of Consulting and Clinical Psychology, 65*, 768–777.

Mueser, K. T., Noordsy, D. L., Drake, R. E., & Fox, L. (2003). *Integrated treatment for dual disorders*. NY: Guilford.

Narcotics Anonymous World Services. (1988). *Narcotics Anonymous* (5th ed.). Van Nuys, CA: Author.

Nowinski, J. (1993). Questioning the answers: Research and the AA traditions. In B. S. McCrady & W. R. Miller (Eds.), *Research on Alcoholics Anonymous: Opportunities and alternatives* (pp. 27–39). New Brunswick, NJ: Rutgers Center of Alcohol Studies.

Nowinski, J. (2003). Self-help groups. In Sorenson, J. L., Rawson, R. A., Guydish, J., & Zweben, J. E. (Eds.). *Drug abuse treatment collaboration: Practice and research partnerships that work.* (pp. 55–70) Washington, DC: American Psychological Association.

Nowinski, J., & Baker, S. (1992). *The 12-step facilitation handbook*. New York: Lexington Books.

Nowinski, J., Baker, S., & Carroll, K. (1992). *12-step facilitation therapy manual: A clinical research guide for therapists treating individuals with alcohol abuse and dependence.* NIAAA Project MATCH Monograph, Vol. 1, DHHS Publication No. ADM 92-1893. Washington, DC: U.S. Government Printing Office.

O'Connell, D., & Beyer, E. (2002). *Managing the dually diagnosed patient.* Binghamton, NY: Haworth.

Ouimette, P. C., Finney, J. W., & Moos, R. H. (1997). Twelve-step and cognitive-behavioral treatment for substance abuse: A comparison of treatment effectiveness. *Journal of Consultation and Clinical Psychology, 65,* 230–240.

Ouimette, P. C., Moos, R. H., & Finney, J. W. (1998). Influence of outpatient treatment and 12-step group involvement on one-year substance abuse treatment outcomes. *Journal of Studies on Alcohol, 59,* 513–522.

Owen, P. L., Slaymaker, V., Tonigan, J. S., McCrady, B. S., Epstein, E. E., Kaskutas, L. A., et al. (2003). Participation in Alcoholics Anonymous: Intended and unintended change mechanisms. *Alcoholism: Clinical and Experimental Research, 27,* 524–532.

Peele, S. (1989). *Diseasing of America: Addiction treatment out of control.* Lexington, MA: Lexington Books.

Prochaska, J. O., DiClemente, C. C., & Norcross, J. C. (1992). In search of how people change: Applications to addictive behaviors. *American Psychologist, 47,* 1102–1114.

Prochaska, J. O., Norcross, J. C., & DiClemente, C. C. (1994). *Changing for good.* New York: Quill.

Project MATCH Research Group. (1997). Matching alcoholism treatments to client heterogeneity: Project MATCH posttreatment drinking outcomes. *Journal of Studies on Alcohol, 58,* 7–29.

Project MATCH Research Group. (1998). Matching alcoholism treatments to client heterogeneity: Project MATCH three-year drinking outcomes. *Alcoholism: Clinical and Experimental Research, 22,* 1300–1311.

Rogers, R. L., & McMillin, C. S. (1989). *Don't help: A positive guide to working with the alcoholic.* New York: Bantam.

Rogers, R. L., McMillin, C. S., & Hill, M. A. (1990). *The twelve steps revisited*. New York: Bantam.

Rotgers, F., Kern, M. F., & Hoeltzel, R. (2002). *Responsible drinking*. Oakland, CA: New Harbinger.

Robertson, N. (1988). *Getting better: Inside Alcoholics Anonymous*. New York: William Morrow.

Slater, P. (1970). The pursuit of loneliness. Boston: Beacon Press.

Spiegel, B. R., & Fewell, C. H. (2004). 12-step programs as a treatment modality. In S. L. A. Straussner (Ed.), *Clinical work with substance-abusing clients* (2nd ed.). New York: Guilford.

Suzuki, S. (1988). *Zen mind, beginner's mind*. New York: Weatherhill.

Tiebout, H. M. (1949). The act of surrender in the therapeutic process. *Quarterly Journal of Studies on Alcohol, 10*, 48–58.

Tiebout, H. M. (1953). Surrender versus compliance in therapy. *Quarterly Journal of Studies on Alcohol, 14*, 58–68.

Timko, C., Moos, R. H., Finney, J. W., & Lesar, M. D. (2000). Long-term outcomes of alcohol use disorders: Comparing untreated individuals with those in Alcoholics Anonymous and formal treatment. *Journal of Studies on Alcohol, 61*, 529–540.

Tonigan, J. S., Bogenschutz, M. P., & Miller, W. R. (2006). Is alcoholism typology a predictor of both Alcoholics Anonymous affiliation and disaffiliation after treatment? *Journal of Substance Abuse Treatment, 30*, 323–330.

Tonigan, J. S., Connors, G. J., & Miller, W. R. (1996). Alcoholics Anonymous Involvement (AAI) scale: Reliability and norms. *Psychology of Addictive Behaviors, 10*, 75–80.

Tonigan, J. S., Toscova, R., & Miller, W. R. (1996). Meta-analysis of the literature of Alcoholics Anonymous: Sample and study characteristics moderate findings. *Journal of Studies on Alcohol, 57*, 65–72.

Trimpey, J. (1996). *Rational recovery: The new cure for substance addiction*. New York: Pocket Books.

Vaillant, G. (1995). *The natural history of alcoholism revisited*. Cambridge, MA: Harvard University Press.

Volpicelli, J. R., Alterman, A. I., Hayashida, M., & O'Brien, C. P. (1992). Naltrexone in the treatment of alcohol dependence. *Archives of General Psychiatry, 49*, 876–880.

Volpicelli, J. R., & Szalavitz, M. (2000). *Recovery options*. New York: Wiley.

W., B. (1958). *Let's be friendly with our friends* [Pamphlet]. New York: Alcoholics Anonymous World Services.

Wallace, J. (2006). Theory of 12-step-oriented treatment. In F. Rotgers, J. Morgenstern, & S. T. Walters (Eds.), *Treating substance abuse: Theory and technique* (2nd ed.) (pp. 9–30). New York: Guilford.

Washton, A. W., & Zweben, J. E. (2006). *Treating alcohol and drug problems in psychotherapy practice*. New York: Guilford.

White, W. L. (1998). *Slaying the dragon: The history of addiction treatment and recovery in America*. Bloomington, IL: Chestnut Health Systems.

White, W. L., & Kurtz, E. (2006). The varieties of recovery experience. In W. L. White, E. Kurtz, & M. Sanders (Eds.), *Recovery management* (pp. 7–43). Chicago: Great Lakes Addiction Technology Transfer Center.

Wilson, W. (1944). Basic concepts of Alcoholics Anonymous. *New York State Journal of Medicine, 44*, 1805–1810.

Wilson, W. (1960). A synopsis of the question-answer period following Bill W.'s talk at the NCCA symposim in New York in 1960. Retrieved May 28, 2007, from http://www.nccatoday.org/conversation.htm.

Yalisove, D. (2004). *Introduction to alcohol research: Implications for treatment, prevention, and policy*. Boston: Pearson Education.

Yalom, I. D. (1995). *The theory and practice of group psychotherapy* (4th ed.). New York: Basic Books.

Index

Index

Index

Index

Index

Index

Index